Edwin Lynn is the minister of the North-shore Unitarian Universalist Church in Danvers, Massachusetts. He is also a registered architect and has had experience as a consultant.

# TIRED DRAGONS

# TIRED DRAGONS

ADAPTING CHURCH ARCHITECTURE
TO CHANGING NEEDS

BY EDWIN CHARLES LYNN

BEACON PRESS   BOSTON

Copyright © 1972 by Edwin Charles Lynn

Library of Congress catalog card number: 72–75540

International Standard Book Number: 0–8070–1132–0

Beacon Press books are published under the auspices of the
Unitarian Universalist Association

Published simultaneously in Canada by Saunders of Toronto, Ltd.

*All rights reserved*

Printed in the United States of America

*To my wife, Marj, and our offspring, Bruce and Sharyl,*
*who often suspected as the book progressed that*
*I was getting more tired than the dragons*

# CONTENTS

# PREFACE

One of the most crucial problems facing churches today is the proper utilization of their facilities. Many people contend that churches should own no property; yet others continue to build elaborate church structures, assuming that religion in the twentieth century will never change. Between these extremes are possibilities in both new and existing buildings for creating efficient and beautiful religious environments. Churches can no longer be constructed as static monuments serving as memorials to the past; they must be conceived as living environments for today's religious community.

As both an architect and a minister I have visited many churches. Some were beautiful but ineffective; others were less attractive but functional. In many, a simple rearrangement of the furnishings, a little effort with a paint brush, or some modest remodeling would transform inadequate rooms into usable spaces. Some congregations were considering building new religious education rooms or totally new facilities, although their present facilities might have been adequate if developed to their full potential. When new buildings were necessary, many churches were planning structures that repeated the errors of the past or duplicated facilities already available in both the secular and the religious communities.

There is a need for a book in which the basic principles of contemporary architecture are applied to the needs of religious structures. I have tried to avoid the failings of the two types of books presently available. The first, prevalent in architectural circles, is filled with decorative photographs of famous churches. The second, common in religious spheres, is the wordy cookbook explaining how to construct a new church in ten easy steps.

In this book I have made every effort to help the reader transfer the recommended principles to his own church situation and to increase environmental awareness within the community. People are becoming increasingly aware of the overall quality of the urban environment, and it is important that they become more sensitive to the possibilities of beauty and function within every environmental setting. The church can be a significant place to begin. Words are not buildings; ideas in the text must be related to the three dimensions of real structures. A number of churches are used as examples; two churches, Christ Church Cathedral in St. Louis and the Interfaith Center in Columbia, Maryland, are presented in detailed case studies.

The purpose of this book is not to invent exotic miracle cures but to apply proven architectural principles to church problems. Fully recognizing that there are many theological and doctrinal differences between churches, I have tried to stress the common functions and architectural considerations. Whether in a Protestant church, a Catholic cathedral, a Jewish synagogue, or a humanist center, the desire for attractive, usable spaces for worship, fellowship, and service is shared by all.

While diagnosing and treating the maladies of churches, I consulted with many individuals. I am particularly indebted to Gobin Stair, who was confident that I could perform the operation, to the many architects and ministers who were generous with assistance and materials, to Marge Starkey for her support and advice, Tal Hindson for his photographic assistance, Shari Gruhn for her editorial guidance, and to my wife, Marj, who performed the difficult task of assisting when needed and waiting when necessary, while I was trying to bring new life to tired dragons.

*Edwin Charles Lynn*

# FRESH AIR

## QUAGMIRE

nce upon a time there were church structures built with dignity, sustained by belief, and strengthened with community purpose. Many of these structures are today's tired dragons, their energies spent, their fire nearly extinguished, their tails drooping. These creatures lie waiting for the daring prince not to slay them, but to restore them to life. Churches were once supported by an influential and affluent urban population. Now they are surrounded by high-rise office buildings that are vacated every weekend, leaving a desert of inactivity. Some are in areas of deteriorating dwellings and oppressed inhabitants who have little interest in a religious message. Many have little time left. The dragons' lung power and circulation are weakening. Their interior condition is hinted at by their exterior. Their once attractive armor of stonework has become little more than scaling skin. Their appendages of towers and decorative elements have lost color and are disintegrating, and their vision is increasingly blocked by boarded windows and locked doors.

Churches have never been known for their fast pace. Their power, like the dragon's, has come from slow but sure-footed strength. Many brave and noisy would-be slayers have attacked them, but they have remained unconquered. New movements, antagonistic leaders, and eddies of social change have spelled trouble for churches, but they have survived—and sometimes gained strength. Their best weapon has usually been their size and fierce display of fire. The noisiest confrontations have been with individual foes and groups, but the toughest battles have always been with the changing environment. The church has adapted when necessary—modifying, absorbing, and adding social changes into its way of life. In the past, the changes were slow to come. Today the churches are in troubled times of rapid change. Everywhere tension is different from what it used to be. Where once there were strong allies,

1

now there are fierce competitors. Where once supporters had power and influence, now they are often weak and ineffective; where once they could sidestep, now they are finding the way blocked; where once they could absorb, now they are finding little room for flexibility. Instead of being integral to their surroundings, churches are becoming increasingly isolated.

Within this bleak setting are some glimmers of hope. A vital spirit lies deep within the church, but new forms of leadership, organization, and facilities are needed to allow its expression in our time.

The most dramatic example of new direction is the convening of the Vatican Councils. After long deliberations many traditional procedures and attitudes were altered, but even more important, a spirit of vitality was released that has given the church new possibilities of life. The Vatican Councils are the most obvious example of what has taken place in many religious bodies. Every synod gathering, presbytery council, and denominational conference is an expression of various efforts to make the church more relevant to the moral and religious issues of our time.

Books about church renewal have become best sellers. *Honest to God, The Secular City,* and *The Comfortable Pew* are in the personal libraries of most active church members.[1] Of course, all do not agree with these works, but these books have provided a challenge and point of departure for the laity in current religious discussions. Nostalgic patterns predominated through the 1950's and justified a material comfort that closely approached decadence. By the early 1960's increasing numbers of young people could find little that was meaningful in the activities of the church. This country had taken a dramatic turn toward urban technological secularism. The trend had been developing for a long time and reached the popular consciousness during the 1960's. The byproducts of science, thanks to technology and mass marketing, have rapidly effected great changes in our physical and mental environment. Technology has influenced every aspect of daily life.

Marshall McLuhan provided some insight into the rapid change and apparent chaos around us. He explained for popular understanding what many technological specialists had known for some time: we have been thrust into a new world in which electronics affects all human behavior. Nonelectronic, mechanical, small-town, parochial religion is irrelevant in the new cultural environment. The electronic world has increased production, allowing men at control panels to operate vast amounts of complex machinery. Through these extensions of man's effort, an unprecedented material affluence has been born, an affluence that has undermined the religious values of austerity and moderation. Excesses are everywhere in urban life: too many things, too many buildings, too much machinery, too many people. The average person in his abundance suddenly finds himself free from bonds of location and family, which have been strong factors in the maintenance of the stability of the church. In our affluent society the most obvious mark of conspicuous consumption is the automobile. It, more than any other product, symbolizes our desire for personal power, fashionableness, and change for its own sake—all values in conflict with the ideals of the church. The automobile gave freedom to the young, breaking down previously strong cultural mores. With the development of superhighways, new kinds of recreation and travel produce additional conflicts with traditional church teachings.

According to Marshall McLuhan's theories of electronic information distribution, television is the principal vehicle of dramatic change. Television's impersonal quality, readily changed programing, precision, and fast pace are reflections of urban life. The medium enters nearly every house. Few people are able to close their windows to its increased stimulation. It creates a new balance of aural and visual relationships, apparent in a changed attitude toward other sources of information. McLuhan states, "The aspiration of our times for wholeness, empathy and depth of awareness is a natural adjunct of electric technology." [2] Individual-centered media such as books, lectures, and sermons lose their effectiveness in a television-conditioned culture.

The electronic media have made much of church life and worship inappropriate. Nevertheless, in a time of machine domination, people want intimacy; in a time of rapid population growth and concentration, people want human community; in a time of specialization, people want individual participation. Only recently has the church realized the magnitude of the effect of the urban environment and the changing needs of its congregation. The situation is so dramatically different that the church finds itself in the midst of the sins and evils of the perennial Babylon, instead of being safely and self-righteously in the hills of the rural people.

In the city spiritual life is given appropriate ceremonial expression, but large portions of the population no longer take it seriously. In Paul Tillich's terminology, our "ultimate concern" has lost a spiritual center. [3] Urban man's allegiance is to the corporate structure or to the union organization. Most people continue to talk about damnation, original sin, and eternal life, but their motivation is derived from this life, here and now. If forced to decide between religious beliefs and occupational advantage, there is little question what most people would choose. This split in identity and loss of spiritual center is nowhere more evident than in the accepted commercial morality of our time, tersely phrased as business ethics.

These changing values are expressed architecturally in enormous skyscrapers, signifying the strength and power of business. Some of the tallest buildings are financed by insurance companies, which, like the church, are concerned about questions of life and death. The insurance company, however, pays dividends on earth. Noted psychiatrist Rollo May summarizes the situation this way:

> I see a sea of skyscrapers, each one surging upward from its narrow base, utilizing nature not to be united with but simply to stand upon, each building rising upward not for spiritual purposes but for achievement, getting to "the top," the spirit of moving "onward and upward" every month and every year, surging on and on to infinity or heaven but caught in the perpetual motion of the everlasting upward drive of finiteness.[4]

The purpose of recognizing these metropolitan trends is not to berate or reject the church but to emphasize that the cultural dominance of the church has come to an end. Polite lip service to religious beliefs and values will continue to be a part of our national heritage, but the presence of religion in every level of society will decrease. At best this offers a challenge to the church, freed from the shackles of superficial religious values. Now a new church can stride forward with new ethical commitments. New religious communities can evolve out of a genuine commitment to honestly proclaimed beliefs in the creation of a better world for all people.

The church will need to resolve the growing conflict between urgent needs and diminishing funds. Like most private institutions, the church historically has relied on the generous donations and bequests of the wealthy. The new church will often find itself in disagreement with its affluent members as it tries to bring humanity and spirit to the technological order. The church will be joining other groups challenging the status quo and criticizing the affluence of the majority while the minority remain deprived. It will probably find itself not on the side of corrupted compromise but in the more appropriate position of justifiable righteous indignation. The literal price it will pay for this new ethical thrust will be fewer bequests and a greater need for everyone involved in the church community to participate in its financing.

The ethical thrust and corresponding projected decrease in income of the emerging church are only part of the changing financial situation. As our culture becomes more sophisticated, many aspects of church administration and maintenance will have to be reappraised. Much of the church's traditional organization has its basis in a money-scarce culture, where volunteer labor and mutual cooperation were important. Churches now call upon experts more and more to maintain their facilities. But this takes money. No longer can a church have a little money and a lot of volunteer help. Not only have cultural patterns limited the contributions of volunteers in the maintenance of buildings, they have also limited the money-raising potential of volunteer efforts. Rummage sales, Saturday night church suppers, and bingo games are not high points of urban social life.

Individual churches are in the same position as the poor. When everyone was relatively poor and goods and services were scarce, the poor were able to survive by self-help and neighborhood cooperation. Now many tasks cannot be completed by the untrained. As technology progresses, the less money and less training a person has, the farther he is removed from the mainstream of urban life. In a less technological and less affluent culture the church was solvent. In today's society, where goods are available but expensive, where services are professional and skilled, it is difficult for the church to survive.

Churches must reevaluate all aspects of their spending. The two most obvious areas that need investigation are the categories of major expense in every church budget. The first is the salaries and benefits received by the professional staff, and the second, and most often overlooked, is the church building itself. Because of loan payments, major repairs, and general maintenance and utilities, the building can consume an even larger portion of the budget than the salaries. A number of surveys have indicated that there is a correlation between the two budget items. Many members of the clergy spend substantial amounts of their time administering not the church but the building. The minister finds himself talking with plumbers, electricians, and property committees.

Since the early 1950's churches have spent enormous amounts of money on elaborate and excessive building programs. These programs were a mixture of optimism and materialism. They were optimistic because new buildings are usually put up in a mood of positiveness and expansiveness. (This may not characterize the committee meetings or relationships with the contractors, but it is generally the mood of the congregation.) Building is a time of looking to the future, of growth, shared accomplishments, and a new era in church life. However, below all these positive traits lies a somewhat disguised materialism. There exists the feeling that the building will permanently express the congregation's religious faith. If the building is large enough and expensive enough, then the congregation's faith can never be questioned. The building can become a sort of idol. In our materialistic culture, we worship not small clay idols but entire buildings, for only they have the magnificence and scope worthy of our homage. In the last vestiges of Calvin's doctrine of good works, the spectacular building is a culturally approved conspicuous consumption to prove that the blessings of a higher power have been bestowed on those that dwell within.

In the 1960's we began to be aware of the failings of large and expensive churches. Congregations found it was easier to get money for new buildings, particularly through memorial contributions, than it was to raise money for maintaining the old structures. Churches found that they could not raise the yearly budgets necessary to provide the services and programs compatible with their facilities. Serious-minded church people, clergy and laity alike, began to realize they were operating religious museums open to the public once a week.

Many members of the clergy realized the church had to be part of the effort to bring about a new morality in American life, and they joined the civil rights movement, criticized the Vietnam War, and questioned the United States military establishment. They knew that moral change had to be as much a part of the American way as technological change. The churches could continue to be museums, or they could be directed to meet human needs. Many clergymen have chosen the latter course and have altered the thrust of parish concerns. An outstanding example of this changed attitude was the decision of the members of the Cathedral of St. John the Divine in New York City to complete as inexpensively and simply as possible the remainder of the church's sanctuary. The cathedral was designed in the Gothic style and construction had begun at the beginning of the twentieth century. Efforts had been made to complete the building as designed, but the cost had become exorbitant. The governing board publicly stated that the church had changed its priorities: the building will be modestly completed, and the church will expand its community-oriented programs.

Some people carry the trend away from church museums to its furthest extreme and contend that all church buildings should be immediately eliminated. Many believe that wherever two are gathered, a congregational expression of religious commitment is being made. There can be little question that small groups can easily meet in homes and rented rooms, and there are exciting possibilities for individual relationships in the new church forms somewhat loosely called the "underground church." To date, however, the underground church has been most prevalent where the overground church is most traditional and unresponsive, particularly in the Catholic church and to a lesser degree in several Protestant denominations. In other words, many individuals are finding the underground movement above ground, both sanctioned and unsanctioned by denominational authorities. One characteristic of the underground church is its pride in the lack of permanent facilities. This is a healthy reaction against building worship. However, many groups have found that lack of a permanent meeting space becomes a hardship, particularly when the group grows and suitable temporary spaces become difficult to acquire.

Church buildings themselves are not immoral. Improper design, motivation, and use are. Buildings should not be sanctuaries from reality. If a church building is not to be fully used by people, it should not be built. However, facilities that are needed and responsibly designed can enlarge the religious life of the church and make a substantial contribution to the community. A usable church building can be of great service in implementing the ethical goals of the congregation. Churches have a long history of providing their facilities for worthwhile community projects such as scouting, charities, Alcoholics Anonymous, and discussion groups. Controversial organizations such as the Southern Christian Leadership Conference, the American Civil Liberties Union, the National Association for the Advancement of Colored People, peace organizations, and the Congress for Racial Equality were often aided in their early stages by the use of church facilities. Well-planned churches have facilities for various community programs related to child care and instruction. During weekdays church facilities have been made available for day care, nurseries, and special projects to help disadvantaged children and working mothers. Churches can provide space that is otherwise unavailable. Community service, however, should not be a rationalization for continuing to build excessive church buildings, but their potential positive contribution does need to be recognized. By altering present facilities, more efficiently planning new buildings, and sharing space with the community, the church can make its structures worthwhile and practical religious expressions.

At the present time there is an important revitalization in the church. This shift from hypocritical platitudes to genuine concerns needs to be strengthened. The proper use of the church facilities can be an aid. We do not need pretentious buildings to serve as idols or museums, but we do need places of rest and meditation, rooms for human interaction, and space for ethical programs. Without these it is difficult to have a functioning religious community.

## AIR

Early in the reign of Pope John XXIII an incident occurred that poignantly expresses the needs of the church today. A Canadian dignitary reportedly asked Pope John to explain the objectives of his papacy in general and those of the Ecumenical Councils in particular. The Pope responded by walking to the window, opening it, and saying, "We intend to let in a little fresh air." [5]

Most churches have learned that letting in fresh air is not easy. Until recently the church in America was one of our most conservative institutions. This conservatism was the result not only of reluctant leadership but also of people's desire for a haven in a world of change. Extreme nostalgia produces neurotic behavior. In the 1970's churches have become aware of this danger and have been searching for ways to deal with reality. However, change is never easy, and as the clergy and laity go to open the windows they in many cases find them locked, painted over, and even broken. The opening itself becomes a major task. In the beginning, the church often must literally open the windows of its architectural facilities in order to let in the needed fresh air. Too often the church building has exuded an ominously pervasive spirit that has subtly continued historical attitudes and restricted innovation.

All denominations need to engage in dialogues about a reanimated church, strengthened ecumenism, and revitalized liturgy. The ideas and theories expressed in debates, discussions, and other exchanges stimulate everyone's thinking and imagination. Students and experienced clergy alike leave such sessions brimming with enthusiasm. However, after the conversations are over and the clergy have returned to their churches, they find that in spite of their efforts much of the church's life continues as before. Some blame the congregation, saying they have lost their spiritual direction. This may, in varying degrees, be true. But one avenue of change often overlooked is the building and its influence on the congregation. A principal cause of the frustrations between theory and practice is the rigidity of the ecclesiastical facility. Unfortunately, the building cannot attend the seminars and has little interest in change. The clergy and membership have to take the initiative to alter it and its use. This is often difficult because churches rely so heavily on ritualistic ceremonies and volunteer services. The volunteer organization of a church depends upon the building to provide the clues necessary for proper functioning. Limited opportunity to train volunteers and other personnel makes it easy to understand why the routine method is always followed and the building's layout has usually predetermined the building's use. Unless the arrangement of facilities and the environment—the offices, classrooms, the sanctuary—are changed, people will continue to experience church life as they always have. This may be a previously undiscovered tenet of the doctrine of determinism.

Clearly, the building is not more important than the spirit of the religious body. Without a sense of commitment, there is a sense of uneasiness as the church faces these changing times. However, understanding the importance of the building can be a significant step in providing direction to a church responding to the needs of people—all people in the church, young and old, as well as those in the community. The church needs to meet the restless challenge of the young; help the forgotten ghetto and rural dweller, guide adults seeking meaning in the spiritual vacuum of suburban living, and give substance to people in their older years.

The architecture of religion needs to express a human orientation. No longer can the church be considered only God's house; it is the house of His people. We can no longer assume that the sanctuary literally houses God's presence and must be maintained solely as a sacred space. We need to develop a flexible attitude toward the appearance and use of every part of the church.

Present changes in religious doctrine and in the use of facilities challenge us all. We are living in an exciting time of religious renewal, of searching and risking. In the search, some ecclesiastical authority will be lost. We can no longer assume that the clergy has the answers to all questions. Clergymen must show humility, acknowledging their ambivalence toward the search for new directions. Humility is exhorted by Jesus and the prophets. Much of the strength of the parables of Jesus is in their intriguing ambivalence, which requires individual search. Unfortunately, much of this vitality has been lost over the centuries. The established church emphasizes the preservation of the orderly religious life set forth by the authority of the church. This conservative emphasis can lead to an emptiness in which only the organization and the letter exist, the spirit having left the people.

The architecture of religious buildings is one expression of the spirit, doctrine, and theology of a church. Nowhere is this more evident than in the dramatic contrast between the Gothic cathedrals of Europe and the Puritan meeting houses of America. In both medieval Europe and early New England, religious beliefs and values pervaded all aspects of living. The social and political environment was integrated with the life of the church. Being a member of the church and of the community were synonymous. Communities were relatively small, and the church's dominance was indicated by its prominent location. The cathedral was built on the top of the highest hill; the meeting house was the central focus of the village green. The church building was the seat of political action, the bastion for defense, the place of learning—in short, the center of community activity. The interior of the church was used for many and diverse functions. The exterior was equally versatile. Spires beckoned far-distant worshipers and served as a landmark for all travelers. Church bells called worshipers to prayer and served as a clock for the entire community.

The medieval cathedral and the New England meeting house both were expressions of religion at the peak of its powers, but there were great theological and liturgical differences between them. These differences were visible in their architecture. In design and construction the cathedral and the meeting house are diametrically opposed.

Most people, through travel and photographs, have a sense of the complexity and beauty of the cathedrals of Europe and many of their American duplications. The Gothic cathedral rose from the theological premise that God is a mysterious and omnipresent force. The cathedral gave expression to this power and mystery through soaring interior spaces and pointed arches that made worshipers feel insignificant. The stonework of the church expressed the permanence of religious faith. Detailed carvings and sculpture depicted the long church tradition of saints and martyrs, biblical personages, and mythical beings. The nave of the sanctuary was without chairs or pews, adding to the vastness of the space. The only warmth in the dark caverns was from the muted light shining through the stained-glass windows and the constant flicker of candles. Henry Adams said of the Gothic cathedral: "To most minds it casts too many shadows; it wraps itself in mystery." [6] The mystery of the cathedral spaces was deepest in the sacred areas, with their elaborate decoration and symbolism, accessible only to the priesthood. The cathedral was a universe of time and space. In detail it depicted the beliefs of people living in medieval cities as well as the grandeur of the sacred powers of the universe. If the universe was ever captured and transformed to beauty and mystery by man, it was in the medieval cathedral.

The New England house of worship differed from the cathedral in almost every detail of its construction. The Puritans dogmatically insisted on the rightness of their beliefs and were bitter because of the persecutions they had endured in England and on the Continent. Their religious architecture clearly showed their disapproval of other forms of worship. Puritans believed that an individual could directly contact a personal God. Life was orderly and without mystery, and God's radiance was everywhere. Man only needed to live according to the morality of the Gospels in order to have the rewards of a better material and spiritual life. Consistent with both necessity and their theological beliefs, the Puritans constructed the well-known meeting houses. The buildings are relatively small, unpretentious, and simple in line and shape. They are white, wooden, single-steepled churches. The interior is bright and usually painted white. Every detail is fixed, and every corner is bathed in light. The windows are clear, large, and are given detail by small panes and flanking shutters. The interior is usually two stories high, allowing for a modest balcony. The ceiling is flat or rounded. Seating is fixed pews with rigid backs and doors opening onto the aisle. Seats were assigned, further indicating the orderliness of God's world. The altar is simple, usually not recessed, and furnished with little more than a cross and candles. The dominant visual and liturgical focus was the pulpit, which was imposingly located on a platform raised above the congregation. The pulpit had its own door, with a lock, the last vestige of clerical sanctity. The raised pulpit denoted the importance in Puritan theology of preaching the Gospel, and the simple altar signified the simplicity of the sacramental rituals of the church. The meeting-house sanctuary clearly expresses the theology of the early New Englanders.

The contrast between the Gothic cathedrals and the Puritan meeting houses exemplifies the interrelationship of theology and architectural design. Where the cathedral was complex and sculptured, the Puritans built simply and without ornament. The cathedral was of stone, utilizing daring construction techniques; the Puritans built of wood with ordinary roofs and flat ceilings. Where the cathedral created an atmosphere of dark mystery and overwhelming awe, the Puritans built a simple structure of light and clarity. Both were valid and beautiful expressions of the beliefs and ideals of a religious people in a particular time and place. To attempt to duplicate these achievements in another milieu would be a perversion of the creative spirit. The essence of both the Gothic cathedral and the New England meeting house was their direct and honest expression of values in practical architectural forms.

Buildings not only express values, they also shape them. In every environment there is a balance of forces. A building can be a source of inspiration or an insidiously destructive force. If the building dominates the attitudes of the congregation, the members become overpowered and lose their religious vitality. A proper balance requires the congregation to respect the integrity of the building, adapting and shaping it to meet their needs. As long as life continues, no environment, natural or man made, can remain unchanged. Church structures are not static forces, but living environments for serving the religious community.

## DEEP BREATHING

The church has taken the easy way during most of the twentieth century, relying on nostalgia, tradition, and habit to continue its functions. It must now face the realities of a changing environment and increased demands for relevance. The church needs to go beyond ordinary breathing to deep breathing, which can release hidden energies. Deep breathing requires drawing fresh air into the center of the body. Deep breathing is performed slowly and requires the full attention of the individual, unlike the unconscious breathing of our daily lives or the hurried and often panicky inhalation before the proverbial desperate plunge. Individuals and institutions both have centers of energy; deep breathing can lead to new awareness and new sources of strength.

Deep breathing in the church is a thorough evaluation of present programs and directions. This does not mean a superficial report by a powerless committee or a summary of church functions by the minister: these are shallow breathing. Deep breathing means reaching into the recess of the life of the church for a thorough look at every aspect of its functions. Deep breathing further requires the full participation of the entire congregation. Until recently it would not have occurred to most church members to think that the purposes of the church needed evaluation. Most felt the church's role was clearly defined by belief and tradition. There would always be a Sunday morning service with music by a choir and organ, sermon and prayers by the minister, and the congregation seated securely in their pews. During the same Sunday hour children would be neatly located down corridors in little rooms designated by grade levels. Throughout the rest of the week the office would be open, the choir would practice, and perhaps a scout troop or two would meet in the basement. This pattern, with its emphasis on Sunday morning worship, is changing and will continue to change.

A cursory review of any aspect of church tradition shows modes of worship and religious life slowly but constantly changing. Even in times of general stability for values and religious beliefs, modest changes were taking place. So the question is not whether churches should change, for churches have always been changing; the only question is how fast should they change. Not only churches, but individuals and organizations, have been affected by the rapidly increasing progression of all forms of change. Alvin Toffler, in his *Future Shock*, clearly describes the effects of change upon all of us:

> Change is the process by which the future invades our lives, and it is important to look at it closely, not merely from the grand perspectives of history, but also from the vantage point of the living, breathing individuals, who experience it. The acceleration of change in our time is, itself, an elemental force. This accelerative thrust has personal and psychological, as well as sociological, consequences.[7]

Toffler goes on to show the influence of change in every aspect of our daily living, pointing out that most of the material goods that dominate our environment have been developed in the twentieth century. The rate of change increases geometrically and will continue to accelerate in the years ahead. Toffler says: "Western society for the past 300 years has been caught up in a fire storm of change. This storm, far from abating, now appears to be gathering force. Change sweeps through the highly industrialized countries with waves of ever accelerating speed and unprecedented impact."[8]

The elements considered most permanent may become transient. Buildings, often considered the most durable of man's creations, have been added to the growing list of things to be discarded in our throw-away society. Toffler's ideas are supported by Buckminster Fuller, the architect-philosopher, who once described New York City as a "continual evolutionary process of evacuations, demolitions, remodels, temporarily vacant lots, new installations, and repeat." [9] Most people consider building operations blocking the streets of the city to be temporary annoyances that will soon disappear to let the city return to some former state of tranquility. According to Fuller, architectural change will not stop but will be a continuing, ever increasing, part of our environment. With their growing realization that the life of architectural structure is limited, planners talk of plug-in modules for a transient architecture. The core of a building would be engineered to last twenty-five years, and the modules would be replaced when necessary.

In this environment churches now need to evaluate existing and future facilities. Just holding on is no longer adequate. Excessive change is not necessarily good, but rigidity, which will not allow even honest evaluation, can be destructive. Unfortunately, rigidity is a common ailment of the tired dragons. Instead of trying a variety of cures, some churches unswervingly dedicate themselves to a point in time of past glories and live out their remaining years bewailing an unappreciative present.

The church has to evaluate its present goals and programs. Humility is the first, most basic, quality of a successful analysis. A restatement of ancient creeds and religious generalizations is not satisfactory. Changes in society and unrest in the churches, reflected in the decline of church membership and influence, have brought some needed humility into the churches. No longer can the dragons proudly tramp around, spewing forth the fire of moral condemnation. A humble church can be a learning church, and a learning church can grow again, to become not a threatening monster but a servant working for the common good.

An evaluation of a church must begin with a diagnosis similar to the self-appraisal necessary in every therapeutic relationship. The patient suffers from both real and imaginary ills. It is a fact that church attendance is decreasing; it is a speculation that the decrease is caused by the moral decline of society. A good diagnosis will clarify the difference between the realities and the illusions. In most cases illusions are so much a part of our thinking that we become extremely defensive when they are questioned. Psychiatrists have found

one of their greatest difficulties in therapy and analysis is getting the patient to
see himself with some semblance of objectivity. Self-deception seems to be a
human tendency. In the fourth century B.C., Socrates laconically restated an
ancient folk adage when he said, "Know thy self." But truly knowing ourselves is not easy. The problem is even more complex in treating the illusions
of institutions, with their collective memories and diverse needs and motivations.

Stacks of books have been written on the inadequacy of the church, yet it
rambles along unabashed. These books are meaningless unless they can be
translated in relevant terms not just to denominational officials and the clergy
but to the members of the church community. Delusions of purpose are particularly dominant in the religious sphere because of the intangibleness of goals
and values. One procedure that will modify this vagueness is to start as close as
possible to the tangible qualities of church life by becoming aware of the specific programs presently supported by the church. It is easy for members of a
church to engage in long discussions about Christian missions or the services
they would like to perform in the community. The embarrassing question is,
Where is the evidence of these good works?

To avoid fostering any illusions the church may have about itself, a good
first step toward self-understanding is to examine the programs of the church.
These will be the clearest indications of the realities of the church's mission.
The simplest way to begin is to list them. It is important that the list be comprehensive, including all activities, from the weekly newsletter to the annual
fund drive. The list does not require a great deal of organization and can be
made by the governing body in conjunction with the minister. To fully understand the total church programing it may be helpful to categorize the activities to be listed. One obvious category is the allocation of financial resources with the percentage of the total budget devoted to each item. The
minister and volunteer committees might also break down their activities according to the percentage of their total time and expense they require. A small
church does not need an elaborate survey to know that almost all its time and
effort are directed toward the Sunday morning worship service. Larger
churches, with more complex programs and attitudes, will need detailed analysis. The purpose is not to make work for the church but to understand the
church on an objective basis.

In most churches there are no accurate records of time utilization and program costs. The typical church has limited activities and has provided these programs regardless of cost. Most churches have not established priorities because they unquestioningly provided a restricted, traditionally determined group of programs. Until recently, a broader range of activities and alternatives has not been considered. Some churches will be shocked to learn the real cost of providing Sunday services. When building capital and costs of maintenance, secretarial and printing overhead, music, and the minister's time are accurately compiled, the cost per seat could easily be ten dollars. Some urban churches with dwindling congregations meeting on extremely valuable land estimate that with the combination of high capital investment and small attendance the cost per worshiper may run as high as one hundred dollars each Sunday. Many people give money to the church under the illusion that it is charity and that their gift is a contribution to good works, when in reality most of the money is used to maintain Sunday morning services and often inefficient weekday operating procedures.

Other institutions and organizations have evaluated their functions and procedures in light of social changes and have striven to more effectively use all the resources at their disposal. Their buildings are being more fully utilized and their personnel are increasingly more efficient. Churches, however, still focus their resources, buildings, and manpower on one weekly worship service. The secretary still runs off the newsletter on the old mimeograph. The minister continues to spend a large percentage of his time driving to social visits with his parishioners. These functions, performed in the past, the church has continued regardless of expense. With a building used so infrequently and with professionally trained ministers used so inefficiently, it is no wonder that a financial crisis has fallen upon the churches.

The church must now face reality and set priorities for its programs. This can be an occasion for creative thinking and innovative planning. The church does not have to deny its former function but needs to plan new and more appropriate methods of operation. Instead of restricting, the new opportunity can expand and strengthen the religious community. The clergy can be used for more demanding tasks, and lay people can become more involved in the total life of the church. The religious facility can become a center of activity enhancing the lives of its members and the community. Whether a church is planning to build or not, a thorough rethinking of its programs and the utilization of its physical and human resources are necessities. Only through objective self-appraisal will the church begin to inhale new fresh air and look to the future, aware of needs and possibilities in the community.

There are a number of ways to formulate goals, and each church must select the one most suitable for its situation. A church with the tensions of conflict will probably need an approach different from that of a cohesive church looking for new expressions of religious life. The approach of a church overwhelmed with the concerns of an urban setting will differ from that of a small-town church suffering from ennui. Most churches have found it is better to establish a special temporary committee representing the full range of church opinion than to turn the task over to the board of trustees or another previously established group. It may also be valuable to ask young people and new or potential members as well as established members to serve on the committee.

Many denominations have specific recommendations and pamphlets listing suggestions or consultants available to local congregations. Other churches have retreat centers with a consulting staff that can help develop goals. In recent years a number of secular consulting services have been developed, and they may also be helpful to churches.

The setting in which the long-range planning committee meets can influence its success. Most planning groups that try to meet on a weekly basis at the church have encountered a resistant and unenthusiastic response. The most successful groups are those that have gone to a new location, such as a retreat or even a gracious home in a pleasant setting, where the committee is freed from the restraints and habits of traditional church patterning and seems better able to think objectively and creatively. Many groups have found that a full-day session including lunch provides the energy and momentum that will sustain the group through periods of briefer, more regular meetings. Other churches have started with overnight weekend retreats, which have been most successful where people attending weekly meetings would have had to travel long distances or where the planning problems are complex. The only danger with the retreat is that sometimes, in the enthusiasm of the weekend, the group can be carried too far away from the practicalities of church life. This is a major difficulty of weekend sensitivity sessions. Individuals become transformed for the weekend, but there is no realistic carryover into their daily lives. A church planning group can overcome this problem by using both the retreat and the weekly meetings to provide a balance of creative and practical recommendations for revitalized church goals.

Many churches and organizations have had most success defining goals in programs that display an awareness of the current situation but are not limited by it. Idea or buzz sessions are usually most effective when there are no restrictions on the possibilities. One of the best approaches is to begin a long-range planning group with a no-holds-barred brainstorming session, with no qualifications or practical considerations allowed. These sessions are most effective in groups of four or six people because everyone can speak spontaneously. During the session the ideas are recorded, and then at a follow-up session their practicality is evaluated and a list of priorities is established. Maybe only one or two ideas from the entire session will prove original or practical, but these may provide a breakthrough in program development.

General statements will have little value without suggestions for implementing the recommendations. Every goal should include a plan for the first step in implementing it. All long journeys begin with a step, and all maps have no value without the first step forward. A proposed goal of "increasing social concern" could easily remain a platitude, with little meaning to individual church members, in the absence of practical suggestions for beginning socially involved programs. A first step might be the development of a day-care center or a drop-in youth center, or it might be as simple as increasing participation in a worthwhile and ongoing community program.

A most innovative total evaluation program for churches has been developed by Dr. Josiah Bartlett of the Wright Institute in Berkeley, California. The program uses surveys, interviews, retreats, and all-church gatherings. In 1970 Dr. Bartlett said his Vanguard Project is "a fresh approach to people, in terms of themselves and their needs, rather than what they can give or do for the church." The program begins with the formation of a special committee of approximately fifteen people. The members conduct a survey of the church. They do not just mail a typical questionnaire; they personally interview present, potential, and former members. The interviews overcome the problems of structured questions and unmailed returns. The interview stimulates an honest exchange and provides a clear picture of the church and its relationship to the desires and needs of a wide range of people. After completing the interviews, the committee meets in a weekend retreat with Dr. Bartlett to discuss the results and their implications. From these discussions, new goals are formulated. The retreat is the high point of the committee members' involvement and is the most exhilarating and constructive part of the project. The next phase involves a return to the total membership for a series of programs in which the committee presents the findings of the survey, the results of its deliberations, and recommendations. Everyone in the church is encouraged to make comments and suggestions for translating the proposed goals into the daily program of the church. The final phase of the project includes acceptance of the goals by the congregation and the establishment of task-force groups to implement them. Ideally the new directions are also translated into a church budget that allows the redevelopment of resources and staff. As the program has grown, it has become evident that an evaluation of the physical environment of the church is an essential part of translating the goals into the programs of the church.

The project is successful because it overcomes the difficulties of the traditional church survey, which gives only a limited opportunity for members to describe their feelings and attitudes. A personal interview can provide the latitude for reactions necessary for meaningful individual responses. By interviewing former and prospective members as well as the existing membership, the project involves not only those presently satisfied with the church but those who have rejected it and those who might join and help shape its future. The weekend provides an escape from normal activities and aids creative thinking, but even at the retreat the interviews provide a constant contact with the real attitudes and opinions of the total church community. The return to the total membership provides the broad base of concern necessary for the implementation of a revitalized program.

There is not one formula for revitalizing the church membership and its programs. Human beings and their institutions are much more complex than surveys and weekend retreats. The essential point is that the church needs to become aware of what it is doing and what it hopes to do. It needs to decide how it can best use its resources—volunteers, staff, facilities—to implement its goals.

# FULL FUNCTIONING

## MULTIPLE-USE SPACES

In every segment of our society emphasis on full utilization of facilities, equipment, and personnel to increase efficiency and productivity is growing. This long and continuous trend is the inevitable result of the Industrial Revolution. The churches, however, have not kept pace. Other institutions have automated; the church is still hand cranking the mimeograph machine. Other institutions have consolidated personnel, giving employees greater responsibility and more specialized work; the church still relies on poorly paid secretaries and good-willed volunteers. The most significant lack of change is the church's inability to maximize the use of its facilities. Institutions, businesses, and industries have for many years been aware of the high costs of construction and building maintenance. During World War II existing plants increased production by working around the clock to fully utilize machines. The resulting saving in overhead helped justify the costs of new and expensive machinery.

Changes have been equally dramatic in retail merchandising. One of the most familiar examples is the simple hot dog and hamburger stand. These stands used to be randomly placed in inaccessible locations. Usually housed in modest or inadequate structures, they were independently owned and in most cases provided lunch and snacks. Now large chain restaurant organizations that have specialized marketing and real estate staffs purchase property at important crossroads, paying premium prices for choice locations. Initial costs are increased by elaborate, sometimes gaudy, structures for indoor and outdoor service. The high total investment in land and construction is justified, however, through the full utilization of the facilities. The crossroad location makes the restaurant accessible to large numbers of people and serves as a continuous advertisement. Seven-day-a-week service is standard, and many of these restaurants are open twenty-four hours a day. Even if the menu is limited, the use

25

of the building is not. It is designed and managed for nearly continuous use, providing food whenever customers want it. Howard Johnson's, for example, serves everything from an early morning breakfast to a late night snack, and every meal and coffee break in between, any day of the year. Some might call this multiple use. In reality the restaurant is not so much engaged in multiple use as it is in the full utilization of its food-serving facilities. Multiple use is a means to an end. The end is full utilization.

In the church, the question of multiple use is not whether rooms should be used for a number of different functions. The real concern is the full utilization of the facility to fulfill the church's mission. Industry, retail stores, and restaurants use their buildings to capacity. In our society costs and wages are based on increased utilization and resulting productivity. It is difficult to justify the high cost of repairing the roof of a building that is used once a week. Various businesses, on the other hand, are consolidating their facilities into seven-day-a-week utilization and are in a good position to pay the increased costs of roof repair because they have compensated for these expenses by increasing the value of the building through greater use. If church classrooms or nursery facilities were used throughout the week, their costs too would be justified.

In most cases, multiple use is the only way that percentage of use can be increased. Full utilization will be more and more necessary to justify the costs of building and maintaining any structure. Industry and retail stores were forced into full utilization to meet competition. One fully utilized restaurant doing as much business as a chain of five poorly managed restaurants in separate locations obviously will have lower maintenance and mortgage costs and a corresponding increase in profit. Churches are not established for profit, and this has lulled them into thinking they are not influenced by cost factors. However, when construction costs go up for Sears, Roebuck, they also go up for the church. If maintenance costs skyrocket for General Motors, they also skyrocket for religious facilities. The church does not have to face the immediacy of competition, but it does have to face the realities of higher costs. Members are beginning to question the extensive cost of church programs and buildings, and new programs for cost reduction will have to be explored. The problem may have little to do with religious commitment, as some churchmen contend, and a great deal to do with poorly managed and inefficient use of existing funds and buildings. Full utilization is not a panacea for every church, but it is a standard by which to judge building performance.

Two factors are basic to the full utilization of any building. The first is the period of maximum use; the second is the period of minimum use. For most restaurants the period of maximum use is the supper hour on weekends; the period of minimum use is in the midafternoon and late evening during the week. Both factors need to be considered by the designers of the restaurant. The maximum-use period of a church is Sunday morning; the minimum-use period is just about any other time. A full-utilization program should consider the maximum use of space during the peak periods and should increase use during the slack periods. A good solution to space needs during peak periods will help to reduce the problems of full utilization during less demanding times. A church needs to seek every possible solution to space problems during its peak use on Sunday morning in order to reduce its overhead throughout the week.

No one builds for peak use. In the past twenty years churches attempted this impossibility, but recently religious attitudes and financial realities have terminated this trend. Planners of other construction projects, such as highways, have peak usage in mind, but highways are never totally designed for the heaviest possible traffic conditions. If they were designed for peak use, we would need ten times as many highways as we now have, or for every lane presently existing we would need another ten lanes. We cannot afford such a luxury, considering the other needs in our communities. Highways would be vain-glorious sights; with forty lanes instead of four, they would look like concrete ghost towns in the middle of the day. Occasionally, after a hard day's work, we would be pleased with the rapid moving on forty lanes before us, but on the day the taxes were due on the bonds and maintenance charges, we would long for the old four-lane road. The space for the forty-lane highway would destroy more of a city than it would help, as it gobbled up acres and acres of usable land. Those forty lanes of bright glaring empty concrete would be the ultimate in man's folly; yet having forty empty silent rooms in our church schools is still acceptable. The future of the church may be similar to that of the highways. Getting bigger is not the answer. We need a new approach. The highway will not be enlarged, but it will be supplemented by new mass transit systems that will carry people quickly and conveniently. We need the equivalent of mass transit in the church to carry us more effectively into areas of community service, church programing, and shared facilities.

In the past, churches not only planned for peak use on Sundays, they went beyond this to build for possible future peak use. In many cases this meant that on Sunday morning many areas were not fully utilized. Some churches had rooms that were never used. The typical approach to building classroom space was to evaluate the size of the present church school, study community population trends, and project needs for the next ten years. Plans would be designed to meet projected needs, and the financial drive would begin. This approach assumed that grade levels, class sizes, and the entire educational process were static.

Peak use as applied to churches is a reversal of the conventional concept of multiple use, which stresses using the church during the week for nonreligious functions. Full utilization during peak periods requires using all available space, regardless of its normal function, to solve the needs of Sunday morning. This practice is typical in most institutions and businesses. In office buildings, for example, elevators are available for passenger service during the peak hours before and after work. Throughout the day and in the evening some elevators carry freight. The interior walls are padded so they will not be damaged by freight. During periods of peak use by passengers the padding is taken down. Unlike elevators in office buildings, most churches have only one critical time during the week: Sunday morning. There are a number of solutions to this problem, but multiple use is the most obvious. Any rooms not used on Sunday morning should be investigated as possible meeting areas for the church school. Reception spaces, offices, storage rooms, and chapels are all potential classroom space, even if padding must be put on the walls.

The second aspect of multiple use deals with the use of church space for functions during the week. Any church that thinks it has a mission of community service cannot help feeling guilty when there are so many needs for space in the community while the church goes unused. In a time of rapidly increasing construction costs it is a waste of community resources to have individual churches with vast areas of unused space, and it is an even greater crime to multiply this by the number of separate denominational churches in any region. Overbuilding is one of the major reasons for the present concern for curtailing new construction. In many situations, church programs and community service funds have been limited because of mortgage and maintenance expenses. A church should not plan any new buildings unless the rooms are to be used for weekday church programs and community service. Anything else is a perversion of the Christian ethic of service, for it involves living in the most exaggerated extreme of religious luxury while others daily live in poverty.

Multiple room use is complex. It requires careful planning. The spaces need maximum use, with minimum friction. Important in the initial planning is thinking through the entire process of access, environmental control, range of usage, and cooperation among groups using the same space. In the daily working arrangements, coordination of maintenance and equipment should be clearly set forth to allow conflicts to be handled routinely rather than in heated arguments.

The ideals of joint usage are exemplified by four neighbors who engaged in what could be considered one of life's most foolhardy ventures. They purchased a sailboat to be used cooperatively. The problems of such an arrangement can be imagined, yet the neighbors worked them out simply and never had any difficulties. They were able to do this because of advance planning and precautions. At the beginning of the year a schedule was made, and each owner signed up to use the boat on specific weekends. Changes after the initial schedule were between the individuals involved. Even more important, and the particular stroke of genius for this group, was investment in an extended insurance policy that generously covered all possible hazards. For an individual owner the policy would have been too expensive, but the cost shared by four people was quite reasonable. Furthermore, each party knew that any damage problems would be handled by the insurance company instead of becoming a personal matter. The wisdom of this procedure was demonstrated early in the season when one of the owners rammed the boat into the dock on an evening with heavy winds. Repairs cost approximately four hundred dollars, but there were no accusations, no battles. The boat was fixed, and the bill was covered by the extended insurance policy.

Successful multiple use requires the realization that conflicts will arise and that advance planning is needed to solve them as simply and conveniently as possible. A multiple-use room should not be thought of as a typical one-purpose room with more than one group using it. Planning must be based on its use by a variety of people engaged in a variety of activities. This often means planning separate entrances, individual heating controls, a convenient kitchen, and toilet facilities. It also means having more than double the normal storage space, both in cabinets and in auxiliary storage rooms. Advance scheduling is essential. It needs to be clearly understood who is using the area, at what time, and in what way. Occasional conferences of the different parties are necessary to review schedules, air grievances, and plan for the future. In some areas, it is not possible to take out an insurance policy, but it is possible to make arrangements about equipment and storage so that problems can be avoided. The creation of a contingency fund for broken equipment can often prevent aggravation when items are damaged.

Cleaning a multiple-use room may be a problem. Rather than rely strictly upon volunteers' goodwill, it is advisable to hire a custodian. In this way, complaints are not between the users but between the users and the custodian. Volunteers who work long and hard at worthwhile projects often are just too tired or unwilling to serve as the group's custodian. Multiple use is most successful when the parties involved do not see it only as a way of reducing building costs. A properly planned multiple-use room may cost more than a typical single-use room, but the total savings will always be much greater than building duplicate facilities.

The need to make optimum use of buildings has rapidly increased because of rising construction and maintenance costs. Churches are no exception and will increasingly be affected by these cost factors. There is no need to panic and proclaim an end to all religious construction, but there is a need to thoroughly evaluate the use and expense of every church-owned facility. Space within the building has to be fully utilized. Old concepts need to be totally reevaluated; old formulas and patterns are no longer adequate.

Much has been said about the merits and demerits of church building at the present time. In the context of this debate denominational offices and religious authorities have written pamphlets and books on building problems and procedures. Many recent publications have tried to update traditional philosophies. In a number of these books is an introductory chapter about the changes in current religious thinking and architecture, but the remainder of the text is a rehashing of the square-footage statistics and traditional programs that have proved inadequate and wasteful in the past. More than words are needed to shift our thinking into new directions. This is one reason that many churches have difficulty updating their facilities. Floors and walls and ceilings speak more vividly and permanently than the easy flow of the spoken and written word.

To break through the old ways a new approach is necessary. A congregation cannot assume that because a building has difficulties it should automatically move to a new location. Increasingly churches will have to stay in their present location and remodel and rehabilitate. No longer can the church divide into neat committees based on previous needs to solve its building ailments. Old committees will come up with old answers. Perhaps they will add a new topping here and there, but the essential solutions will be the same. New committees must be organized if the present typical construction is to be curtailed.

A new program is necessary to create an environment for the entire church and community. We have to discard the old categories of room use based on Sunday morning scheduling and during-the-week emptiness. No longer is it acceptable to give lip service to community service and design churches to be used only on Sunday. We can no longer talk about flexibility and then allow long rows of unused classrooms. We have to rethink the entire life of the church. In the twentieth century most churches, regardless of denomination, have designed buildings based on a standardized pattern. The room names are familiar and each connotes a definite Sunday morning use. Not one of the rooms is in any way community related. In most churches a few rooms are used during the week, but the emphasis has always been the Sunday morning functions. A list of typical rooms in the standard tired dragon would include the following:

| | |
|---|---|
| narthex | first-grade classroom |
| sanctuary | second-grade classroom |
| chapel | third-grade classroom |
| flower room | fourth-grade classroom |
| choir practice room | fifth-grade classroom |
| parish hall | sixth-grade classroom |
| women's parlor | seventh-grade classroom |
| office | eighth-grade classroom |
| minister's study | high school classroom |
| nursery | kitchen |
| kindergarten | service areas |

Over the years some of the names have been changed (perhaps to protect the innocent), but the rooms have remained essentially the same. The narthex has been renamed the entry; the parish hall has been changed to the fellowship hall; the women's parlor now is called the lounge. In religious education there has been the Akron plan, the Atchison, Topeka and Santa Fe Plan, and numerous other varieties and changes, but the emphasis in every case has been strictly on Sunday morning use. In recent years many churches have discarded traditional architectural styles, but most of the changes have been only on the surface. Inside the building the walls are as rigid as ever, and various functions are performed much as they always have been. If there is to be any substantial change in church life, it must begin with an environment of change, an innovative program that organically relates to the needs of the church today. It is important to remember that this new program is to be used by both new and existing churches. Too often revitalization implies a new building, but this is not the intent. Many recent books on contemporary church architecture make occasional reference to existing buildings, but their tone and direction point to new buildings. Nevertheless, many new buildings are unnecessary. A tired dragon could easily begin the transition to a full-functioning program with modest changes.

In spite of all the words written and spoken about the need for change in religious architecture, when building time comes, most churches end up with a design not unlike that used fifty years ago. The reason for this is the false assumptions of planning committees that consider their function to be designing a church and church school for Sunday morning. As long as this assumption is accepted, churches will be similar to those of the past. A full-functioning environment requires a program that leads to a fully utilized and vital church community center. The building should not be designed just for Sunday morning, with other activities squeezed in during the week. The building, old or new, should be designed to be used throughout the week by church members and the community. This presents a challenge to the church. It in no way implies that the Sunday morning worship service is not important. Indeed, for the foreseeable future Sunday will remain the focus of church activities; most services and religious education programs will continue to be conducted on Sunday. In the full-functioning environment, however, greater consideration is given to the total daily life of the church community, and facilities to be used throughout the week are provided. A full-functioning program limits unnecessary construction and emphasizes the full utilization of every space.

The full-functioning program requires a religious facility that serves as a church community center—a building where young and old are welcome at any time to use a variety of resources and participate in diverse programs. The full-functioning program requires the building to provide activities seven days a week. It incorporates a flexible attitude toward scheduling and room allocation on Sunday mornings. The full-functioning program recognizes that community service should not be an afterthought but should be integral to the life of the church and must be designed into its environment.

The change from planning for one hour on Sunday morning to designing a full-functioning environment of seven-day-a-week religious life creates new space designations:

| | |
|---|---|
| meeting and worship space | media room |
| reception area | projects room |
| minister's conference study | regional service room |
| education classroom office | two kitchens |
| early childhood unit | unfinished room |
| adult program lounge | service areas |
| study library | |

Many of the rooms are adaptations of old spaces to new purposes; others indicate new dimensions within the church. In the following sections each space of the full-functioning program is described and explained. The meeting room, including fellowship space and the chancel area, is considered separately in the next chapter.

## RECEPTION AREA

The reception area should reflect the changes taking place within the rest of the church. If the community is using the building throughout the week, the church office is no longer limited to minor administrative tasks. It serves as an important greeting area. Like all reception areas it should be near the major entrance. It is not important to place the receptionist near the formal sanctuary entrance, which is used mostly for Sunday and special services. The location of the receptionist there has determined the location of many church offices, which are accessible only through long corridors and narrow doorways. The offices are often completely filled with clutter from the unorganized efforts of volunteer workers. Many give the illusion of activity but also reflect the actions of a completely unorganized administrative staff. Stacks of four-year-old sermons, three-year-old newsletters, and two-year-old orders of service collecting dust on cabinets do not speak well for the alertness and ability of the church to deal with this year's problems. The office can no longer be the church secretary's private domain. As a reception area near the main entrance it will be open to the entire church.

The reception area should seem spacious and pleasant. A glass partition between the lobby and the office will combine some privacy with two-way accessibility. The room should have a wide door designed to remain open most of the time. Too many churches have interpreted the designation "office" too literally and have created rooms similar to the principal's office of their childhood grade school, the most prominent feature of which was an imposing counter. Perhaps the church's use of it comes from battle weariness or a subconscious desire to duplicate the returns and complaint counter of the local department store. In any case, a church office does not need the barrier of a thirty-six-inch-high counter. It needs to be informal and inviting. Open space and a reception desk where the secretary can both do her work and help visitors are preferred.

In an existing building a church office not near the major entrance should be relocated there. Some secretaries may feel that their little corner niche tucked away in the farthest recesses of the catacomb is the only place where they can accomplish their work. But if they understand that they are not only secretaries but are also receptionists, they may welcome the move. When the office is changed to a reception area, the clutter should be cleaned out. Depending upon the size of the church, the office can be designed with cabinets for storage. A large church may need a separate room adjacent to the reception area to serve as a storage and work room. The reception area should be large enough to accommodate the receptionist's desk and file cabinets and a work table to be set up for special projects or meetings. With sufficient space and a neat appearance, the office could be used as an auxiliary classroom.

Transforming the church office into a reception area may seem unimportant. For many churches, however, the change will signify the gradual transformation of the church into a center of activity for the members and an important resource for the community.

## MINISTER'S CONFERENCE STUDY

The minister's conference study gives expression to the increased counseling role of the minister. In recent years the study has become less a retreat and more a room where the minister meets with members of the church. This trend will grow as the minister decreases parish visits and encourages members to meet with him at the church. A pleasant office can create an atmosphere that is as hospitable as in a private home. The room can provide a comfortable setting for conversation and individual counseling. It should be large enough to include a desk and an area with comfortable occasional chairs around a small coffee table. This setting encourages informal conversation and breaks down barriers between the minister and visitors. Too often members of the clergy have isolated themselves with artificial barriers such as pulpits, imposing desks, and even clerical garb. Increasingly they will have to be more receptive if they are to be effective in helping and communicating with others. A major first step is the creation of a gracious and hospitable conversation and conference area within the office. This area could be used on Sundays for small church school classes, depending of course on whether the minister uses the office on Sunday morning. During the week the conversation area would be an ideal setting for small discussion groups.

The usual location of a minister's study, adjacent to the reception area, allows the secretary to coordinate appointments. However, some ministers have been extremely pleased with an office somewhat removed from the work area of the church. These offices were along the same corridor as the reception area but not in the midst of the administrative unit. Communication with the secretary was easily handled by intercom. These ministers felt that because so many volunteers and visitors come into the administrative area a greater sense of privacy was needed for both counseling and productive work. The main lesson to be learned from this innovation is there are no inviolable rules of planning. As the functions of the minister and the church change, new ideas should be explored. Regardless of location, the minister's conference study will increasingly be used for conferences and counseling and should be designed to encourage uninhibited communication.

## EDUCATION CLASSROOM OFFICE

In this century religious education programs have gradually developed, and religious education has become a main concern in most churches. Some Sunday school superintendents have been given an office, but churches have never been sure the space was justified. As a result, the office is usually just large enough for a desk, filing cabinets, and storage shelves. It is often so small that it becomes a storage area rather than a functional office. The church's ambivalence toward the director of religious education is indicated by the various places his office has been put. If, when the building was designed, the director was a woman, the religious and cultural assumption was that she should be with the children and her office was located in the classroom wing. If the director was a clergyman, the assumption was that he is an executive and should be in an office in the administrative suite. This distinction should come to an end.

In the full-functioning environment the office of the director of religious education should not be hidden among the maze of classrooms or buried in the administrative suite. In a church of medium size, whether the director is a man or a woman, the office should be near but not in the administrative suite. The room should be accessible from a major corridor. The most important requirement for the director's office is enough space for use both as an office and as a classroom for ten or twelve youngsters. This would allow a large, satisfactory office for the director and would provide a room for small classes. The room could be used as a small meeting or conference area during the week.

Planned and furnished with care, the education classroom office can function as a versatile and active area within the church.

## EARLY CHILDHOOD UNIT

Every community needs preschool programs for children between the ages of one and six. Nursery schools and kindergartens are becoming more important, day-care centers are desperately needed, and in some communities Headstart programs have been limited because of lack of space. Each of these programs needs to be provided because young children need beginning skills in order to adjust to first-grade classes. Children enjoy the social contact in nursery school and kindergarten and develop and learn in stimulating surroundings under trained leadership. Day-care centers and child care programs are vital to the well-being of family life in many areas of a community. According to a HEW publication:

> In supplementing parental care, daytime programs for children are necessary under a variety of circumstances. With the increasing need for women in the labor market, more mothers are working. A large number of these mothers represent "one parent families" where the mother is the sole breadwinner. Physically, emotionally, and mentally handicapped children and their families often benefit from daytime programs as well as those from economically and culturally deprived homes. These programs frequently make it possible to keep children at home when the mother is ill or cannot, for other reasons, assume her full parental responsibility. Daytime programs offer stimulation, development of intellectual capacity, and opportunities for social adjustment so important to children.[1]

Adequate facilities for these programs are scarce. Public schools often do not have the room, other forms of community space are already in use, and available vacant buildings are often too dilapidated, and remodeling too expensive, for preschool care. Thus the many partially used church facilities can be an important source of space for these programs, and churches embarking on a construction program should consider building early childhood spaces that will meet community needs, which in every case will be well suited to church school needs also. In some cases the church will initiate and develop the total preschool program; in others various organizations will develop and operate the center, using facilities provided by the church. In *Day Care: How to Plan, Develop and Operate a Day Care Center,* the authors state: "Day care centers located within larger building units such as churches, public schools, apartment buildings, community centers, are often more economical to maintain and often have the added advantage of being within walking distance of the children's homes." [2] Ronald W. Haase supports this point of view in *Housing for Early Childhood Education:*

> The early childhood education center is the place where the child begins to grow beyond family and home, where he encounters those experiences which contribute to his awareness of himself as a member of a larger community. The location of the center must therefore be accessible to the residential community it serves—convenient, obvious and inviting.

Ideally, it should be within walking distance along safe streets. An alternative is the provision for safe delivery by private car and the proximity to public transportation.[3]

The variety of locations, accessibility by car, and convenient parking can be provided by the church. Even more important is the fact that the church already has fully developed space for preschool programs. No other institution is so well prepared. Operating costs should not be a hindrance because most programs are self-supporting or community subsidized and the church is usually fully compensated for the use of its facility and for utilities and maintenance. The combination of available space and the opportunity to serve the community make weekday early childhood programs an excellent project for churches.

The changing emphasis from Sunday to weekday programs makes it necessary to plan early childhood programs as a single planning unit. The old division of rooms into Sunday crib room, nursery, and preschool room is no longer valid. The space for these functions should be connected to provide for flexible use by the church and the weekly programs. The coordinated arrangement of space can allow a greater variation of total educational use. The church school can decide how to use the rooms on Sunday morning according to the number of infants, toddlers, and older youngsters that are present. In some cases different age groups can share some space for a portion of the morning.

The early childhood unit would allow a similar flexibility for community programs. Whether the area is used for a half-day nursery for learning basic skills, a private kindergarten in a community without public sessions, or a day-care center, the program can most effectively be organized if a variety of spaces are available. Community nurseries and kindergartens can use adjoining rooms for dividing noisy and quiet play, neat and messy activities. Many programs prefer or require a separate area to allow a child to rest and a space for parent conferences and administration. A total unit could provide crib space and nursery and preschool rooms on Sunday. During the week a private kindergarten could use the crib room as an individual rest space, the nursery area as a play space, and the preschool room for adult-directed activities.

Another alternative, depending upon community needs, would be to develop the entire unit—crib room, church nursery, and kindergarten—as a day-care center, with the crib room still a rest area and both larger spaces serving as a total environment for activity, with different interest areas located throughout the rooms. If the rooms were isolated, such flexibility would be difficult, if not impossible. It is also important to realize many community programs require a substantial amount of space in order to have classes large enough to meet operating costs. One isolated room probably would be too small, but several adjoining rooms used together could provide space for the program.

Ample indoor space is needed for play and recreation and for equipment. Most building codes require a minimum of thirty-five square feet of floor space for each pupil. However, space footages need to be flexible. Some rooms and situations require more space than others. Ruth E. Jefferson, director of the Pinellas County License Board for Children's Centers and Family Day Care Homes in St. Petersburg, Florida, explains the need for flexibility:

> Authorities differ on indoor floor space recommendations, but the range from 35 to 60 square feet per child will provide a fair-sized room for a group of from 15 to 20 children. If the group is small the space per child should be increased in order to provide adequate space for the equipment, its use, and for the varied activities of the children. If the same room is used for lunch and afternoon naps as well as for the morning program, it is important that the space be generous so that transition activities can take place smoothly.[4]

The early childhood unit should be easily accessible. Parents should be able to safely leave and pick up their children. Ideally, they should be able to let their children off at the doorway. A teacher should be at the door to guide the children. The early childhood area is most suitable when it can be separated from the rest of the building and have a separate entrance, heating controls, and toilets. This will allow effective building control and economical maintenance. The area should be near a kitchen facility. Serving snacks and drinks is important in most preschool programs, and in day-care programs it is imperative. The unit should be gaily decorated. It should have large windows and an adjacent outdoor protected play area. The most important consideration for the use of the room by more than one group is extensive storage space, including not only an auxiliary storage room but storage cabinets for small articles. The total amount of storage space will be considerably influenced by the relationship between the church and community programs. If large equipment is shared, less storage space will be needed.

In an existing building the nursery and preschool programs may need to be relocated. In many old churches children are tucked away in some far corner of the basement so that their exuberant sounds will not disturb adult services. This buried location is usually far from entrances, legally unacceptable, and notorious for uncontrollable heating. The early childhood unit should be near an entrance, at ground level if possible, and where heating and cooling can be managed. Decoration of the room should take into account its use by youngsters. It should not be painted sleepy green but should be white or a light color, with bright accents of color. The room should be decorated with drawings, pictures, paintings, and mobiles to create a three-dimensional environment.

The traditional concept of the individual crib, nursery, and preschool rooms needs to be reevaluated in light of changing educational patterns and community needs. These rooms need to be considered within the context of a total early childhood unit. The church can provide important assistance in the daily needs of member and community families through early childhood programs within the church facilities. These programs are a natural extension of church life; they are child centered and well within the capabilities and finances of any church. They do not require elaborate technical facilities, or do they require huge amounts of investment capital. The combination of available facilities and the opportunity to serve the needs of the community make the weekday nursery, kindergarten, or day-care center an ideal and necessary program for the church.

## ADULT PROGRAM LOUNGE

The increase in adult programs in every church makes space for these activities imperative. Many churches use religious education rooms for adult programs. These rooms are filled with children's furniture and decorations. The setting is funny for the first few meetings, but the novelty soon wears off because everyone has to sit in miniature chairs at a tiny table, with their knees in front of their faces. Another room often used for adult programs is the lounge or women's parlor. In many churches this is the most unused room in the entire building and in some cases is more a monument to the past than the sanctuary is. Too often the parlor has served as the collecting place for gifts to the church. The chairs are often antiques, beautiful to look at, valuable, but not suitable for creating an informal atmosphere. The walls are usually decorated with paintings of historical figures. In many churches the key to the room is guarded by the women's service group. When locations are sought for adult programs, the parlor is always mentioned, but getting permission to use it and acquiring the key are more difficult than singlehandedly slaying a dragon. The lounge is the stronghold of the traditions of former times.

New churches have planned adult lounges that have overcome many of the problems of the women's parlors, but these new rooms still have inadequacies. They are usually too large for small group discussions. Too often it is necessary to furnish them with sofas so large that they cannot be conveniently moved. Instead of having a friendly atmosphere, the room becomes rigidly formal. The adult lounge is better than a third-grade classroom, but not so good as it should be.

Some members have performed a flanking movement past the women's parlor and the classrooms and have begun to meet in individuals' homes. To the surprise of some, these settings have proved more conducive to informal programs than the church. Residential game rooms, family rooms, and living rooms are designed for adult activities and conversation, and even the most formal areas have a scale and style more supportive of human interchange than the typical institutional setting. Residential rooms usually have well-designed informal seating. The decor is usually simple, and the floors have some carpeting. The hostess usually provides cold drinks or coffee, adding a pleasant dimension of hospitality. Many have found houses so compatible that they have become the permanent site of adult discussion programs.

Meetings in the home do present some difficulties. Most significant is location. It is easy to get lost in a suburban tract of look-a-like houses. Even though residential interiors are well suited to informal adult activities, houses are not designed for easy access and convenient parking. Churches should provide a setting combining the best features of accessible and convenient public meeting space with the qualities of a home environment.

The adult program room should not be a memorial to the past, nor should it be a children's school room. It should be designed for active adults. The room need not be completely carpeted, but it should have some carpeting to absorb sound and soften the harshness of most institutional settings. Wall decoration should not be limited to historical remnants but should include contemporary design. The room should probably be about the same size as a large living room or game room. The recommended conversational unit is from eight to twelve feet in diameter.[5] The room should permit a convenient arrangement of furniture for small groups and for larger groups of up to twenty-five people. A large round coffee table is particularly conducive to informal discussion. The table can be used for books, papers, and coffee cups, and yet does not have the rigidity of the typical full-height rectangular arrangement. In general, the furniture should be comfortable but light enough to be easily moved. A friendly atmosphere can be encouraged by varied styles of chairs, instead of the uniformity of institutional furniture. The room should be cheerful and comfortable, with individual lamps similar to those in a residential game room; rows of fluorescent lights completely destroy the desired informality. A feature that is inexpensive and provides excellent lighting flexibility is a rheostat switch, which will allow the lights to be dimmed and brightened.

In an existing building one of several rooms may be adapted for adult programs. A religious education room can easily be converted for adult use, and it still could be used on Sunday mornings for religious education. On Sunday morning, children would meet in the adult atmosphere. The room that is probably most closely allied to an adult program environment is the church lounge. These rooms are usually large, well furnished, carpeted, and have interesting amenities such as fireplaces. The principal difficulty with them is that they are usually not well separated from the rest of the building. To be used as an adult program room the lounge needs to be isolated, so that a group meeting there will not be disturbed by every entry and exit into the church.

The area for the adult program should not be used just for informal discussion groups. If properly arranged, it can be used for a wide variety of church and committee meetings. We have too long assumed that committee meetings are work and should be formal and dull. Every church has a conference room suffering from many of the defects of the women's parlor. It has a large immovable table at its center. These rooms remain unchanged over the years and have the consistent failing of being inadequately lighted and decorated. Meetings of the board of trustees, the religious education committee, or the worship committee are always held there. In this setting individuals take on the airs of corporation executives, thinking they are making momentous decisions, while all they are deciding is the type of lock to put on the front door. The church needs creative ideas and informal human conversation rather than pretended earth-shaking pronouncements. Everywhere people are becoming aware of the need for more informal planning meetings. Robert's Rules of Order notwithstanding, meetings with formal agendas and dull reports are disappearing. New agendas are being devised placing important business first, followed by lesser categories, to ensure that the important issues will be considered. Even with administrative changes many boards and committees still find their meetings very stiff, and as long as they are conducted in the stodgy setting of the conference room, they will remain so. More church meetings should be held in the informal setting of the adult program environment, whether it be an adapted lounge, a modified conference room, a redecorated classroom, or a room specially designated for adult meetings.

The atmosphere of the adult program lounge will encourage the honest exchange of views rather than pompous rhetoric. The room will combine the warmth and hospitality of a home setting with the convenience and accessibility of a well-marked public building. An informal adult program lounge designed for small and medium groups can be a significant asset to the church in developing a religious community.

## STUDY LIBRARY

Many churches have developed their own libraries. Often used as wall decoration in parlors and lounges, they consist of the membership's attic discards and rummage sale leftovers. The classic color of the bindings is black, with a thin layer of dust. The books usually are not arranged in order, and to find one contemporary selection, the potential reader must push aside nine volumes of collected local essays or turn-of-the-century histories. In most cases there has been little attempt to retain the dust jackets, feature popular writings, or make the books attractive in any way. In recent years public libraries have learned that their purpose is not only to preserve books but also to encourage people to read them. Many church libraries are still in the era of preservation rather than circulation.

The church can learn not only about books but about architecture from the dramatic changes that have taken place in libraries in the past fifty years. Most early libraries were conceived as public benevolences, donated to a community by wealthy prominent citizens as their memorial. A sense of sanctity permeated the entire library; even the books had an air of holiness. The mood was hushed, not only to allow others to read but to revere the accumulated knowledge of Western man collected in honor of the departed. In recent years libraries have come to realize they should be not public monuments but necessary and vital resources in the community. They are learning centers, and this change has been reflected in their architecture. No longer are libraries austere pseudo-temples; they are convenient buildings welcoming the public. The change from closed stacks, in which only staff members were allowed, to open shelves was significant and reflected the dramatic change in values. No longer were books considered so precious that only trained personnel could handle them, and no longer were people considered so careless that they could not be trusted. The church, like the libraries, needs to emerge from the ominous hush of the past and become an inviting and active place.

If books of current interest are available, the library can become a vital part of the church's mission. The church library needs to have a balance of fiction and nonfiction, philosophy and religion, light and serious works. The church has the opportunity to extend its stimulation by creating an up-to-date library, which will be an important part of the educational direction of religious life. New books can be featured on the library shelves and at special tables set up in the lobby or fellowship hall. Many large churches have book sale tables where a variety of books are sold as a convenience for the members and as a fundraising venture for the church. If the minister, study discussion groups, or others related to the church refer to particular books, these should be available in the library. A church library can easily afford a wide variety of paperback books; they are inexpensive, convenient to carry, and attractive.

Like all rooms in the full-functioning environment, the study library could be used as a classroom on Sunday morning. It would be an ideal classroom setting for one of the intermediate groups. The study library could serve the church members and the community throughout the week and the church school during the hours of peak usage.

The room would add another important dimension to church life. With increasing numbers of people of all ages engaged in the educational process, the church building can become a place for individual study. Many find it difficult to study at home, and school and public libraries are often crowded.

A church study library would be quiet, familiar, and convenient. The church would provide adequate parking, usually missing from public institutions. In most cases, the individual would not need much reference material. With the use of paperbacks and the free circulation of books from larger libraries, a place for quiet study is much more important than a large collection of reference books. The church can provide amenities such as hot water for coffee and a generally more human atmosphere than the large institutional library. Depending upon the size of the church, special keys could be made available for members who apply to use the room on an individual basis. The room could also be available with moderate supervision during the weekdays and evenings and could be open to the entire community as well. In contrast to the usual rows of darkened windows characteristic of many churches during the evening hours, the lighted windows of the church study library would be heartening and inspiring.

## MEDIA ROOM

The electronic communications media will increasingly become a major influence in our daily living. This is especially true for today's young people, who still need to be aware of the past but also need experience and training to cope with the future. Values and beliefs will be shaped and influenced by the media, and religious groups must face this new challenge. In the words of Marshall McLuhan:

> Today in our cities, most learning occurs outside the classroom. . . . This challenge has destroyed the monopoly of the book as a teaching aid and cracked the very walls of the classroom. . . . Today we're beginning to realize that the new media aren't just mechanical gimmicks for creating new worlds of illusion, but new languages with new and unique powers of expression.[6]

A great deal is being written about adapting to the media through the use of audio-visual materials. The media approach is considered the wave of the future. However, it usually sinks in the classroom because it is not buoyed up with technical competence. Media use requires retraining of the teachers and, equally important, changes within the building. Teachers need to develop the skills of full media presentation and become knowledgeable about available equipment. Many viewers, both children and adults, have struggled with a muffled soundtrack or an out-of-focus picture. Most rooms used for films have poor ventilation and no light control. If audio-visuals are to be used successfully, higher standards of presentation are needed. This is true in public schools and in the church.

Media presentations are not intended to replace the work of individual church school teachers with individual children. In the future, religious education will still emphasize the individual. Films should be a complementary activity, not a substitute for a church school program. It is unreasonable to expect every church school teacher to be able to operate technical equipment. Several trained people who are particularly interested and skilled in this area should be responsible for media presentations.

A media room in the church can serve many functions. It is unnecessary to adapt every church school room for film showing. One well-designed room can effectively serve the needs of the entire church school. Short filmstrips require little preparation and can be shown in any space. Films require much more preparation and would be best presented in the media room.

A media room should be designed for convenient and proficient presentation of films, overhead projections, and taped and recorded sound. It needs acoustical sound control, with particular attention to absorption surfaces and insulated doorways. The interior lighting should be variable, controlled by a rheostat, and exterior lights should be controlled by darkened window shades. The room should be supplementally wired to provide full voltage requirements, and a wide flexibility of outlet locations should be provided by plug-in strips. A full range of audio-visual equipment, depending on the size and budget of the church, should be available—film projectors, slide projectors, screens of various sizes, tape recorders, overhead projectors, video recording equipment, quality speakers, and slide and tape coordinating equipment. A special room with wide shelves should be provided for storage. Standard equipment would include projector tables and other accessory furnishings.

The purpose of the room is to provide not only a space for film showing but an environment for experimentation. Strobe lights, volume sound equipment, and other kinds of audio and visual equipment could be utilized. The room would lend itself to the creation of a totally electronic environment and could serve as a workshop laboratory throughout the week. Many contend that all forms of education should be oriented toward the future. A media room could be a step toward providing all persons in the church with an opportunity to become aware of the communication and expressive possibilities of the electronic media.

An extension of the media room would be a photographic darkroom. With the increased interest in photography and the expense of and limited space for constructing individual darkrooms, it would be natural for the church membership to build one cooperatively. Like all shared ventures, the darkroom should have an adjacent room or large cabinet for the storage of individual supplies. In some cases the church could provide the developing equipment and enlarger; in others the church would provide the space, and the equipment would be purchased by the photographic club or each individual would provide his own. Some might argue that a photographic darkroom has no relationship to the church. However, the church of the future will increasingly emphasize its function as a cooperative community, whose members share their special interests and talents, united by a common faith. It is well within the tradition of most religions to work cooperatively on various endeavors.

The media room and darkroom would provide a stimulating environment for a photography group, film experimentation, and total media presentations. The media room would be used by church school during peak periods on Sunday mornings. It would be assigned to a class, especially one likely to make extensive use of films or other media. From time to time other classes could also use the room for film presentations: the occasional need to change the location of the class would be compensated for by the convenience of the simple preparation for film showings. The media room could become one of the most exciting and most-used rooms in the church.

## PROJECTS ROOM

Contemporary religion should be concerned with the development of the whole individual. Creative sensibilities as well as spiritual and intellectual dimensions should be awakened. Through a program for art and hand-crafted projects, self-expression and self-worth can be enhanced, and individuals can become more appreciative of the struggles of artists and gain new insights into artistic works. In *Art and Religion,* Von Ogden Vogt stated, "The very nature of artistry is activity. Works of art are described as creations. Whatever may be said about the appreciation of beauty, art is the production of beauty. Artistry is expression, liberation, outgoing effort, authorship, origination." [7] A working knowledge of the arts is more meaningful than the typical art appreciation course.

The term "projects" is used to indicate the range of activities possible. The projects room should provide facilities and surfaces for work with ceramics, collage, painting, sculpture, weaving, carving, woodcraft, and other artistic materials and media. Work in this area could be stimulated by scheduling classes for children and adults in the week, during the day and evening. It is much easier for one art instructor to travel from a nearby school or college to the church than it is for twenty people to travel to the outskirts of town to attend a class. Another advantage is that the participants can continue their projects at the church during free periods.

The projects room would also be available for those not attending formal classes. One of the difficulties many people have in undertaking art projects is the inconvenience of setting up equipment at home. Many people, particularly in apartments, do not have adequate working and storage space. Good lighting is also a problem. Many novice craftsmen feel they would be better stimulated if they had others with whom to work. If a projects room were established within the church, two members could plan to meet during a scheduled free period and work together. Another convenience of the church location is the possibility that babysitting will be available in the building during the day. Usually the local arts and science center or the university has no facilities for babysitting. The project room at the church would enable the young mother to find meaningful and enjoyable creative activity outside her home.

The projects room should be large enough for work areas of all kinds. It should be well lighted, with natural light from a northerly or easterly direction. Its artificial lighting should be at a higher intensity than in other areas of the building. Extensive storage space is needed: two walls completely lined with shelves from floor to ceiling. Some of these could be open, but most of them should have simple doors. These units do not have to be elaborately finished cabinets; they can be simply and economically designed. To most craftsmen there is nothing more precious than the initial venture into the realm of creativity. Some would guard their first efforts in a bank vault if possible. Because of this protective instinct, generous space to store projects between work sessions is imperative. The storage area is basic to the success or failure of the projects room. If people feel free and secure in leaving their materials and work at the church in storage cabinets, the projects room will become an active vital area. If, however, work is damaged during the week, and materials lost, the room will lose much of its value. Thus it is far better to provide too much storage space than not enough.

Like other rooms in a full-functioning environment, the projects room would be used during the peak period on Sunday as a class area. Some churches provide alternate programs of study and activity, and the projects room would be a natural environment for the activities curriculum. It could also serve as a large, well-lighted classroom. If there is proper storage for equipment and uncompleted work, the room could be used for every group in the church school.

The projects room could be the most active room in the church throughout the week. It would provide a place unmatched in institutions or the home for individual creative effort. Perhaps from the easels of the new projects rooms, new emblems and insignia for the onrushing dragon rejuvenators will be designed.

## REGIONAL SERVICE ROOM

The regional service room is to be used as a base of operations for both church-initiated service projects and community organizations. It could be a center for church members working on programs related to ecology, education, or any number of issues important to the well-being of the community. A separate service room would allow for active involvement without interfering with the reception area and administrative unit. Depending upon the extent of the church's involvement, community organizations could share the room. It could be a local center for well-established community programs such as the Red Cross, nurses' auxiliary, and the League of Women Voters. In some churches the room could be the center for peace groups, civil rights organizations, and planned parenthood programs. The various groups would work out a schedule, allowing a number of organizations to use the room.

The regional service room should be equipped with cabinets so each group could have its own locked storage space. A separate storage area would also be available for the church school class. The room would, of course, also be a classroom. It would be smaller than some of the other rooms, with a capacity of fifteen or twenty students. The room should be equipped with adjustable tables to be used during the week by the various service organizations and on Sunday morning by the church school.

The regional service room is not intended to be the sole contribution of the church to regional concerns. It is just a practical and inexpensive way to house diverse organizations related to the interests of the church. Church members participate in many organizations both in the church and in the community. For the church to use the equivalent of one classroom for a variety of these organizations is quite reasonable. This arrangement is certainly much more sensible than the vacuum in space and in involvement that exists in churches. Many active people feel the church should be more responsive to community issues.

Each church should establish its own procedures and policies for the regional service room. The church may well decide to provide modest but needed community programs. The regional service room in no way implies that the remainder of the building should not be used for community work. Other rooms in the full-functioning environment can be used for scout meetings. The projects room may be used for an arts program; the adult program lounge could be set up as a regional clinic. In a full-functioning environment, the entire church serves its members and reaches out into the community.

In contrast to organizations formed for special causes, the church is often weak and inactive. However, cause-oriented groups also have problems. The emotional intensity of the individual at the peak of involvement is difficult to sustain, and support for a particular concern can diminish rapidly. By combining the intense commitment of many small organizations with the long-range institutional commitment of the church, a merger can be made that will enhance the contribution of both to social concerns.

## TWO KITCHENS

Group dining has always been an expression of unity. Throughout the Bible and within our religious heritage are examples of shared meals and feasts to celebrate human community and the bountifulness of life. The celebration of Thanksgiving shows the significance of dining as a shared experience. The first Thanksgiving began with religious services followed by three days of festivities. There was no question of whether it was a religious or a secular activity; it was a community sharing together the fruits of their labors in the sight of their God.

The changes taking place in our culture are reflected in the changes in our dining habits. We have long had a strong family tradition reinforced by common dining. The entire family used to gather at the table, with the seat at the head of the table occupied by the head of the household. Everyone was expected to be at the meal. Eating together was basic to the family and social structure. This tradition has been weakened by changing social and economic conditions. Teenagers have increased spending power, and there has been a corresponding rise in the consumption of hot dogs and hamburgers. In an affluent society the young people become less dependent upon the family for their meals. Hamburger stands are not causing the disintegration of the family, but they represent an element in contemporary society that conflicts with the traditional functions of common purpose and sharing in family life.

Attitudes toward church suppers also reflect changing values and living patterns. The importance of commercial restaurants has rapidly increased. The fastest growing are those serving modestly priced foods, catering to young families. More specialized restaurants, which provide exotic settings, cocktails, and gourmet menus, are also expanding. People are willing to spend money for elegance and variety in their dining. Except in small towns, church suppers are disappearing. At the serving end, in the kitchen, young church women are increasingly reluctant to spend their weekend preparing suppers at the church. Many women work or have other responsibilities and are not thrilled by a weekend of kitchen tasks.

With the changing attitudes and the decline of church suppers, it is necessary for the church to have a flexible kitchen arrangement. Instead of one overly equipped kitchen, present needs call for smaller, more strategically located kitchen areas. There is still a need for a principal kitchen, but equipping it with expensive commercial refrigerators, special cooking areas, steam trays, warming pans, and other elaborate institutional cooking equipment is no longer necessary. Even at the peak of supper success, the purchase of this equipment was questionable for a once-a-week meal. It has been speculated that to truly amortize the cost of the kitchen and its equipment the church women would need to charge more than five dollars a meal. Churches are now becoming aware that providing space for fund-raising events that bring in pennies does not justify expending dollars for mortgage payments.

Because of the trend toward light meals and prepackaged and home-cooked foods, the church kitchen can adequately function with several home-style ranges and residential refrigerators. Often these can be donated or purchased at discount prices. Many women feel more comfortable and can work more efficiently with familiar home appliances than with complicated specialized equipment. Residential equipment is flexible and can be moved and replaced simply. The new kitchen must have enough space for several women to work at one time. In the past the kitchens were overdesigned and became too large. Many newer kitchens, however, are too small. Just because the kitchen uses residential equipment, it should not have the space limitations of a kitchen at home. Whether for a casserole meal, a pancake breakfast, or a full supper, there will be several people in the kitchen and they will need room to move. There should be plenty of counter and floor space and an ample work area. Two sinks or a double sink are a necessity. The one additional piece of equipment the church might consider is a dishwasher, depending upon the amount of suppers at the church.

The second or auxiliary kitchen might consist of a small unit combining a stove, refrigerator, and sink, or it could contain individual appliances. The auxiliary kitchen can be located in a variety of areas, depending upon the total plan of the church and the location of the principal kitchen. It could be placed in the religious education wing, where punch and crackers can be prepared, or in the adult lounge area, where light refreshments could be served during the week. To perform the simple task of boiling water for coffee it is more convenient to go to a small kitchen nearby than to travel down long corridors to a large kitchen full of complicated specialized equipment.

With the increasing importance of the nursery and preschool programs, the kitchen or the auxiliary kitchen should be located to service the early childhood unit. In the future, the preschool spaces will be used more than any other. Most nurseries and kindergartens provide snacks, and day-care programs provide hot lunches. Church members might prepare a supper once every two months, whereas the day-care facility will be preparing a hot lunch every day and definitely needs adequate kitchen space. These needs will have to be coordinated into the total kitchen plan.

There has to be variety in the implementation of the two-kitchen concept. Perhaps a small church could justify only one kitchen, but it should consider the community nursery and preschool center as well as fellowship dinners when determining the location of the kitchen. The basic principle of the two-kitchen concept is to be aware of the changing patterns of dining and food preparation. Large institutional kitchens are no longer necessary or justifiable;

smaller kitchens equipped with residential appliances are satisfactory. A second or auxiliary kitchen in part of the building away from the main kitchen can greatly simplify ordinary kitchen tasks and make possible the full utilization of the building.

## UNFINISHED ROOM

Few building programs purposely include an unfinished room. There is the occasional addition or new building constructed with the hope that the membership will someday complete the unfinished rooms. Even though initially unfinished, these rooms are finished as soon as possible, depending upon the enthusiasm of the member hand-crafters. The unfinished room of the full-functioning program is left unfinished permanently, not to save money or allow volunteer completion but to provide a neutral background for a constantly changing environment.

In the past religion taught children to take care of church property. Even in their most active exercises children were supposed to maintain self-discipline so that the building would not be marred and would continue unchanged for another hundred years. This attitude has prevailed in many public education programs, and in their own home children are placed in adult settings and told to respect them. With home, school, and religious environments so restrictive, young people seek other, more relaxed and informal, settings. The church could provide a constructive solution to this situation by allowing at least one room to remain unfinished and be available as a constantly changing environment for the young people, a room in which they can create an environment of their own. It would not have to be limited to youth use, but it would be primarily for them.

In a new building the room would probably be unpainted and might not have a finished floor. Young people would be encouraged to develop the environment in any way they saw fit. Murals could be painted or applied to the walls, floor and wall colors selected, and any other decorative ideas implemented. Many churches already have rooms that could easily be turned over to the young people. This does not mean that young people are required to use only their room but that the unfinished room is theirs for their own development. Such a room could give the young people a sense of identity as a part of the church and foster responsibility for maintaining their meeting space.

Many adults might be startled by the vivid colors and imaginative furnishings, but the unfinished room might be just what is needed to stimulate the tired dragon.

The unfinished room would provide an environment of endless developmental possibilities, as does in fact the total full-functioning church program. The full-functioning environment itself remains unfinished to the degree that it stimulates the church to adopt, adapt, and create new full-functioning environments.

## SERVICE AREAS

The location of service areas, often called the auxiliary spaces, such as entries, corridors, and bathrooms, can play an important part in the full utilization of the building. Poorly planned corridors and improperly placed bathrooms can limit the varied functions within the church. The entry should not only be inviting, it should provide a key to the circulation of the people within the facility. This area can serve as a means of separating different groups according to their purposes. In all architectural planning, whether for a public library, a professional office, or a social service agency, control of the entrances is an essential design element. In the case of churches this means designing the passageways to restrict access in the building to limited areas.

The children in the early childhood suite should not be able to run around the entire building but should be limited to their own area; a nonmember attending a community meeting only needs to use the portion of the building where the meeting is being held. A waiting room adjacent to the main meeting room can make the room especially appropriate for community use because the remainder of the building can be isolated. This type of separation can encourage the church to expand its policies of community use because only portions of the building are needed for each program. Reciprocally, most organizations using the building would prefer to limit their responsibilities while they are there.

Closely related to the control of entrances is the necessity of coordinating all elements of planning. Many buildings have carefully controlled and separated entrances but have toilets in the basement or down a long corridor, thus forcing the entire building to be opened for every gathering. If the toilets were located in the entry area, the meeting room could function independently. This may mean, especially in large structures, that more than one set of toilet facilities for men and women will be needed: one set to serve the main meeting rooms used by the church and a variety of outside groups and another set in the early childhood suite to allow the same type of independent use of these rooms. The building does not need toilets for every room. In fact, in a small church one set may be adequate, but it is important that they are located so that they can support the development of a full-functioning environment. Large churches would almost always be best served by toilets in different locations even if installing them meant slightly higher costs. Someday building codes may allow both sexes to use the same toilets, which would facilitate more variable and less expensive planning.

Perhaps the most significant of the many service areas in the full-functioning environment are the storage areas. In order for different groups to share space, it is necessary to provide adequate storage for each. This cannot be too strongly emphasized. Although shared space requires some additional expenditures, largely for storage to ensure smooth operating, in the long run the shared space is money saving. It is also important to distinguish between the storage traditionally available in abundance in church basements, which collect everyone's discards, and the active storage necessary for full functioning. Our concepts of storage need to be expanded to include self-storing equipment. As an example, individual self-stacking chairs can remain in a room and require only a minimum of space. In the early childhood area, storage cases with connecting hinges that join the front, leaving only the solid backs exposed, are another effective, self-contained way to store equipment. There is still no substitute for a nearby storage room to place unsightly, bulky items out of the way. These areas can be held to a reasonable size as long as they are limited to the storage of items in continual use. Items used once a year should be stored in less valuable secondary areas in remote parts of the building.

Some rooms can be turned into foyers, and doors can be added within existing corridors to provide the limits necessary for restricting access to portions of the building. In some cases, additional toilets may be necessary to allow more controlled building use. These are never inexpensive, but if held to a minimum they may provide new functional capability to an entire wing of the building. Depending upon available space, the church might even convert a room into a storage area to serve several areas, thereby allowing increased vitalization and use of the other rooms.

Service areas are more than filler spaces between rooms; they are important life lines of service necessary for the full functioning of the building. They should be planned with care and consideration of the intended use of the facility. With minor alterations to limit circulation, most churches could expand their policies of community building use. Equally important, division of storage into active and inactive and more self-storing furnishings can enhance the utilization of the full-functioning environment.

## RELIGIOUS EDUCATION

The full-functioning environment will in no way limit religious education programs. In many situations it will enhance them. The rooms in the full-functioning environment create a wide variety of possibilities for religious education. No longer are the rooms designated for all time as the third-grade or the fourth-grade room. Each year every unit of instruction is assigned to the most suitable rooms. Grades one through twelve will use various rooms, depending upon the curriculum of the church school. Many churches are using a varied schedule within their church school program to provide variety for the children and shorter instruction periods for the teachers. With so many time demands and diversions, retaining good teachers for a full year is difficult. Teachers now work in teams and accept unit assignments of eight or ten weeks. With this increased flexibility in teaching and programs, the rooms also need to be flexible. If the fourth grade is going into a curriculum unit using films, the media room would be the natural location for the class. If they are to work on artistic activities, the projects room would be ideal. If the class is to be engaged in biblical or historical studies, the study library or adult program lounge would be appropriate. Room flexibility would permit adaptation to variations in class size. In a mobile society predicting class size from one year to the next is not always easy. In previous rigidly fixed classrooms one area would be designated the fourth-grade classroom and designed for twenty-five students. One year the class might have thirty-five students and the next only twelve. One year the room was too small; the next it was too large. A full-functioning program would allow more flexibility. A small fourth-grade class could easily use the education classroom office for a study seminar, and a large fourth-grade class could use the adult program lounge. Variation in available areas allows a suitable allocation of rooms according to function and class size.

A church with a full-functioning program is well suited for the complete utilization of the facilities on Sunday morning. The following list is a sampling of the rooms allocated for church school classes in a curriculum based on grade levels:

| Class | Room |
|---|---|
| nursery | community nursery |
| kindergarten | preschool area |
| first grade | projects room |
| second grade | media room |
| third grade | regional service room |
| fourth grade | educational classroom office |
| fifth grade | adult program lounge |
| sixth grade | study library |
| seventh grade | reception area |
| eighth grade | minister's conference study |
| high school | unfinished room |

Another trend in religious education is the development of the activity-centered curriculum, in which classes are fixed not by grade level but by general age and interest. One class may study the Old Testament and have children in grades four through six. At the same time another group of fourth-, fifth-, and sixth-graders will be working on special constructions in the projects room. At the same time, some of the sixth-graders will be learning about audio-visual materials through an in-depth study of a biblical character through films. The activity-centered program is based on the assumption that children learn best when motivated by their own interests. The Bible can be approached in creative ways through hand-crafts, writing, role playing, and individual study. Reading and lecturing are not nearly so effective. Some decry the new ways and long for the good old days, but because of television and improved educational techniques used in public schools, children expect a competent and engrossing presentation.

A building designed or altered to provide a full-functioning program is ideally suited to activity-oriented teaching. The following schedule shows the room allocation of a typical activity-centered church school unit.

| *Activity* | *Room* |
|---|---|
| nursery | community nursery |
| kindergarten | preschool area |
| "Hello People" program (grades 1–2) | regional service room |
| projects (grades 1–4) | projects room |
| New Testament study (grades 3–4) | study library |
| Bible films (grades 3–6) | media room |
| introduction to the Old Testament (grades 5–6) | adult program lounge |
| music and religion (grades 6–8) | education classroom office |
| comparative religions (grades 7–8) | unfinished room |
| contemporary issues discussion group (grades 9–12) | reception area |

A large church may need additional classroom space to provide adequate rooms for all the classes. It may need more than one of each of the full-functioning rooms. Possibly it would need two adult program lounges or, if there is a large teenage enrollment, more than one unfinished room. The same is also true of the preschool area, the nursery, and the projects room. Another possibility is to follow the current trend in public education and connect several of the rooms together into one large space.

The full-functioning program is based on the principle of the complete utilization of the facilities. The specific rooms that have been mentioned are suggestions; churches may have their own ideas or special interests that can expand program possibilities. The essential point is that no room should be built only as a Sunday classroom.

A special children's chapel has deliberately not been recommended. With the emphasis on small, intimate sanctuaries and increasing family services, the average church should be able to comfortably use the main sanctuary for all forms of worship services.

Some may argue that the emphasis on weekly activities in the building will detract from the program of the church school and that children will not feel at home in a room designated for other purposes. In reality, a full-functioning environment will make the children more, not less, appreciative of the church. They will see it as a place of excitement and activity rather than as a hollow building visited under duress in uncomfortable clothes once a week. The atmosphere of the various rooms will encourage activity, learning, and experience in the place of meaningless memorizing. Children will become aware of activities within the church and the community. A fully equipped nursery and kindergarten, justified by full use during the week, will be an exciting environment for young children. The projects room and its atmosphere of constructive activity and creative direction will stimulate groups of all ages. Young people will appreciate the films and sound equipment in the media room. They will enjoy the relaxing comfort and freedom of the adult program lounge and the adventure of the unfinished room. The full-functioning environment is adaptable to both grade-level and activity-centered curricula. The full-functioning program improves the environment for religious education and enhances the quality of religious life.

## FULL-FUNCTIONING ENVIRONMENT

No church has to immediately implement all these suggestions for the full-functioning program. They are a goal. If a church plans to create a full-functioning environment, it can establish a long-range plan, developing a new program area each year.

A community nursery is desperately needed in many communities and would be an ideal first step. Churches are perhaps in the best position to create these centers for children because of their already equipped preschool facilities and convenient parking. Or other programs can be initiated, depending upon the particular circumstances of the area. A church in a community with a large number of people attending local colleges may decide to begin by developing the study library, which does not require a lot of money; it requires only a change of attitude within the church. An existing classroom or lounge could easily be converted into a study by the addition of tables and chairs and reading areas. The book collection would not need to be large, for the emphasis would be on developing a study facility. Another church may set up a media room first because of the enthusiasm and knowledge of a particular member or group of members for audio-visual equipment. Many churches already have much of the equipment in their possession, and for them the media room would be a place where it could be stored and used. Like the other areas, the media room does not require a large expenditure of money; it requires a change in attitude. In many old churches the unfinished room may already be in existence. What is needed is a new attitude that will allow young people to be responsible for its use and decoration.

Clearly, the major ingredient in implementing the full-functioning environment is a genuine concern within the church for improving church and community life. This concern must be translated into a policy allowing new uses of existing facilities. Providing the programs of the full-functioning environment may encourage some churches to work together. As an experimental venture two churches might jointly fund and promote a projects room and a community nursery, one church starting the community nursery in its facility, the other church beginning the projects room. The combinations are endless. These modest additional functions could easily fall within present budgets.

Some might object that a church is not a community center and should not provide a variety of activities. The crux of the argument is clear. The full-functioning program in no way subtracts from the religious life of the church. Religious education is improved, and worship will be enhanced through the members' having a greater sense of being involved in the religious community. The full-functioning program can only add to the total life and vitality of the church. As in the past, the church is most effective when it is a focus of community activity. It can no longer pretend to be an economic power wielding substantial influence over the decisions of industry and government. This power is now concentrated in corporate headquarters and organizational bureaucracies. The church can no longer pretend to be the sole patron of the arts or the curator of creative enterprises. Community cultural centers, independent theater companies, and museums now foster and support the arts. Nor is the church the center of learning, the fountain of science, or the mainstay of healing. What it can be is a vital force in the daily lives of its members and the community. At a time when the centers of power have become overwhelming and dehumanizing, the church is a place where the individual is still important. With a full-functioning program the church can be a place for individual growth and community service. It is more than a community center, for it has a spiritual base. A full-functioning church creates a human community, sharing in the sacraments and emphasizing the validity of the individual in the democratic self-direction of church policies. The full-functioning church can become a daily center enhancing individual human potential. The study library is more than a public library because it infuses into life and learning the living assumptions of religious existence. The projects room is more than an arts center; it is an affirmation of art as an integral part of life. The full-functioning church is deeply personal and has as its educational aim the stimulation of awareness in human life. A church serving as a center for the entire community can become the focus of human activity again.

# STIRRING

## CELEBRATION AND PARTICIPATION

Worship services provide spiritual inspiration and the symbolic expression of beliefs. They are the wellspring of unity within the religious community. The history of Western church architecture shows the evolution of religious values reflected in church design. At the present time, some people want to behave like early Christians, who clandestinely met in homes, underground, and in a variety of obscure and often undesirable locations, because of continuous harassment and persecution. It is fanciful to pretend that Christians, even in the underground Christian movement, are being persecuted today. A return to basic Christian principles and the resulting reduction of physical luxury are worthwhile but should not delude worshipers into the belief that a service in a home is superior to one held in a church. Similarly, meeting in an adapted early basilica or a Gothic cathedral is not inherently superior to meeting in a modern church facility. Previous generations imitated the forms of Gothic cathedrals because of their need to imitate the grandeur of the past. We have to be careful that we do not fall victim to such eclecticism. A return to basic Christianity does not require facilities that copy the cathedrals or the ancient catacombs. We need to stop reaching into history for both grand and ungrand solutions for our religious structures.

Instead of looking backward, church leaders and members need to look to the present and the future. They should evaluate theoretical and practical theology and its application to contemporary religious environments. At the present time all denominations are increasingly emphasizing the community of believers and their participation in all aspects of religious life. According to John Scotford:

> The aim of the Liturgical Movement in the Roman Catholic Church has been to involve the congregation in the Mass, and a similar ideal has in-

spired many Protestants. The common goal is to transform passive acceptance to active participation. Instead of sitting in the pews and listening to the minister or observing the priest from a safe distance, the congregation should share in the action. How this can be brought about is a pressing practical problem for both Protestants and Catholics.[1]

Congregational participation was a problem for the early Christian church and was a goal of the Protestant Reformation. Today, clergy are concerned less with placating an angry God than with helping people find their spiritual and ethical resources. The minister is no longer the only person with healing powers; the members of the entire religious community can minister to each other. Many denominations have long traditions of lay involvement, and they are being extended, while in other denominations significant experiments in lay participation are beginning. These changes are significant; no longer is involvement limited to the prudential affairs or property maintenance of the church. The laity are now beginning to share in the total spiritual life, becoming more active in the conduct of worship services, visiting the sick, and helping the indigent of the community. The worship service is no longer considered just a ceremony performed by the clergy for the congregation; it is an experience in which the clergy and the congregation participate together. This change in the role of the laity needs to be expressed in the design of existing and new religious facilities.

In his recent book *The Feast of Fools,* Harvey Cox discusses the need for increased festivity and fantasy in our culture, indicating the significant changes toward a more festive mode in our churches:

> Even in the churches dance, color, movement, and new kinds of music dramatize the recovery of celebration. In short we may be witnessing the overture to a sweeping renaissance, a revolution of human sensibilities in which the facilities we have starved and repressed during the centuries of industrialization will be nourished and appreciated again.[2]

The church should be not an escape but a source of renewal and courage for facing the challenges of everyday living and the concerns of the larger community. It is not necessary, nor is it desirable, for the worship service to be depressing or foreboding. Sermons need not be threatening; they can be informative. Music need not be somber; it can be uplifting. Singing need not be ponderous; it can be joyful. Worship does not have to be a passive ritual; it can become an act of redemptive joy, celebrated through the full participation of the assembled religious community.

The emphasis on celebration and participation requires an evaluation of the basic elements of the worship service, which in turn will influence the religious environment of the church. One of the major barriers to change in the worship setting is the vague feeling that the church should somehow be "churchy" or "worshipful." These terms lead to the excessive monumentalism and benign nostalgia characteristic of the tired dragons. Churchiness implies lack of conviction and understanding. It denotes careless attitudes and sentimental feelings. The churchy church is the one we think we remember from our childhood. For some people churchiness is an attempt to return to childhood rather than to acquire a meaningful belief. It is an attempt to retain forms of worship that are no longer appropriate. Churchiness implies the absence of participation and celebration. It implies passivity rather than activity. It implies duty rather than spontaneous joy. A meaningful worship service and worship setting can be created only when terms like "churchy" and "worshipful" have been eliminated. Music is not churchy; it is music. It either stirs the emotions and is appropriate to the service or it is not. To judge it on the basis of its churchiness is to deny its reality and leads to the noninvolving background music of the supermarket. If Christianity is to have any meaning for people's lives, it will not be because the building and the worship service are churchy. Too often churchiness has led to the copying of previous styles or to frenzied efforts to discover authentic early rituals and architectural settings. Instead of searching for the basics in the ancient traditions, clergy and laity should concentrate on the basics of the present time. Serious thought should be given to the essentials of communication. Instead of long dissertations about pulpit heights, today's means of communication, public expression, and symbols in the religious community should be thoroughly considered.

The design of spaces for worship should not be determined only by historical or even theological requirements. If a speaker cannot be heard, the historical correctness of the placement of the pulpit will be of little value to the congregation. If the organist and choir are limited to traditional selections, then the musical expression of the Good News will be old sounding and droll. When communion and baptism are not given symbolic and visual expression within the religious setting, their value and importance are dissipated. All words shared by the religious community and congregation are meaningless when every architectural element of the church limits personal involvement in the worship service.

This chapter is an examination of the basic elements of the worship service and its setting to determine what is most suitable for today and the future. Where should the congregation sit? How can we improve communication within the worship service? How can we give creative expression to the joys of song and music? Can communion and baptism be given an appropriate architectural expression? How can all these elements be brought together in a way that is beautiful and meets the demands of a full-functioning environment?

## SEATING

Emphasizing celebration and participation makes the area designed for the congregation especially important. Books and articles about the sanctuary usually discuss pews or seating areas tangentially. In today's church the design has to begin with the congregation. The seating space is important because it comprises a large portion of the sanctuary. This in no way means that the communion table, baptismal font, and pulpit are not important; they are basic to the worship area. However, so much attention has been given to them that the seating area is usually considered as an afterthought. In a participatory service the location of the congregation is a primary concern.

Seating has been considered an extension of the chancel area. The concept of sacredness and sacred space has been applied to the chancel and gradually extended to the pew area. In the Middle Ages, when the church was the focus of every aspect of life, construction of a cathedral took many centuries. We have tried to achieve with money and sophisticated construction technology what medieval builders accomplished with time and belief. The modern church became a monument both to God, and to the church's major benefactor, instead of a living space for people. The chancel furnishings, the altar, lectern, baptismal font, and pews became static just as the statement of God's eternal presence became rigid. Eternal became confused with inflexible.

An obvious fault of these monumental churches is the large area occupied by pews. In the past the church's seating capacity was determined by planning

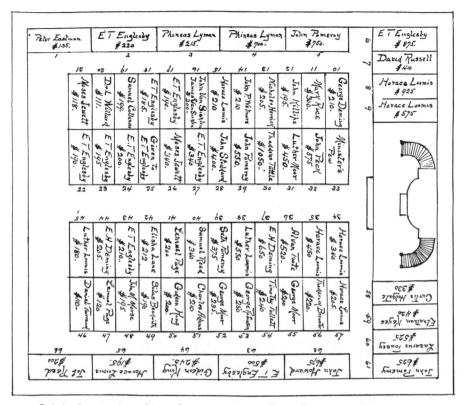

*Original proprietorship of pews, 1816, First Unitarian Universalist Church, Burlington, Vermont*

enough space to accommodate crowds coming to hear a spectacular guest preacher or to attend regional conferences. The ordinary needs of the local congregation were not considered. Even during Sundays of maximum attendance many churches are not filled. The empty pews are an inefficient use of space.

Some people consider pews part of the Christian tradition and will object to changes affecting them. However, the most cursory review of history reveals that every element in the church has experienced a variety of placements and functions over the centuries. In the early Christian churches there were no pews or chairs; people stood during the service. This practice is still followed in Eastern Orthodox churches. In this country, pews were added to the early meeting houses, which were used for town meetings and assemblies as well as for religious services. In the New England community, the seating was a natural extension of the wooden meeting houses. Pews were constructed like boxes with four sides and a door. In the earliest churches, they were purchased and were a principal source of church revenue. Wealthy and prominent citizens bought the most prominent pews. The social structure of the community was apparent from the pew arrangement. Edward Sinnott stated in *Meetinghouse and Church in Early New England:*

> A great . . . shock . . . to our ideas of Puritan democracy comes when we examine the seating plan of a typical meetinghouse and understand what it was that determined the station that a particular individual should occupy therein. Just as some seats were evidently much better than others, so were some people considered superior to their fellows, and it was the essence of the Puritan's social philosophy to give the best men the "foreseats" and to reserve for lesser individuals those that were further back or less desirable in other ways.[3]

The worldly order expressed in the arrangement of the Puritans' pews is a basic ingredient of religious life. A sense of order has always given meaning to religious beliefs; doctrines or myths of origins have structured the universe. Order and doctrine are basic to every religion. The religious prophet embodies an ideal, but the ideal is unattainable for ordinary humans. The church modifies the demands of the prophet, acts as intermediary, and sets attainable goals. Churches do this by providing orderly frameworks of belief, conduct, and education. An understanding of this basic quality of order in all religions gives some insight into attitudes toward worship. Many people profess to come to church to be ethically motivated, but in reality large numbers of them come to sustain a sense of peace, harmony, and order.

In the context of order, pews have taken on a theological importance. Their symmetry symbolizes the desired order—not the extreme social order of the pew renters and purchasers of colonial times but the order of religious tradition. However, to sit securely in the pews, smugly oblivious with present changes is inconsistent with a revitalized, meaningful religious belief. Architects have created fancy building shapes and spectacular roof structures; clergymen have inspired changing worship forms. Nevertheless, congregations have refused to change their attitudes, and their immobile seats confirm their rigidity.

The obstacles are difficult to overcome. Until the rigid pew structure is changed, the church will not substantially alter its present course. The pews are where the people are, and unless they are willing to alter their patterns, there is little hope for the tired dragons. This does not mean that by destroying all pews we would have a revitalized church; it only means as long as pews are worshiped, there is little hope for a relevant church.

In the past, changes in pew design have come slowly, and designers were always looking into a rear-view mirror. At each stage of their design, pews have incorporated superfluous elements of earlier designs. The original pews in meeting houses were constructed as family boxes. Seating was on three sides and the door on the fourth. In time, the impracticality of seats on three sides with some not even facing the pulpit led to a more modest box arrangement having seats on only one side, facing the pulpit. The box was elongated so that everyone in the family could face forward. At first, two boxes adjoined each other, each having an access door from the aisles. The two adjacent sides formed a middle divider. Eventually the divider was eliminated, and the pew spanned the distance between aisles. Eventually, the inconvenience and the limited value of doors became evident. Even in the absence of doors, the high front, back, and sides of the pew were retained. Later, it became obvious that without the door, the high ends on the aisle sides of the pew were unnecessary. The original purpose of the high ends was to provide a frame for the door. With more time, it was realized that the solid back of the pew was cumbersome and unnecessary. The pew slowly was streamlined and now usually consists of a seating surface and a back rest, often as separate pieces supported by brackets. Some churches have moved one more step by using pews that are not fastened to the floor. Others have shortened pews to the length of three or four seats, making them more like chairs.

The history of the modifications in pew design tells the story of changing theological ideas and design tastes. When we look back over the varying styles, it is evident that each time period did not see its own limitations. One group kept doors no longer necessary; another kept pew ends when there were no doors to hold; and still another retained the solid backs of the pew box long after they were not needed. These details are not significant in themselves, but each pew style indicates how different periods preserved elements of the previous time that had little or no function in the next.

During all these changes the rectilinear arrangement of the pews and the resulting building design were not questioned. The layout of the aisles was standardized, and the church added rows of pews at the rear and on the sides, depending upon construction limitations and expected seating capacity. This seating arrangement has been used by all styles of religious architecture in this country, from neo-Gothic to sentimental meeting house. Such unquestioning use of inherited styles is inadequate in the context of congregational seating and participation. Paul Tillich, in his essay "Contemporary Protestant Architecture," emphatically sets forth the need for a more congregationally oriented design:

> The plan of the church is, of course, of first importance. A plan adequate to the Protestant purpose would be, preferably, a central one in which members of the congregation look at each other, and in which the minister is among the congregation for preaching and leading the liturgy. The place for the altar should not be removed, but preserve the character of a table for the sacramental meal in which, ideally, all members participate.
> Churches that retain a central aisle leading to a removed altar as the holiest place, separated from other parts of the building, are essentially un-Protestant. With the abolition of any kind of hierarchical dualism between laymen and clergy, between a secular and a holy role—in short, because of the fundamental Protestant concept of the priesthood of all believers—these remnants of the Catholic tradition are religiously inadequate for a Protestant architecture. No new church should have them, and existing churches should be transformed as much as possible away from this old direction.[4]

Only in the past decade has there been an extended effort to experiment and improve seating arrangements. These efforts have dealt with two closely related aspects of the problem. The first is the type of seating, and the second is the total seating arrangement. If a church uses individual chairs instead of pews, the possibilities for arrangement are greatly expanded. If a church uses fixed pews, their arrangement must be carefully considered. The type of seating and its arrangement should not be an afterthought but should be one of the first considerations in the construction of new facilities, for there is a direct relationship between the basic architectural shape of the room and the seating arrangement. The type of seating selected and used by the church will strongly determine the total worship environment. Rigidly fixed pews are no longer suitable for worship stressing celebration and participation. No one would contend that seating can make a person religious, but it can have symbolic importance. If a minister is encouraging his congregation to be flexible and adapt to this changing world and his listeners are seated in self-righteous, unadaptable pews, his message is denied.

There is nothing religious or even Christian about sitting in a pew. At best, it can be said that the pew is churchy, but this very concept can no longer be a part of meaningful religion. Clearly, a chair is for sitting and is not in itself religious. This realistic attitude toward seating could provide a symbolic transition from the ideals of worship to the actions of daily living. We should not think we are better persons because we sit in pews. There are no pews in real life. When decisions are made throughout the week, they are made in chairs at home or in the office.

Many churches used pews in the past because of the convenience of working with established church-furnishings dealers. All that was necessary was contacting an experienced seating "expert," who, armed with many catalogs showing his company's products, would provide pews. Typical of the impressive catalogs is one offering ten valuable tips about seating, each leading to the selection of pews. Nowhere in the list is there any hint of the possibilities of different types of seating. The church is led to buy the standard pews, with an occasional modern wrinkle. The simplicity and convenience of ordering pews, however, are far outweighed by the inconvenience of the resulting immovable seating in what could have been usable space and by the total expense. Even though many manufacturers of church furnishings are conscientious, business has to be concerned with profits, which are best realized from repeat sales and standardized products. It is, unfortunately, in the interest of the manufacturers to maintain the status quo with traditional church pews, which isolate the church market from the diversified and more competitive seating companies. The problem is not with the companies but with their limited vision of church design and furnishings, which has inhibited new approaches to seating. Perhaps manufacturers will eventually widen their vision of religious life, but at present they are a stagnating influence. A church working in conjunction with an architect is in a much better position to select a style of furnishings most appropriate for its needs. In some cases architects may work with a church-furnishings company and in others with general seating manufacturers.

One reason churches have been unwilling to use individual seating is the bad example set by some churches that have used chairs to save money rather than to provide appropriate seating. Too often the church turns the selection of the chairs over to someone who can get a bargain, and the church ends up with cheap chairs that are uncomfortable and ugly. Other churches have used folding chairs, which are inadequate and not indicative of the potential of flexible seating. Individual chairs need not be clumsy, distasteful, or temporary. In existing buildings individual chairs can provide the flexibility necessary for full utilization of the present spaces, allowing much greater variation in arrangement, aisle location, and seating capacity. Individual chairs can have the same dignity as pews but without rigidity. Great care should be taken in selecting chairs. They are an important element in overall design and can influence the appearance of the sanctuary as much as the walls can. An existing church making the transition from pews to individual seating needs the advice of knowledgeable persons even more than a new church does. The selection of chairs for an existing sanctuary requires sensitive blending of design with the fixed elements. Individual chairs can be stacked for convenient space-saving storage and left in a room without being an ugly distraction or consuming space unnecessarily. Chairs with interlocking features for aligning and with accessories for communion cups, book racks, and kneeling benches can be purchased.

The setting for the chairs is an important criterion of selection. Plastic, vividly colored chairs can detract from the dignity of the worship setting. Wood provides a warm appearance and a naturalness compatible with the desired simplicity and dignity of worship. Whether the frames are of wood or metal, the seat and back surfaces should be in neutral colors. Deep, muted colors or blacks and browns are appropriate in most settings. In general, gaudy reds, yellows, and blues are distracting and can make the sanctuary seem more like the waiting area of an airline terminal than a space for worship.

The principal advantage of individual chairs is the varied seating arrangements they allow. For typical Sunday services of modest attendance, the seating can be arranged so the room appears comfortably full, neither crowded nor empty. Nothing is more discouraging or disheartening than 150 people in a sanctuary with a seating capacity of 700. The empty pews imply 550 people are missing. The atmosphere in the same church, even though oversized, with 200 individual chairs set up and 150 people in attendance, would be positive. If

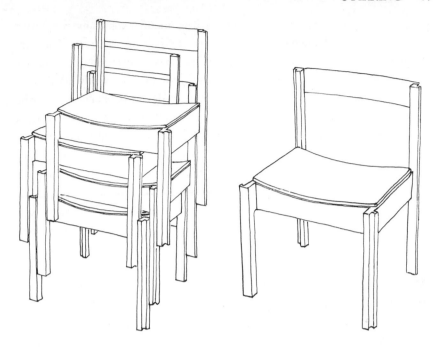

church attendance rises to 500 at seasonal worship services, such as Christmas and Easter, chairs can easily be added.

Flexible seating is not limited to varying the seating capacity; the individual chairs also allow rearrangement of the seating for different focal points. If intimacy is required, the chairs can be arranged in a semi-circle around the communion table. If space is needed near the chancel for a dance presentation, it can easily be provided. If audio-visual presentations are part of the service, the seating can be adjusted. If a special performance of combined choirs or a small musical ensemble is planned, the seating can once again be expanded or contracted, adjusted and rearranged, to the setting most suitable for the performers and the congregation.

Seating arrangements in existing churches are of crucial importance in the full utilization of sanctuary spaces. The present large areas of space cluttered with unused pews is one of the greatest offenses to a relevant religious environment. These spaces must become more suitable for contemporary worship and for increased functioning. There are many approaches to these changes.

In some churches, the initial alterations will be modest, for many people are still wedded to the building and, in particular, to their favorite pew. These irrational, sentimental attachments will be the major obstacles to significant change. In old churches, there is more seating than is presently needed. A minimal and simple solution is to remove some of the pews. They need not be discarded but can be stored and, if attendance increases in the future, returned to the sanctuary. Many churches have side aisles that are never used and are awkwardly located. Whole sections of pews can be removed from one or both sides of the church, creating generous areas that can be used in a variety of ways. Pews can also be removed from the rear of the church. In the typical, rectilinear sanctuary, these pews are the most remote from the pulpit and communion table. The removal makes the seating more compatible with present needs and eliminates the seats that most limit participation in the service. The rear area can be used as a gathering place at the end of the service or as a location for display tables, and even if unused, the area can enhance the interior with its spaciousness and grace. If the chancel area is poorly designed or limited in space, the front pews can be removed, opening new space and arrangement possibilities. In most churches, the front pews are unnecessarily close to the pulpit, and people sitting in them are either blasted out of their seats by the minister's oratory or acquire severe neck cramps from straining to see the speaker in the raised pulpit. The removal of some of the front pews will open up space in the front of the sanctuary, which then may be redesigned to create a more appropriate chancel area. In some churches pews should be removed just to allow better walking circulation. There are churches in which more than half of the pews are empty on Sunday, yet the rear and front aisles are so narrow that one can hardly walk along them.

The advantage of pew removal as a form of church renovation is that it allows the preservation of the historical and architectural integrity of the building while meeting the contemporary needs of the church through convenient and inexpensive adjustments to the sanctuary. A more thorough solution is the complete removal of all pews. This would make the sanctuary a room for meetings and allow more variety in worship services. If a church is unwilling to discard old pews, or even relatively new ones, they can at least be made portable by unfastening them from the floor. Most pews are solid and heavy enough to stand independently. If a broader base is needed for stability, it can be added to the present support area. The unfastened pews would be stable for seating, yet flexible for relocation. A further variation would be to let pews in one area remain fixed in place, while pews in another are made movable.

Like the use of individual, more flexible chairs and pews, total seating arrangements have also received increased attention in recent years. The first changes began with an adaptation of the traditional three-part sanctuary. The pulpit and communion table were projected out into the sanctuary area, with the seating divided into a main and two side sections. The arrangement retained the formality of the traditional rectilinear plan but increased congregants' sense of participation by providing them with seating surrounding the chancel. With the extension of seating into three areas of the sanctuary, the logical next step was the development of the semi-circular arrangement, which has proved very successful. It combines the advantages of compact space and proximity to the chancel for increased involvement by the congregation. Another variation is seating in the round, completely surrounding the chancel. The plan has the advantage of providing seating near the altar area in every direction and the disadvantage of awkward pulpit placement. Much has been written about the symbolic value of the religious community's surrounding the communion table. Many churchmen have expressed satisfaction with circular seating, which stresses the equality of the communicants. Instead of looking in one direction toward the minister, the members have an opportunity to look at the communion table and at the entire congregation. In theory this stress on unity is appealing, but in practice it is not too satisfactory. Many people feel awkward facing another group of people and are not sure where to look. It is interesting that many writers who say that the choir should be removed from the front of the church because of the awkwardness of the choir and congregation staring at each other recommend seating in the round.

The ideal solution, whether in an existing or a new church, is a compromise between the circular arrangement and the traditional one, with economy and symbolic emphasis given due consideration. The seating arrangement that most successfully achieves this balance is semi-circular. Semi-circular seating gives the congregation a sense of participation by combining closeness to the worship center and a physical sense of unity. Semi-circular seating avoids the rigidity and distance of rectangular seating and eliminates the difficulty of cross-vision among the congregation. With the semi-circular arrangement, the worship focus is effective yet more flexible than with seating in the round. The congregation faces forward, and all the major elements of the chancel are directly in view. The choir problem is easily solved by placing the choir members at the end of the area next to the organ or other accompanying instruments in the front of the church, while at the same time seating them as part of the congregation.

Flexibility can be added to semi-circular arrangements by the use of movable individual seats. With movable chairs, the seating could be changed for special worship services and other occasions. A sanctuary with movable seating and a semi-circular arrangement would provide a practical solution to seating for all types of churches as well as the flexibility needed for easy adaptation to future needs. The combination would, further, provide a sanctuary setting conducive to increased participation and a greater emphasis upon worship as celebration.

## SPEAKING

No longer is the authoritative voice of the preacher unquestioningly accepted. Exalted oratory no longer moves many in the congregation, nor is it the most effective means of communicating religious and moral concerns. The lofty pulpit is no longer an unquestioned source of absolute truth and moral preachments. Today clergy, perhaps more than the congregation, realize the importance of mutual communication. Social conditions clearly indicate that preaching has not elevated morality.

A minister needs to speak directly and honestly to the congregation, not because he is better or more holy but because he is committed to the spiritual enrichment and improvement of human life. He is a man speaking among men. He is willing to stand with them, not above them. He does not need, nor should he want, the props of an exaggerated, elevated position to make his words seem righteous.

Just as the design and construction of religious architecture are not isolated from the economics and values of contemporary society, so communication within the church is influenced by the standards and patterns of the larger community. Television is the most obvious innovation in communication. Everyone is well aware of the significant impact of television. Even though most adults use the medium as a diversion or an escape from their everyday concerns, television is a major source of communication. Its visual orientation is a new experience: if a picture is worth a thousand words, then television with its millions of pictures is worth volumes of books.

Television does have its limitations; there is much the medium cannot do. It does not allow direct participation, sharing, or mutual communication. Experiments have used phone-in and write-in response techniques, but they are limited. Even with its limitations, however, television is a convenient and effective source of stimulation and education.

A church can fill a unique role in the area of communication by providing opportunities for mutual exchange in contrast to the one-way direction of the mass media. Communication is more than speaking. True communication requires, at a minimum, an active listener as well as a speaker. If no one is listening, a speaker's words have little value. Some preachers have conveniently assumed people were not listening because their truths were too profound or too shocking or too moral. These preachers projected the responsibility and the inadequacy onto the congregation, condemning their lack of receptivity. Now the burden is on the minister to communicate effectively. With mandatory attendance and the pressures of social conformity no longer forcing people to attend church, those who do attend are coming because they want to. The total number is small, but the interest level can be high. People want to hear, see, and be a part of the worship service. An increasing number want to participate and have an opportunity to express their viewpoint and feelings.

The emphasis upon increased mutual communication requires a change of attitude by the clergy and the parishioner. The change needs to be reflected in the architectural setting. Many people no longer want to come and be shuttled to the dark shadows of the rear pew. They want to be involved. They wish to hear without straining, see without stretching, and sit without discomfort. Increased attention will have to be paid to the desires of the congregation.

In the context of mutual communication, the pulpit takes on a new significance. It is no longer a symbol of authority or a shield separating the clergy from the congregation. It can no longer be an object of reverence. Many members worship the pulpit from which the minister speaks but resent his ethical demands and call for a new religious commitment. They care more about where he speaks than about what he says. With the changing attitude of the ministry and the understanding of the congregation, the pulpit will have a different significance.

The pulpit is no more nor less than a place for speaking in the setting of religious worship. Like other pieces of chancel furniture, it should have a pleasant appearance and fit in with the total worship setting. It need only be high enough to allow the congregation to clearly see the speaker. It need not be imposing; in the future, it will not need to compete visually with mammoth sanctuary spaces. When seating areas are reduced, the pulpit can be modest in size and still be an effective focal point. To enable flexibility in the use of room space and in the worship services, the pulpit should not be fastened to the floor or permanently built into one location. It need not be a flimsy, obviously portable stand. It can be provided with hidden wheels and stops that allow movement. The pulpit need not be moved every other week, but it should have the potential for movement.

In existing buildings it would be worthwhile to consider installing a pulpit appropriate to today's communication. The existing pulpit could be modified for a new location and made more serviceable, or it could remain in its present site and be used for special and formal services. A new pulpit could be added for use during the weekly services. If it were portable, it could be moved to the side when not in use.

The lectern is another element used in spoken communication in the church. In the days of imposing pulpits the lectern provided a practical solution for conducting the service. In the dogmatic symmetry of former times the lectern also provided a convenient balance to the pulpit. All these considerations are now irrelevant because pulpits are no longer reserved only for high oratory and symmetry is no longer the guideline of ecclesiastical architecture. To build a permanent lectern in a new church would be inappropriate and a restriction on future congregations. Some churches may desire to have a lectern, but it should be portable, usable in a variety of locations. In existing churches flexibility may be obtained by altering the design of the lectern or, at least, by not being dominated by its presence. In churches where the pulpit now serves adequately throughout the service, the lectern may be removed, opening new possibilities of chancel arrangement.

In the future, it is quite possible that ministers will not be limited to speaking from fixed locations. Traditionally the static location was an unquestioned expression of the order expected both in architecture and in theology. In our time even major speakers before large audiences are using portable microphones and are moving away from formal lecterns to give more animated presentations and direct communication. In the future, it is possible that the minister will not speak from the pulpit each Sunday. He may stand directly in front of the congregation and perhaps even go among them. This movement by the minister would indicate that he is not above the congregation but with them. A further extension of this mobility would be the introduction of dialogue in the worship service, allowing people to ask questions and present their point of view. Providing an opportunity for congregational response would mollify many objections to the minister's speaking on social issues. A minister cannot dictate social consciousness, just as he cannot dictate righteousness. He can only persuade and convince, and open forms of communication are effective for this.

Individual churches and denominations will have to decide the type of communication that is most appropriate for their services of worship. Clearly the trend within society and the church as a whole is toward greater emphasis upon mutual communication as the most effective means of stimulating and encouraging the spiritual and ethical awareness of the congregation. Many of the physical barriers between the speaker and the congregation will have to be removed or altered. Congregants will increasingly require a physical setting more conducive to their participation in all aspects of the service. Each of the elements in the sanctuary should be designed with enough flexibility to allow change without a major construction effort. A grand pulpit frozen into the architecture of the church is not only unsuitable for today's worship but imposes an unnecessary limitation on communication for future worshipers.

## SINGING

The sound of singing and the music of instruments are closely related to the speaking and listening of the clergy and the congregation. Music is sound. Traditionally it has been sounds ordered and composed in harmony and beauty. In recent years, a broader definition of the purpose and organization of music has emerged, broadening the arrangement of sounds acceptable as music. The human voice has the ability to make noise. This articulated sound can be structured into language, which can be further enriched to create poetry and music. Singing is an extension of speaking using a fuller range of sound and adding a desirable grace. It is important and necessary to worship. Spoken language lacks a dimension necessary for reaching deep into the human soul. Music, with its combination of intellect through language and emotion through sound, provides an important release and motivation. The value of music has long been recognized; the early Greeks defined it as "remembered inspiration." The combination of melody and harmony cuts deep into our consciousness. Throughout the Old Testament, there is much evidence of the importance of music in the daily lives and celebrations of the Judaic tribes. The psalms of David give expression to the joy of music, especially Psalm 100: "Make a joyful noise unto the Lord, all ye lands."

Making a joyful noise through music is closely related to participation and celebration in worship. "Make a joyful noise unto the Lord" is perhaps the best expression of celebration in biblical literature. All occasions, from public events to religious sacraments, are enriched by music and song. Song uplifts the spirit and lends unity. Music is a portion of the service in which everyone can participate, not just by listening or responding, but in a full-hearted expression of thanksgiving, dedication, praise, and joy. Even the poorest singer, when joined by the full congregation, can enjoy the emotional expression possible through song.

Because of its penetrating power, music can be not only an expression but a source of values. Plato stated in the *Republic,* "When modes of music change, the fundamental laws of the state will change with them." [5] The laws of the state changed long ago, and the irrelevance of many nineteenth-century hymns is evident. There is no relationship between much of our church music and the contemporary situation. Many popular and folk songs are more honest expressions of present life than the church hymns are. They have become the true hymns and have deeper meaning for large numbers of people.

There is no more obvious place for music to express important values than in religious life and worship. If religion is an expression of values and beliefs, it should have a vitality that speaks to living today. Traditions are important but must be balanced with present realities. Some traditional music should be continued, but it needs to be balanced with contemporary selections.

The singing of traditional hymns provides an important link with the past. However, for many middle-aged and young people, the hymns do not have significance. Cultural patterns have changed, love ballads and the top forty have replaced hymns as meaningful music, and many young people have difficulty singing the old hymns. It is well known that most hymns are based on tunes and lyrics of past centuries, and young people are not only unaffected by the hymns but are actively against the use of music that has so little relationship to both the concerns and the musical style of the present. Diversified music is needed in the church if a wide range of people is to be encouraged to participate. New hymns and songs must be added to the old. Just as the concept of the sacred in architecture must change, so should the concept of sacred in music. A bad tune written a century ago is not a good tune today. Appropriate contemporary songs with suitable words and singable melodies should be added to the musical repertoire of the worship services. It can no longer be assumed that members of the congregation know either the old hymns or the new songs. To implement the broader range and greater variety of music the congregation will need guidance.

The seating of the congregation can hamper or aid in the adoption of new music. A large, rigidly seated group almost out of its own momentum continues to use the same hymns because to change direction of such a monolithic grouping is more than most musical directors and clergy can tackle. A smaller congregation with flexible or semi-circular seating has a much better opportunity to learn new music and adapt to changing forms. The congregation and music director in these small groupings are likely to be in dialogue, learning from each other, rather than routinely presenting a standardized service of worship.

If new music is introduced into the worship services, it may become desirable to change the patterns of musical leadership. In most churches the musical director is both the organist and the choir leader, and no one attempts to lead the congregation except indirectly through the organ music and choir's singing. The choir is often so far removed from the congregation that their singing is of little help. In the past, there was no reason to be concerned with these problems because the entire congregation since earliest childhood had been singing the same hymns, and in adult life everyone knew them well. A couple of new hymns might be introduced each year, and the congregation could easily learn them, or if a new hymnal was introduced, large numbers of the congregation would attend hymn sings to learn the new melodies. With today's busy schedules even the choir members probably would not come to a hymn sing.

Because of these changes in attitude and the need for new music, someone will have to spend time directly leading the congregational singing. This may be the choir director, who, during the hymns, particularly new ones, comes to the front of the congregation to lead. This, of course, implies there is a separate organist. The choir may join the director to help the congregational singing. Another alternative is to appoint a congregational song leader to lead the members while the music director continues with the choir. There are a number of alternatives, with the essential goal being direct leadership of congregational singing when new music is introduced.

Some churches, through the prodding of the younger members, have attempted to introduce increased amounts of new music but did not think through the total process of change. No one altered the setting or musical leadership practices, and as a result, the congregation sang so poorly at the initial singing of the new music that the once-spirited newcomers became discouraged and gave up their efforts.

New directions require new methods. The extensive introduction of new music is most likely to succeed with modified seating and new forms of musical direction. Many churches are unwilling to expend the energy these changes require. The introduction of new music is a good example of the interrelationship of the elements in a church. The physical setting, the architecture, and the furnishings have a strong influence, and each is related to the church leaders and their functions, which in turn are closely related to the congregation. It is easy to see why so many churches think it is easier to just lumber along than to give forth the effort required to provide change. This interrelationship of elements in the church is one of the reasons clergy and young people have so much difficulty in making even the simplest alterations. Any change relates to other changes, and the total process must be thoroughly considered. Wishing for change does not make it happen; that requires energy and hard work and a thorough realization of the influence of the environment.

A choir may considerably help to revitalize a church's music program. If the members of the choir are familiar with the new tunes, they can provide important leadership during the singing period. To be most helpful, the choir should be located close to the congregation. In most churches the choir has been located in a host of places, depending upon the ideas and fashions of religion and the congregation at the time of construction. The difficulty with the various locations is their permanence. The choir has never just sat somewhere; it has always had an elaborate nest. If located in the chancel, the choir is enclosed in decorative wooden dividers and partitions and is as immobile as the organ. At the time of construction, these encasements were a compliment to the permanence and importance of the choir in worship, but now they are solid barriers to needed change. Many churches cannot bring themselves to remove the choir from the specially constructed loft, even though they know the choir would function more appropriately in another location.

There is a long and varied history of choir locations, and as a result, an equally wide and varied number of choir arrangements. The varieties may be summarized into four basic categories: divided chancel, front loft, rear loft, and front side. Each location has its own history and its problems in adapting to a worship service of celebration and participation.

Locating the choir in the divided chancel began in this country in the first half of the nineteenth century through the influence of the Cambridge Movement. The ideas of the movement were propagated by the New York Ecclesiological Society, founded in 1848. The first landmark of the movement was Trinity Church, in New York City. The principal tenet of the group was the adoption of medieval worship practices and architecture. Like all reversions to the past, the movement disrupted the progressive growth of religious expression. Many of the elements adopted had little relevance for nineteenth- or twentieth-century worship. The placement of the choir in a divided chancel expressed this backward direction. In the medieval period, the divided chancel was necessary for antiphonal singing.

When divided chancels were made for use in parish churches of the past century and again in this century, circumstances were much different. Choirs of the past one hundred years did not regularly sing antiphonally, and at the present time most choirs find the divided seats a definite obstacle to singing as a unit. Even more significant, the built-in permanence of the chancel gave it a new sanctity. Its new location implied that the choir served a clerical role in the service rather than as part of the congregation. The choir's role continued to grow in importance until it completely dominated the music of the worship service and placed the musical participation of the congregation in a subordinate position.

The history of the influence of the Cambridge Movement shows one example of the relationship between values and functions and, in turn, function and environment. Each works on the other. The founders of the Cambridge Movement considered the medieval period the high point of Christianity and wanted to return to the theological values and worship practices of that time. As an expression of those values, a corresponding environment needed to be created, resulting in the copying of medieval cathedrals even for the smallest parish churches. To adopt medieval theology and worship without the building would have been inconceivable, and to adopt cathedral architecture without the worship would have been inconsistent. In both values and environment, it is obvious to us now, the supporters of the Cambridge Movement made a gross error in trying to return to a Christianity several hundred years removed. It was not only an error for them but has been a curse on churches since. Once such decisions are frozen into lofty arches and divided chancels, it is difficult and expensive to thaw out the damage. Many churches today are still suffering from the unfortunate sanctuary constructions and divided chancel choirs of this pseudo-medieval pietism.

Another choir location providing an equally formidable obstacle is the front loft and platform. This location has two origins. The most important is the influence of revitalism that dominated Protestantism in the mid-nineteenth century. Traveling evangelists performed anywhere, from campsites to city auditoriums. With the influence of this new nonliturgical religious form, new values and environments emerged. In revivalist worship, the most important factor was the strength and power of the evangelist to call forth individuals in public testimony of their belief. The emotions of the service were enhanced and aided by a strong and inspiring choir. The mood was emotional and the choir was essential.

The evangelist movement influenced much of the church architecture in this country from the middle of the nineteenth century. The chancel and the imposing pulpit were discarded. Liturgy and symbolism were unnecessary when the service stressed the personal experience of the worshiper and his public affirmation of belief. A platform, much like a stage, was used and allowed the evangelist the physical mobility necessary for coaxing, speaking, and drawing the worshipers forward. The choir, serving as emotional reinforcement, stood directly behind the evangelist.

The choir was also placed in the front of the church, perched in a loft above the central pulpit in copies of the meeting houses. These lofts contained both the organ and the choir. If a loft above was impractical, the organ and the choir were squeezed into small niches behind the pulpit. These have proved more inadequate than lofts, for they are always small, and the organ and choir do not have enough space.

Whether the location is the front stage, niche recess, or loft, many churches are now faced with inappropriate choir settings. In each case, the choir and the congregation have to stare at each other throughout the service; this is both an annoyance and a distraction. Even more important, the choir is removed from the congregation. In these locations the choir members become performers removed from the worship, rather than fellow worshipers leading the members in song.

A third choir location is the rear loft. It preserves the traditional appearance and arrangement of the front chancel or platform area and yet provides a centrally located, separate area for the choir and the organ. The rear location also eliminates the staring contest between the choir and the congregation and prevents the organ from becoming the dominant visual focus of the sanctuary. Because of these advantages the rear loft has been reintroduced to some recent church buildings. However, the rear loft, in new and old buildings, shares the same flaw by contemporary standards as the first two locations because the choir is still completely removed from the congregation. (The theory at one time seemed to be that music should descend as if from angels, although the angels too often made earthly sounds.) Another difficulty of the rear location is the congregation's desire to turn around and watch the organist or choir when they perform. This is bad for their necks and a not very dignified or suitable form of participation.

The fourth location of choirs, in the front and to the side of the chancel area, is the most successful for present-day worship. The choir is in the front of the church but is not the center of attention and not engaged in direct visual confrontation with the congregation. The choir can be seen while performing but is close enough to the congregation to assist during the singing of the hymns. The religious visual focus remains the center of the chancel, and the choir has a more appropriate supportive position. One difficulty with this location in most churches is the potential imbalance of having the organ and choir on one side of the chancel area and emptiness on the other. Another is that the choir and organ require considerable space and are often cramped in the limited space between the pulpit and the side wall. This problem is especially acute in the typical, narrow, rectangular sanctuary. However, in spite of the space limitations, if an existing church has a front side location for them, the choir and organ are probably in the best of the four possible positions for flexibility and appropriateness in contemporary worship.

With all this moving from one place to another in the sanctuary, the choir has acquired an affliction known as choir virus. This virus is characterized by weakened voices and reduced attendance. The choir once gave out strong rich tones of quality music. Now its sounds are raspy and its direction unclear. As the choir gets weaker, it succumbs to delusions of grandeur and repetitious renderings of musical selections. The choir might once have been full spirited and joyful, but the sounds have become melancholy. Paid, semi-professional choir members are hard to find. Voluntary choirs composed of church members have been growing. Some of these choirs have been immensely successful, and others have led to a new low in church music.

The combination of travel distances and busy schedules makes it difficult to get a talented and responsible group of men and women to faithfully attend weekly rehearsals and Sunday services. The changes are not as noticeable in large active churches where some members are still paid and where a qualified director is an inspiration to the group. In churches where music has been emphasized and is a focus of church activity, the choir tends to remain strong. But in the average medium or small church, the choir is suffering from an acute case of choir virus.

Formerly, the choir dominated much of the music and all the singing in the worship service, but if the church is ever to cure the virus in its midst, the choir should take a rest, allowing other forms of music to be part of the service. The choir should recuperate. Instead of increasing their grand isolation, the choir members now need to join the congregation in full participation in the worship service and use their voices to provide occasional anthems and leadership in congregational singing. This change should be expressed in the worship environment, with the choir placed to be an integral part of the congregation.

In some churches the choir seems literally glued to the organ. It may be difficult to move the organ, but the choir members are movable. If the choir is presently in the front loft, either facing the congregation or as a part of the chancel area, existing churches should attempt variations in the location. These need not be permanent arrangements but will be experiments in ways of uniting the choir and the congregation. One possibility is to have the choir sit in the front pews, joining together with the congregants in hymn singing and then standing and turning to face them during the anthems and choral responses. The choir might also walk to the front of the church or gather at the chancel area and return to the front pews. The major objective of these arrangements is to work out a smooth transition during the movement of the choir. Another alternative location for the choir is the side section of pews nearest the organ. The choir would then need only to partially turn to face the congregation. In some churches, particularly those with wide sanctuaries, slight modifications in present seating would approximate a semi-circular arrangement of the choir and the congregation. In churches with the organ in the chancel or at the rear of the sanctuary, moving the choir closer to the congregation would require experimenting with other forms of musical accompaniment. A piano or other instrument in the front of the church would free the choir from the static location of the organ. There is no reason for all music to emanate from one instrument, the organ, in one location.

Initially, the church could attempt a variety of experiments to see which locations are suitable and maintain the dignity and beauty of the worship service. If one particular pattern is suited to the church, it can be incorporated on a permanent basis. The various experiments have the advantage of not requiring immediate architectural changes in existing buildings. The main concern is to not let the existing architectural arrangement dictate the function and location of the choir when they may no longer be appropriate. Because a choir loft was built into the building many years ago does not mean that the choir is stuck there forever. As we have seen before, architecture can limit possibilities. In many situations, the architecture does not have to be altered; it can just be avoided. In most churches, if the choir begins to sit with the congregation, there is no reason for the choir loft not to remain in its present form. To close off the loft or in some other way modify it may be awkward and an unnecessary expense. The movement of the choir is an example of how a changing function can be accomplished in existing environments.

Churches will not hurriedly abandon their present procedures, but they should begin some tentative diagnoses and experiments. A worship service of celebration and participation requires a choir that is able to understand its new functions in leading congregational singing.

Even in new buildings little progress has been made in the solution of the location of the choir. Many churches are still building choir lofts, merely repeating the past, rather than fully considering the alternatives for expressing contemporary worship. Each church, old and new, should give expression to the basic premise that the choir is part of the congregation and the gathered religious community. The choir should be located with the congregation to fully participate in worship, yet separated enough to be able to sing together as a group.

The location that best achieves this is within the fan-shaped congregational seating area of some of the new churches. At the Melrose Congregational Church, in Melrose, Massachusetts, the choir is placed in the center and to the rear of the congregation. The choir's only separation is its placement on risers. This location makes the choir an active part of the congregation, able to provide excellent leadership in all forms of singing. The congregants have a new sense of involvement in the music of the church with the choir gathered with them. Another variation of the fan-shaped arrangement is placing the choir at the end of the seating area, close to the chancel yet within the congregation. In this location, the choir can be close to the organ or accompanying instrument, easily seen by the congregation during anthems and solos, and still part of the congregation to provide leadership for singing.

Many variations of the function and placement of the choir are possible. Many present-day experiments such as multiple and dispersed choirs may become common or may be rejected. In any case, it is important to provide flexibility. In existing churches, historic choir loft and built-in locations should not limit the placement and function of the choir. Inflexible isolation and a false sense of grandeur led to the present malady of choir virus. In new churches, the choir should not be permanently boxed into an arrangement that prevents change and variety.

Flexibility also needs to be applied to other areas of the choir's activities. One of the most static and money-consuming architectural requirements of the choir is the practice room. Ironically, many of these rooms were built to save money. It was thought that the cost of heating the sanctuary could be saved by providing a small room for rehearsals. In many ways it was the height of luxury to build a room to be used so infrequently. In a new, full-functioning building the room could not be built with its present limited concept. In the future, sanctuaries will be smaller and will serve more adequately as a practice area. Another rationale of the choir room was to provide a place for robing, but even this does not justify the room. Choir robes can be stored in cabinets. Choir members can put the robes on in almost any convenient location, whether it be the church office or even in a secondary corridor. We no longer need to pretend that the choir members drift in from outer space to sing angelic tunes only to drift away again. The choir members, like the minister and the congregation, are human beings who wear robes as part of their singing function.

In existing churches, the present choir practice room should be converted for additional use as a part of a full-functioning environment. Many existing choir practice rooms are hardly used and are little more than storage rooms for old hymnals. Often only the egotism of the choir director stands between full utilization of the space and continuing it as a solitary choir room. One of the solutions, in both new and existing buildings, is to develop it into a music room. The room can serve all the functions of the choir practice room for rehearsals, robe storage, and dressing, but in addition it can serve as a music practice and listening area for the entire church. It could provide, on a scheduled basis, a church instrument practice area, relieving many homes from the piercing initial sounds of the violin or the vibrations of a teenage rock group. It could also be used as a listening area, with outlets for phonograph and tape recordings.

The next practical solution for churches would be to expand the concept of the media room to include the functions of the music room. Electronic equipment and sound control are already part of the environment, so expanding the room to include robe storage and practice facilities would make it a very serviceable room. Just as members may come to the full-functioning church center for meditation, study, and creative projects, all individuals should be able to come to the church to both practice and listen to music. The practice room is thus transformed from dead storage space used occasionally by the choir to part of the full-functioning environment, serving not only the choir but the everyday musical needs of the entire church membership. Whether it be the placement of the choir during the worship service or in rehearsal, congregational involvement and choir flexibility are necessary considerations.

The music of the church must become more vital if it is to express the joyousness of the Good News in services of celebration. Eighteenth-century anthems and nineteenth-century hymns are inadequate expressions for present-day worship. New music is needed, not necessarily to replace the old but to broaden the range of sounds and singing within the church, representing

both the richness of traditional music and the vigor of twentieth-century creativity. The choir should be moved from its drafty loft to become part of the
congregation, sharing in the worship and providing the needed leadership for
congregational singing. Only long-range changes can ensure revitalized worship services with a music program that expresses the spirit of celebration and
the total involvement of the congregation.

## MUSIC

The singing and the instrumental music of the church are related by function
and location. In terms of the basics of sound, our voices are used for speaking
and singing; they are our extensions into the world of sound. As a further extension, man has combined invention with sound to create musical instruments. One of the most powerful and wide ranging of these instruments is the
organ, which in the West is closely identified with religion. For many, it is
impossible to conceive of a worship service without organ music. This music
has become so much a part of churchgoing that for some parishioners it is
more an attribute of churchiness than a means to spiritual awakening.

In a return to basics, it is important to realize that an organ provides music
and that there is nothing more religious about its music than about any other
music. It is now part of the tradition of Western religion, but it is not inherently religious. The organ did not exist during the time of the writing of the
Scriptures; its importance is strictly a cultural phenomenon. Much of its identity with worship is sentimental rather than meaningful, and in some cases its
melodious notes smother rather than inspire. The organ has been successful in
the past because its wide range of sounds provides a variety of tones unequaled
by other instruments. The immense power and vibrance of the organ was
needed in many large churches and was an ideal accompaniment for large
groups of singers. Its overwhelming size and permanence were favorable at
the time for its incorporation into religious structures. Many felt that a large
organ built into the building would ensure quality music in the church for all
time.

What was once called permanence is now rigidity. The musical versatility
of the organ has been its strength, but its architectural inflexibility is now its
weakness. When everything within the church was fixed, from theology to
pulpit and pews, the static quality of the organ was no problem, but with

changing theology and more variety in worship, its immobility is a definite handicap. The organ now dictates to many existing churches their entire worship program and environment. When other changes have been accepted and modifications made within the building, the organ often stands alone without alteration.

Every church needs to thoroughly consider its long-range plans for the organ. If the organ is to be used for concerts, it should be well maintained. There is a limit, however, to the number of churches that can justify organ concerts. Among old and young alike, organ music is not at the peak of its popularity. Its only uses seem to be within churches, organ guilds, and roller skating rinks. The typical medium-sized suburban church probably does not have the type of organ that can be used for concerts. Every church has to watch that it does not become inflicted with organ fever. Case histories include individual members willing to donate $25,000 for a new organ, yet unwilling to contribute $250 for a worthy church-sponsored community project, or the music director who is unwilling to spend $250 for new hymnals while planning to spend $15,000 for organ refurbishing.

A major step forward would be a realization that the organ is not the only instrument appropriate for worship services. In the earliest days, the organ was one of many instruments. The emphasis was on the simple, melodious chants, and the major function of the organ was to provide music for processions and the pitch for the chant singing. In time, the organ became larger and gradually took over the music of the church. The progress of the organ is similar to that of the choir. As the organ was given more emphasis and its prominence in the religious setting and worship service increased, its influence grew out of proportion, and correspondingly the role and contribution of other musical instruments were diminished.

The earliest meeting houses had no organs. The Puritans shunned any musical instrument in the worship service, except the pitch pipe for congregational singing. They believed the organ to be an "instrument of the devil." The earliest organs in this country were small and copied from instruments in England. The organ began to swell in size in this country, as in Europe, and at the end of the nineteenth century had reached a new peak. During the period of extensive church building in urban areas, large organs were common and were designed to match the grandeur of the buildings and to provide the soul-stirring music. The organs tried to become substitutes for entire orchestras and had stops and sounds for every instrument. During this period, the pipe organ dominated the field.

Later the electric organ was developed and became extremely popular. Superior merchandising and successful advertising by the electric organ industry expanded the market into many churches. Where the pipe organ companies were often small, unorganized, and musically esoteric, the electric organ companies were large, aggressive, and provided a product that was less expensive and more flexible than the pipe organ. In recent years, the pipe organ regained some of its lost ground as organists and musicians began to speak out against the inferior musical quality of the lower-priced electric instruments. The higher cost of pipe organs can be overcome in smaller churches by the use of a free-standing one-manual organ, which provides a full range of sounds for accompaniment and background music. It is, of course, limited in its use as a solo instrument. Another way to reduce the cost of a pipe organ is to purchase a used one. Recently, societies of organ enthusiasts have been formed to assist, on a nonprofit basis, churches interested in acquiring small, used pipe organs.

The role of the organ will probably diminish in the next decade, so large expenditures for maintenance or rebuilding of existing organs are ill advised. Many churches are considering replacing their present organs; such expansion should be avoided. However, the organ can be moved. Many old churches are remodeling their chancel areas to provide a greater sense of congregational participation in the worship service and during the sacrament of communion; this provides an ideal opportunity to relocate the organ. People often conceive of organs as large numbers of permanently placed pipes, but in many cases the visible pipes are false and the functioning pipes can easily be relocated. The keyboard can also be moved and placed as far as twenty-five feet from the pipes. The difficulty in most churches is not the organ, but the encasing woodwork and floor construction, which need to be modified.

Magnificent organs of the future will be found in a few specialized churches and universities. More modest religious settings make many other musical instruments appropriate for worship. Other instruments have a more expressive tone that speaks directly to many people, particularly to the young and the middle-aged, who do not see religion as the grand, awe-inspiring force it has been in the past, impressing the individual by the strength of its tradition and the power of its omnipresence. The organ, with its floor-shaking tones, was a symbol of that power. In contemporary society, where people expect new ideas and sounds, the use of the organ at every service makes the music stale and ineffectual. The emphasis in contemporary worship is upon the sounds of individual instruments such as the violin, cello, flute, and harpsichord. String and wind instruments can perform both traditional and contemporary music, with even jazz selections being very well received. Other instruments such as the recorder and guitar bring a similar individual as well as plaintive quality to the worship service. Each of these instruments provides tones and musical selections as valid for religious music as the organ. Some of these instruments were used in religious services in previous times, but in each case, churches became stricken with organ fever and gradually all other instrumentation was eliminated.

Smaller instruments are not only more appropriate for the feelings and needs of today's worship service, they are more flexible than the organ. Just as the choir should be able to move, the instruments of the church should have flexibility. The organ is often played not only out of habit but also to justify it as one of the church's major investments. More individual instrumentation eliminates excessive expenditures, for the musicians can provide their own instruments. This will allow the music of the church to vary. In every way, individual instruments provide more flexibility and limit long-term costs. The format of the service may stay the same, but the elements within can change weekly. With the increased variety of music within the service, the organ will play a lesser role, although it will continue to serve as an accompanying instrument for hymns, choir, and the performance of postludes and preludes. With a more balanced musical program, using individual instruments and the organ, initial investment in the organ should be restrained. There is no need for future congregations to be trapped into paying for music they no longer desire.

Too many people think the only alternative to organ music is rock music. They have been deafened by the presentation of young people in an "experimental" Youth Sunday service and have decided something safe, like organ music, is the only suitable music for worship. However, there can be little doubt that rock music will have a place in the religious musical repertoire of the twentieth century. It is the musical form expressive of life today. A lively, active church with new young families and a full spectrum of age levels will need to be open to all possibilities. No church will convert to hard rock as its major form of music for worship, but neither should every church be limited to organ music. In the near future, the new music in the church will probably be not the highly publicized rock but modest contemporary musical forms.

Another dimension of the future of music within the church is the use of recorded or taped sound. Some congregations have successfully used recorded sound during the worship services. It is particularly appropriate when a range of sound is required but cannot be provided by the musical talent available to the church. Recorded music is suitable for music from the full range of the orchestra and special sounds that can be duplicated only in recorded form. The possibilities of recorded or taped music are vast and have only begun to be explored in worship services. An amplifier and speaker system can be installed inexpensively in medium-sized churches. Sound systems should not replace live performance of music, but they will become another alternative in years to come.

In the twentieth century, there are many instruments as appropriate as the organ for worship, and these have been neglected by the church. String and wind instruments are seeking a place in services of worship. Folk instruments such as the guitar and recorder are making a contribution in congregationally directed services. In some cases, jazz and rock will take a larger place in the repertoire of worship music, and recorded sounds will provide a solution to the specialized musical needs of some congregations. Not one of these forms of music will supplant the organ in the near future, but each will increase in importance. The principal task of churches today is to modify the expenditure and attitudes that have allowed the organ to take over the worship music of the church, relegating all the other instruments to the background. A vital worship service requires a wide range of music so that we will not be trapped into sentimentality and can truly make a joyful noise.

## COMMUNION AND BAPTISM

Each element of the liturgy has a long and varied history that has been expressed in the constant change of architectural elements symbolizing it. Church histories show that what seems permanent in one generation is deemphasized or modified in the next. With the present increase in the rate of change in our society, variations in religious practices will become increasingly common. Religious life has been based on consistent principles, but their ceremonial expression in physical representation have always been adapted to current needs. We need to be more fully aware of this variability. In every aspect of the worship service there is a diversity among denominations. Seating, speaking, and singing vary, and so does the performance of religious rituals. The intention here is not to examine the many denominational variations but to emphasize basic principles applying to the physical structure of the worship environment.

The act of communion is the most important and architecturally significant ritual. It has several different names: the Eucharist, Holy Communion, the Lord's Supper, and the Mass. The symbolic setting is called the communion table and the altar. Regardless of terminology, in both the liturgy and architectural setting, communion is being given new emphasis by all denominations.

The new Methodist hymnal has a revised communion service; the Episcopal church has introduced a new liturgy on an optional basis; and the United Church of Christ is developing a new order for the celebration of the Lord's Supper. The Catholic church has also made a number of significant changes that have been officially expressed in the reforms resulting from the Vatican Council. In each case, the sacrament has been given a more prominent place in the worship service.

The present emphasis on communion is a continuation of a long tradition. The Eucharist began in the third century of Christianity as a celebration in the manner of the Last Supper. The participants sat together around a simple table. After the acceptance of Christianity in the Roman Empire, homage to martyrs of earlier times became a part of the communion service, and the simple tables were changed to cabinets to hold the relics of the martyr. In the medieval period, the repository altars held not only relics but a variety of sacred objects, and their size increased considerably. The altar was eventually placed against the rear wall of the chancel area, and was enlarged until eventually it covered the entire wall. Located against the rear wall, with the deep chancel and separating screen, the altar was far away from the worshipers.

After the Reformation many churches removed the elaborate altars and returned to the simple tables of early Christianity. They were placed forward in the chancel area in accordance with the new emphasis on congregational participation. With the expansion of Protestantism, many variations were instituted and have continued to the present. Some churches removed the pews and placed tables in the sanctuary area to reenact the early Christian ceremony. In the seventeenth century the first altar rails were built, to protect the table from irreverent treatment. Later the communion table was removed from its forward location and placed back against the rear wall, with the railing remaining at the front of the chancel even though it no longer had a definite function.

In this country, Protestantism has long been ambivalent about the sacrament of communion. The early Puritans and Congregationalists gave little emphasis to it and placed the altar table in an insignificant location on the floor below the pulpit. It eventually became a repository of flowers and collection plates. Churches having a more complicated liturgy, such as the Anglican and Lutheran, continued to emphasize the altar, adhering more directly to the practices prevalent in Europe. Many revivalist churches rejected the altar altogether, considering it a vestige of Romanism. Because of their emphasis on conversion through spirited preaching and exhortation, revivalists thought the communion table was insignificant and used it primarily as a decorative element.

The trend today toward the community of all believers has effected the removal of the altar from the rear chancel wall and its placement in a free-standing position closer to the congregation. The new location allows the presiding clergyman to face the congregants as he consecrates the communion elements. Where possible, the altar area is open on three sides, creating an intimate feeling of congregational participation. The first churches using a free-standing altar retained the surrounding railings, but to allow an even greater sense of involvement, the railings are now being removed. The free-standing altar surrounded by congregational seating has also been instituted in new Catholic churches as the result of the liturgical recommendations of Vatican II.

An existing church should thoroughly evaluate the placement of its altar. If the altar is against the rear wall of the chancel, for both liturgical and architectural reasons its relocation should be considered. In some churches, the altar could be modified to be used as a free-standing communion table. This renovation should not be attempted by volunteer help but should be undertaken by a master craftsman. In some cases, part or all of the rear-wall altar could be retained in its present position, if removal or modification is too difficult, and supplemented by a new altar. A church involved in remodeling or relocating needs to think through the implications of various altar locations. Moving the altar or adding a new communion table in a more central location will affect the other elements in the sanctuary. A communion table in a forward location may require the removal of some pews in the front of the sanctuary or at least the relocation of the choir if it is in the chancel area.

Over the centuries the communion table has moved forward and backward, toward the clergy and away from the congregation, and back again. In recent years, by being returned to the center of the worship space, it has taken its most forward position among the congregation since the third century. The communion table as the worship focus has been increasing and is becoming a dominant feature of sanctuary design. The central communion table serves as a meaningful symbol of spiritual fellowship within the congregation. The location dramatically emphasizes the act of communion as one of both celebration and congregational participation. John Scotford, writing about innovation in the Lord's Supper, stated:

> The emphasis has shifted from a gloomy preoccupation with man's sin to a joyous acceptance of God's love for man. As a boy I found the communion service fearsome and depressing and begged off from attending whenever possible. In those days any who felt unworthy or who for various reasons did not wish to participate were given "an opportunity to retire" during the singing of a hymn, and many accepted the invitation. Today those who come to church on communion Sunday seem glad to stay through. Shadows have given way to sunshine.[6]

The church should use prudence in emphasizing the communion table. If the Eucharist is celebrated weekly, a strong focal point may be desired, but if the church performs communion only on a monthly basis, it is much less appropriate as a dominate symbol. Some churches have become so involved in giving literal and permanent expression to the centrality of communion that the altar has been carved from stone and built as an integral part of the floor system. Such a permanent position is even more limiting than placing the altar at the rear of the chancel. If the communion service changed, many buildings would have to be torn apart to make even the most modest alterations. The communion table can have permanence and dignity without becoming a fixed part of the building. Even if it is not to be moved, it does not need to be fastened down. If the altar is of substantial construction, it will stand by itself and will still be movable. Too many people misunderstand the nature of flexibility, thinking if something is designed for flexibility, it will be made of balsa wood for lightness or have balloon tires for mobility. This is not the case. The communion table should be designed so that it can be moved. It may have an appearance of permanence, but it should be independent of the building's structure. The history of altar placement clearly shows the need to provide opportunities for flexibility for future generations. The altar at St. Mark's Church in Kansas City, Missouri, is constructed of stone, yet six men can move the altar to another location. At the North Christian Church in Columbus, Indiana, the altar is constructed of ten solid but separate elements that can be used in a variety of shapes as well as relocated within the sanctuary. A flexible arrangement can provide a more usable church facility and, if used with discretion, more meaningful and beautiful worship services. John Scotford, who has spent most of his life working with churches and architectural problems, at the age of eighty said:

> We could enrich the life of our congregations by offering the Lord's Supper in many different forms. There should be large celebrations in the big church and small observances in a chapel, the lounge, and the homes of the people. At times it should be brought to the people in the pews, at other times they should kneel at the altar rail. Some services should be largely musical, others should proceed with few words and much silence. Through a wise use of the Supper of Our Lord it can both widen and deepen the Christian commitment of its people.[7]

Baptism, like communion, has a varied history and a wide range of individual interpretations. With these variations, the architecture and design of the baptismal area and font have also altered. In each period, the value placed on the rite has influenced its architectural placement and construction. Baptismal fonts have been located both prominently and inconspicuously in the chancel area, in side rooms adjacent to the entry, in the center of the entry, in side chapels off the main sanctuary, in separate buildings, and in separate baptismal areas in a variety of locations throughout the church. In some periods, baptism has been considered the most important aspect of Christian life. The Leaning Tower of Pisa was designed as a place for administering baptism. In other times, baptism had a minor role, as in the New England meeting houses which had no formal baptismal font. In this century, many churches assigned baptism to a minor role, and baptismal fonts are small and placed in insignificant locations. At the present time, the rituals and symbols of worship are receiving new emphasis, and even some churches with little liturgical formality are giving renewed attention to the ceremony of baptism.

Theologically, baptism is essential for entrance into the Christian faith. Baptism in the early church was a rite performed at the earliest possible date so that salvation would not be denied the child in case of early death. Baptism also became the naming ceremony of the child, enforcing its early performance in the present time. Along with the renewed emphasis upon baptism, there is concern that the rite may be unduly early. The ritual of baptism has a strong appeal to parents, but its meaning to the youngster is in question. New approaches are being explored in order to make the act more meaningful. In many churches, this was accomplished in the past by the act of confirmation, in which the young adult confirmed the decision of faith made in his name by the parents. Other denominations have always limited baptism to adults, believing the decision was so basic to the Christian faith that it needed to be performed with the full understanding of the baptized. These variations indicate not only historical differences but also present-day varieties of emphasis and meaning. Every church should clearly evaluate its beliefs and attitudes toward the sacrament of baptism and their symbolic and architectural expression. The basic sacrament will always be a part of the Christian faith; however, flexibility is needed in consideration of its role within the total context of the church. This does not mean that the baptismal font has to be on wheels and weigh five pounds so that it may be moved at a moment's notice. The baptismal font can be large; it can be heavy; it can be designed with dignity and a sense of permanence; but it should not be permanently fastened to the building structure.

Each church should make a list of questions similar to those asked by John Morse in his *To Build a Church*. The answers will influence the type of architectural and design solution appropriate to the beliefs and feelings of the clergy and congregation. Morse asks:

> Is Baptism the infusion of God's grace by means of the priest, without involving the congregation at all, or is it the dedication of parents who covenant with God to raise the child in the Christian life? Or is it the act of the congregation in accepting the child into the Christian community, an acceptance that will later be confirmed by the covenant of the child when he is able to make the decision in his own behalf? Or is it the covenant of a person who voluntarily enters into a relationship with God and His Church, dying to the world and being raised to a new life of faith and

obedience? Is the congregation a necessary part of Baptism or can it take place just as well in a side room, or in a hospital, or the family living room? May only an ordained clergyman perform the act or does the clergy function simply in behalf of the congregation? When these questions are not faced, decisions are based on historical recollections, the personal preferences of the architect, or mere chance.[8]

Much has been written about the symbolic importance of entering the Christian community through the rite of baptism. Some churches have interpreted this symbolism literally and have placed the font at the front entrance to the church. The church needs to be careful that in any architectural expression of symbolism it balances theological and practical considerations. The placement of the font at the entry is logical theologically but runs into difficulty in the practical use of the building. The entrance functions essentially as a building circulation area, and a baptismal font can become an obstacle, rather than a symbol, if it is not carefully designed. The Catholic church has traditionally solved this problem by placing the baptismal font to the side of the entry, in a separate room. The difficulty with this location for most Protestant churches is that congregational participation in the ceremony is limited.

In recent years, there have been some ingenious solutions to the problem of combining the dual functions of the baptismal font as a symbolic entry into the Christian faith and as a focus in the worship center. The main entrance of the Emmanuel Presbyterian Church in Chicago is designed with glass between the lobby and the chancel. The font is located in the chancel, near the glass. The congregant can see the baptismal font upon entering the church and also as a visual symbol within the sanctuary. The difficulty with the plan is the long entry corridor required, which would be unsuitable in most churches. In the Grace United Methodist Church in Friendly, Maryland, the baptismal font is to be located in a special side aisle adjacent to the multi-purpose worship space. In this location, the font is near the entry and still visible to the congregation during the service and the ceremony of baptism.

In some churches, the baptismal font has replaced the lectern on one side of the altar. This is a reasonable compromise to maintain the major religious symbols in the total context of the worship center. It is also the type of alteration that can easily be made within existing churches. Other churches, particularly those using token amounts of water in the ceremony, can utilize a baptismal font composed of two elements, the supporting stand and the sacramental bowl. The total font can be placed in a variety of locations throughout the church, and during the ceremony of baptism the bowl can be removed and brought to the center of the sanctuary. This solution provides both permanence of location and functional flexibility.

Churches that require total emersion need more complex architectural solutions. A standard approach is locating the baptistry behind the rear wall of the chancel, which provides some convenient construction advantages but is a completely inadequate expression of congregational participation. More effective solutions have been covered pools in the chancel, sanctuary, or other appropriate areas. Some churches use portable covers over the pools. Other churches have left the pools open as a constant and beautiful symbol. If designed with dignity and located in an area open to the congregation but not too obstructive, the open pool can be the most successful solution. One of the most outstanding examples of the open baptistry is the North Christian Church in Columbus, Indiana. The pool is located in a separate chapel open to the entrance area and is designed with elegant stone and grille work. The total cost of such a space, however, is increasingly prohibitive and may be overly luxurious. A modified form of the same concept might provide a successful solution for other churches. The most ecumenical and practical solution to the question of baptistry has been achieved at the Interfaith Center in the new city of Columbia, Maryland. The center was designed to provide religious facilities for five Protestant denominations, Catholics, and Jews. One of the unique design and religious dimensions of the center is the baptistry, which is located in the large entry that unites the spaces of the religious groupings. The baptistry is used by both Catholics and Protestants. It is near the entrances to the church areas and, with the generous spaces of the entry, is able to maintain a sense of importance and dignity. The shared development of the building has also provided a well-designed baptistry that is of modest expense to each of the participating groups.

The baptismal area is increasing in theological and symbolic importance in our churches. It will therefore be placed in more prominent architectural locations and be given greater design emphasis. The congregation will need to think through its genuine feelings of baptism and work closely with the architect to give expression to their beliefs. They must be careful not to apply its symbolism too literally or rigidly and to allow for changes within the total context of the religious community.

## FELLOWSHIP

In the past, church members in a small town or city parish saw each other throughout the week, and church events were an integral part of the community. Because people were members not only of the local church but also of the local community or neighborhood, relationships were not limited to Sunday morning and were a part of everyday life. Now church members rarely see each other except at church-sponsored events. With the broader range of interests, leisure activities, and more specialized careers, church members have much less in common than they had in previous eras. The problem is further compounded by the mobility that is characteristic of our time. In a single year, 36 million Americans change their place of residence. There is in many churches a constant influx and outflow of members. The stable population that formed the basis of a smoothly working volunteer church organization has been dissipated. New forms of church organization are necessary to deal with the changing conditions.

A church membership drawn from a constantly shifting population of unrelated individuals must face the task of bringing these people together on some meaningful basis. Participation in the worship service alone, even though it is the central focus of the church community, does not provide a broad enough spectrum of personal relationships. A church needs to provide a full range of human experiences. The members want to be involved in the exchange of ideas in discussion, special programs, art activities, and social gatherings. These forms of interaction are an increasingly important part of religious life. However, because of past and present inadequacies of these auxiliary church activities, fellowship is a much abused concept in the religious tradition. It has been used as a rationalization to cover a multitude of avoidances of primary religious and ethical needs. In many churches, particularly in suburban locations, the social life has received such strong emphasis that churches have become little more than tax-exempt country clubs. But the fact remains: religious communities have always been based on a social as well as on religious unity. One of the principal tasks of the church today is to provide opportunities for the full range of human relationships in order to develop a sense of fellowship and community among the congregation. The challenge of this task is to do it without losing sight of the ethical and religious ideals of the church.

Fellowship is best expressed in the full-functioning environment in such rooms as the adult program lounge, the study library, and the projects room. Each of these spaces provides settings for small groups of individuals to get together. In this respect, the broad category of fellowship permeates every part of church life and its facilities.

The parish hall is the traditional expression of fellowship within the church. In some churches, the room has even taken on the name of fellowship hall. Parish halls have been designed in all shapes and sizes. They are located in prominent positions with elegant furnishings and in badly neglected left-over basement spaces. The parish hall has probably received more attention and experimentation than any other part of the religious structure. Architecturally, it has been divided, expanded, and contracted; functionally, it has been used for religious, educational, social, and community gatherings.

The parish hall seems to be an area that is either very well or very poorly used. In many churches, the hall is the one room that comes closest to being fully utilized. This is especially true in halls that have been converted into classrooms for use on Sunday morning and are still used for a variety of church and community activities throughout the week. In other churches the parish hall is probably the least-used room in the entire building. Some churches do not even use the room on Sundays and only occasionally during the remainder of the week. This problem is compounded in buildings that have both a large upstairs parish hall and another hall downstairs. Usually, the downstairs hall is developed because of the pressures of church school growth and the convenience to the kitchen for large adult gatherings. In these situations, the upstairs parish hall probably is idle most of the time. In the same building, there may be a full-functioning basement hall and a nonfunctioning parish hall upstairs.

The location of the room and the needs of the church will determine the most appropriate function of the existing parish hall. It may be that it is best adapted to programs of the full-functioning environment such as a community nursery or adult program lounge. If the parish hall in existing churches is to become fully operable, it needs to be adapted to provide for an increased variety of functions. Dingy walls, stale curtains, and echoing confines are no longer adequate for a fully utilized area. Bright walls, clean surfaces, and sound-absorbent materials can transform a room from an old basement or nondescript upstairs hall to a colorful, pleasant environment. The major consideration is for the church to recognize the potential of the parish hall as a vital part of the religious community and to be willing to both improve the space and use it as a part of the full-functioning environment.

The past concept of the parish hall is inadequate for new churches. One of the principal functions of the parish hall was to provide a room for church suppers and receptions, but these are not at the height of popularity at the present time. Even though many parish halls were well used in existing churches, the space will need more stringent design requirements in future buildings. Many churches will find that the spaces designated as the sanctuary will serve the same functions as the former parish halls. The fellowship hall can be designed as an extension of the sanctuary to provide overflow seating for worship services, as well as space for supper, classes, and other church functions. Jewish temples have long been designed with the fellowship halls coordinated with the sanctuary, for the synagogue has long been a social as well as a religious gathering place. The secular life of the larger community was not integral with Jewish religious life. These needs, combined with traditional Jewish concepts of fellowship in religion, made the design of space for social life in the synagogue a necessity. The adjacent social hall also solved the seating problem caused by fluctuating attendance at worship services. The Jewish tradition places a strong emphasis upon participation in the high holidays. At these special services, attendance far exceeds the weekly average. To solve this problem synagogues have placed fellowship halls in a variety of ingenious locations in relation to the sanctuary. The social areas have been placed side by side, behind, in front, and at all angles to the sanctuary. The goal in every case has been to provide an area that can be used as conveniently as possible for the expanded seating of the worship space. In the future, more churches will need to design their building to provide for the variations in attendance related to seasonal worship.

The fellowship area can provide space for a full range of programs during the week and even on Sunday morning and still provide overflow seating on special Sundays. In the past, churches have designed their sanctuaries for the highest possible attendance at Christmas or Easter. Churches can no longer afford, nor desire to build, for these special services. An adjoining fellowship space, divided by folding doors, can provide an economical solution to the expanded seating requirements of these services.

A somewhat different and innovative solution to the fellowship area has been designed for the Melrose Congregational Church in Melrose, Massachusetts, a church with more than a thousand members. In smaller churches, one multiuse room is an adequate and economical solution to the needs of both fellowship and worship. In other churches multifunctional auxiliary spaces for overflow seating, similar to those in synagogues, are practical. However, in very large churches, there may be so much activity that more carefully delineated spaces are necessary. At Melrose the fellowship area is the central entry, designed to serve both as the entry and the fellowship space.

Most church entries are restrictive, their only purpose being to provide circulation space. The multiple functions of the fellowship area in the Melrose Congregational Church allowed the practical development of a very generous and inviting space. The area serves as a gracious entry to the church and as a place for a variety of functions, including conversation and coffee hours before and after worship services. The gracious setting of the area encourages and enhances the quality of fellowship within the congregation. The area is large enough to accommodate two hundred tables and is ideal for dinners and receptions. Throughout the week, the room is used for fairs, art exhibits, and meetings. Its location, convenient to the entrance of the church, makes the area ideal for community groups; there are no problems with people wandering all over the building trying to find the parish hall. The area can be divided into three sections. The entry to the sanctuary is in the center, and both sides are flanked by areas that can be separated into classrooms or meeting rooms. It might have been better if the sanctuary and fellowship space were connected by folding doors, allowing the fellowship area to provide overflow seating for special occasions. However, the basic principle has been adapted by providing folding doors for overflow seating in the adjacent chapel and adult lounge. On Sunday morning, services are held in the sanctuary and the social hour in the fellowship area. The convenient fellowship gathering space before and after services helps create a more unified church membership. During the week the areas are also used together. One evening a drama was performed in the sanctuary, and the fellowship area served as the convenient social gathering space. At other times during the week each of the rooms can be used separately.

In a time of increased human separation, relationships within the church will be increasingly important, and the church organization and the facilities will need to reflect this emphasis. Existing parish halls will need to be redecorated and more fully utilized to provide for membership gatherings and a full range of programs. New churches will give greater emphasis to the fellowship hall as a place of weekday activity, fellowship, and auxiliary seating for worship services.

## MEETING AND WORSHIP

We are in a period of experimentation in religious life and worship, and this is reflected in our church environments. James White, author of *Protestant Worship and Church Architecture*, stated:

> At the present time the churches of this country are at the beginning of what may be a great new reformation. Indeed, historians of subsequent centuries may look back upon our period in time as one of great renewal and strengthening within the church just as we now consider the previous century as one of tremendous work in the expansion of the faith.[9]

This period of experimentation is filled with both vitality and uneasiness. The very uncertainty of the future is an important impetus to the experiments of the present. Rev. White goes on to say:

> Perhaps no other phrase sums up the various features of the new reformation as does the term "Liturgical Movement." At its heart are the results of great Biblical, theological, historical, and ecumenical stirrings of our time. It is through the liturgical movement that this new ferment enters the life of the parish church. It would be impossible to distinguish completely between the liturgical movement and the other great movements of our time. The liturgical movement tends to be an application and expression of the whole twentieth century reformation where it most directly affects the life of the Church.[10]

The present search is leading to an emphasis on the basics of religious faith and a return to the modes of the early church. Each denomination is looking back to its origins to gain a new sense of purity and strength for its continued mission. Part of this return to basics includes an evaluation of the essential elements of worship. The worship service and worship center will become more flexible. Most parishioners do not want every service to remain the same year after year. Even within the most disciplined traditions the number of variations is increasing, dependent upon ministerial leadership, congregational membership, and regional and metropolitan influences. The basic elements remain the same, but their use in relation to each other is changing. These changes will be reflected in the visual focuses of the worship service. Some associate a flexible worship space with a prefabricated building, but a religious space can be permanent and still allow flexibility through the varied use of chancel furnishings and congregational seating. A pulpit built into the structure cannot be altered without great expense, but a free-standing pulpit can be moved, allowing greater possibilities of communication. In the past century, churches carried monumentalism and sentimentality to the extreme; it is now time to return to basic considerations. The church needs to provide a setting of beauty and dignity to give expression to the eternal chain of life and religious affirmation. The most practical solution is to create a full-functioning worship space. These spaces are not all-purpose rooms; nor are they one-hour-a-week sanctuaries. They are areas where the religious community can meet as a united body.

The basic elements of the worship service come together in the room traditionally called the sanctuary. This area has usually been divided into congregational space and sacred chancel area. The seating of the congregation can be in many forms, shapes, and sizes; the chancel is equally characterized by a variety of arrangements, emphases, and furnishings. In existing buildings, it is possible to improve or change these elements individually, but because of the interrelationship, coordination is increasingly important. Seating must be considered in relation to the pulpit, and the pulpit in relation to the communion table. Similar to the need for a long-range master plan in the total construction of the church facility is a need for a master plan in the remodeling or altering of the sanctuary area. A master plan would allow one element to be changed at a time within the context of an overall plan to be implemented over several years. A long-range sanctuary plan would eliminate change for its own sake and would lead to a better-integrated worship setting.

Along with a reevaluation of elements of the sanctuary, there have been some experiments in the design of the total setting of the worship space. New buildings have incorporated many changes in seating and chancel design into the total concept of the religious environment. Similar to the other aspects of the full-functioning program, the basic premise of each of these design solutions is increased utilization and flexibility. In the best examples, this is done not only to save money but as a clearer expression of the role of worship in the total life of the church, in the individual lives of the members, and their contribution to the larger community. Worship cannot continue to be isolated in rigid sentimental environments. A full-functioning environment for worship requires a space that can be used for more than Sunday morning services and an occasional wedding. The six unused remaining days, instead of symbolizing the joy of the Good News or the sacredness of belief, have come to mean the irrelevance of the institution in the daily lives of its members. Instead of representing the foundations of daily religious values, the continually vacant sanctuary denotes the tangential quality of religion in everyday life.

The worship area needs to represent the values of a fully utilized environment. As an expression of this need for a revitalized religious community worship center, the traditional name of the sanctuary could be changed to the meeting room. The term "sanctuary" seems inconsistent with the more varied functions of the worship space. "Sanctuary" in our time connotes removal from society and escape from daily living. In the medieval period "sanctuary" did not mean removal but denoted a place of worship that was an integral part of daily life. If the concept of the sacred was a more continuous part of our thinking, "sanctuary" would be more acceptable, but it has come to mean a specialized part of an already isolated religious orientation. There are many possible names for a revitalized sanctuary. Some churches now use the term "worship space" or "sacred area," but both of these designations indicate an overly restrictive use of the area. The highly successful church architect Patrick Quinn has designed within a modest budget a church of good design and exciting spaces at Chico, California. In the Church of Our Divine Saviour he has introduced a new designation for the main area of the church. Called the people space, it is the focus of the church building, with auxiliary spaces radiating from the central core. Other possible titles for the sanctuary include the great hall, all-purpose room, multipurpose area, and assembly space. Each of these possibilities seems too prosaic for a house of worship, with the possible exception of the great hall, which is too pretentious. The liturgical churches such as the Catholic and Anglican continue to use the traditional term, nave, which has validity but is not reflective enough of the present broader concepts of the area.

The simple change in designation to the meeting room may help overcome some of the restrictions churches now place upon themselves. The term is consistent with the expanded functions of the space and clearly expresses the emphasis upon participation in worship and fellowship in the religious community in the context of commitment and celebration. The *the* is important, for the room is not just an ordinary meeting room, which one might find in any building, it is *the* meeting room. The meeting room still has the qualities of a special place for worship and the gathering of the religious community. The meeting house is a more closely related historical reference, with its emphasis upon religious community. The meeting houses were simply designed and easily adapted to a variety of functions, including all forms of church and community meetings.

There is no magic in mere names. If a church calls the space the nave or sanctuary or all-purpose area and uses it as a full-functioning environment, the title is unimportant. Here we shall use "sanctuary" for existing churches that are already named. "The meeting room" could be a more appropriate future designation.

The church community would be strengthened by the use of the meeting room for a wide variety of activities. A shared supper would have deepened meaning. A business meeting might be more attuned to the religious dimension. The church would be less likely to fall into the hypocritical position of investing in munitions stock at business meetings in parish halls and praying for peace in their sanctuaries. By conducting business and worship in the same space, the membership would be constantly reminded of the importance of ethical considerations in all aspects of church life. The room would take on the qualities of a special place, not because it is called the sanctuary and is used for Sunday morning worship, but because the religious community has shared together the full range of experience within the space. They will have worshiped, dined, discussed, and decided together as a community within these walls. They have known the exaltation of beautiful music, the power of prayer and the sacraments, the anguish of decision-making, and the simple pleasures of conversation. Religious life need not be fragmented into isolated compartments, symbolized by a separate worship space removed from the other activities of the religious community. All essential gatherings of the church will occur in the meeting room, whether it be for the sociability of a supper or the drama of a Christmas candlelight service.

Instead of standing dark and filled with empty pews six days a week, the meeting room will be a center for a full range of human experience. Communication, meditation, and aspiration will not be limited to a few hours on Sunday but will be an integral part of the seven-day-a-week life of the religious community.

The meeting room will provide a single space for all the large gatherings of the church. The room is a combination of the traditional parish hall and the sanctuary. By joining the two together, the advantages of both are united. The sanctuary is no longer isolated to Sunday mornings, and the parish hall is a more integral part of the religious life of the church community. Relatedly, the financial savings are obvious in initial investment, maintenance, and repairs, freeing funds for programs and mission projects rather than mortgage payments and heating bills. The sanctuary is no longer a monument to the past but a living environment in the realities of the present. The return to basics has led to the desire to replace rigid pews with flexible individual seating, and ancient encased chancel furnishings have been released from the bondage of the building. Now the meeting room itself can be liberated.

In the past decade, many churches have built a parish hall as the first step in the development of their facilities, with the plan of eventually constructing a large and imposing sanctuary. After many years, they are still finding it impossible to finance the building of the sanctuary. To some churches this is a cause of dismay, but it may be a blessing in disguise. The parish hall, as it is used in most churches that do not have a sanctuary, meets the criteria of a full-functioning environment. It is used on Sunday for the worship services and throughout the week for church meetings, social gatherings, and community groups. Almost inadvertently, the parish hall was designed with the flexibility necessary for complete utilization. Because of the traditions of parish hall use, with tables for suppers and flexible seating for various meetings, the room was not furnished with fixed pews. Similarly, the church knew, or at least hoped, that they would be relocating in the future sanctuary, and the pulpit, baptismal font, and communion table were also designed so that they could be moved. The difficulty with many of these parish halls is their design, which is too stark for total use.

At the present time, a worship space is needed that combines the flexibility of the fully utilized environment with the beauty of a worship setting. There is no reason for flexibility to be in one room and beauty in another. The basic shape and size of the parish hall are similar to today's more limited sanctuary spaces. The parish hall is used six days of the week, and the sanctuary is used on the seventh. It is inevitable and natural that one quality room be built to serve the church seven days a week—a room that would require little more than half of the total construction costs of a traditional parish hall and sanctuary and, equally important, require only half of the maintenance and repair expenses.

Some of the objections to the parish hall as a worship space have been the general inadequacy of the room design as well as the too-obvious temporariness of the furnishings. Often inexpensive metal folding or plastic chairs were used, and chancel furnishings were inadequately designed. A combined parish hall and sanctuary would make available money to purchase quality chairs, and the design of the ecclesiastical furnishings could be substantially improved. People who are critical of the parish hall as a worship space are basing their objections on the unimaginative, all-purpose rooms that unintentionally have become permanent worship settings. If the rooms had been initially designed as full-functioning worship spaces, they would be much more satisfying. There needs to be a planned compromise between the practical flexibility of a parish room and the inspiration and artistic quality of the sanctuary space.

The basic elements of the worship space should be flexible enough to allow changes when needed for special services and future alterations. The additional possibility of adapting the worship space to a full range of church functions and selected community programs varies with the individual congregation. Each church will need to determine for itself the degree of flexibility desired within the structure. A church with a strong liturgical tradition may limit the use of the sanctuary to more restricted programs, while a church dedicated to community service may feel every space within the church should be used by the entire community. The size of the church is an important consideration. A large church may find that its schedule of weddings, funerals, and worship services is so extensive that attempting to use the sanctuary for too many other functions would become an excessive burden. Conversely, a smaller church, with limited financial resources, may have no other choice than to design one area that can serve the worship and fellowship needs of the congregation.

In recent years, a number of solutions have successfully combined the best qualities of sanctuary and parish hall design. These solutions meet the requirements of the full-functioning environment and still preserve the quality of religious space. There are two basic approaches to more adaptable worship space. The first divides the worship space into two or more sections, providing a separation between the chancel and seating areas. This solution is especially appropriate for liturgical churches where the preservation of the sanctity of the chancel is of prime importance. The proposed Grace United Methodist Church of Friendly, Maryland, and the Catholic church in Vettelschoss, Germany, are examples of this design. The second design uses one space as a multiple-purpose area, for worship and a variety of other church and community programs. The Hope United Presbyterian Church in Creve Coeur, Missouri, is a modest-sized church using this approach, and the First Congregational Church in Melrose, Massachusetts, is an example of the same principles applied to a large congregation.

The first design, dividing the sanctuary into a seating space and a chancel area, allows both areas to be used for a variety of functions. The seating area has all the advantages of a multipurpose room, providing space for a full range of activities throughout the week. The chancel area is equally well used, serving as a place of daily meditation and prayer and as a setting for small weddings, funerals, and worship services. In some ways, this two-part sanctuary design is an adaptation of the traditional concept of the chancel as a separate space for the worship of the clerical orders (a type of chapel) and the nave as the seating area for the people. The significant difference for contemporary worship is that the chancel and seating area are both designed for full use by the members of the congregation. The pulpit is located in the all-purpose area, and individual chairs are used for flexibility. The communion table, baptismal font, and other sacred elements are located in the chancel area and serve both the larger meeting space for worship and the smaller chapel. The organ console is placed in the chancel area and serves both the all-purpose space and the chapel. Some choirs have used the seating of the chapel during the worship services. However, this location is not recommended, for it removes the choir from the membership. Even in the two-part design, the choir should still sit among the congregation, providing leadership in singing and participating as members in the worship service.

The separation of the chancel from the all-purpose area overcomes some of the difficulties churches have with a single multiuse sanctuary. Many people, particularly in more liturgically oriented churches, feel the chancel should be restricted, having more dignity and sacredness than other areas within the church. It is also felt that some activities that occur in a multipurpose room are inappropriate in the context of the sacramental symbols and, therefore, a separation between the areas is desirable. As an expression of this separation the chancel area could continue to be called the sanctuary, and the larger seating area could be called the meeting room.

The major difficulty in the two-part sanctuary design is providing an adequate seating arrangement. If the separation between the all-purpose area and the chapel is not carefully handled, the design can have the undesirable effects of removing the members from the center of worship and discouraging congregational participation. Churches in the past purposely divided the sanctuary into two parts in order to preserve the chancel area for the clergy while the members were relegated to the nave. If the contemporary plan is to be successful, the transition between the two spaces needs to be handled so the mistakes of the past are not repeated. Keeping the sanctuary to a modest seating capacity and designing a square-shaped space can help prevent the isolation of the chancel area. The difficulty of separation can be further overcome by designing a communion table that can be brought into the all-purpose area for the communion service. The same flexibility could be built into the baptismal font. These arrangements for flexibility would provide the two-part plan with the best qualities of a worship space, the dignity of a sacred area would be continued, and at the same time the congregation would be encouraged to actively participate in the worship service.

The opening between the seating area and the chancel can be designed in a variety of ways. It is important that it be along the length of the widest side to allow access to the chancel. The opening itself can be divided by opaque wood folding doors or movable translucent decorative screens. Another possibility would be an elegant curtain that could be drawn to separate, but not completely close off, the areas. The relationship between the meeting room and the chapel, and their separation, would need to be worked out by each church.

The Grace United Methodist Church in Friendly, Maryland, is developing a multipurpose room and chapel design. It has added an additional feature, which provides a unique solution for the location of the baptismal font. A passageway serves as an entry to both the chapel and the sanctuary and is also to be used during the worship service for baptism. The pulpit is located within the all-purpose area, allowing better communication and eliminating the inappropriate separation of the clergy from the congregation. This innovative design was developed for a long-established black community that required seating for approximately 200 for worship services and fellowship facilities that

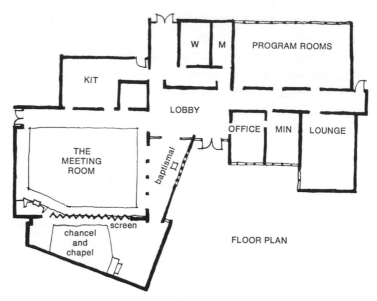

*Floor plan, Grace United Methodist Church*

would permit seating for 150 at supper. The church has a limited budget, and by utilizing the main hall for both purposes, the architect estimates a saving of about fifteen hundred square feet of floor space and lower costs. The church has not limited multiple functions to the meeting area. The sacristy has been eliminated, the kitchen is used for flower preparation, and the general office has cabinets for paraments. The kitchen will also be used for the storage of the table carts. The church has selected interlocking chairs, which can be used both for meetings and for dining. The concept is summarized by the architect, Benjamin Elliott:

> We have developed the plan to make multi-use of space. The main hall would be utilized for both fellowship and worship. The rolling slatted door closing off the chancel area while the room is being used for fellowship purposes. When the door is open, the character of the space will change, revealing the chancel and choir. The baptistry passage and pulpit remain a part of the multi-purpose room, representing the interrelationship of religious and secular life. During the week people would be encouraged to pass through the baptismal passage into the chancel, which would then become a small chapel independent of the fellowship hall.[11]

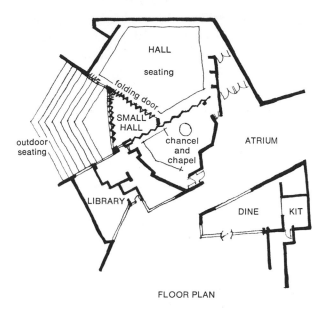

FLOOR PLAN

*Floor plan, Vettelschoss Catholic Church*

The Grace United Methodist Church is just the beginning of the increased experimentation necessary for more flexible sanctuary design. Another example, in a far different location, is the new Catholic church in Vettelschoss, Germany. The architect, Justus Dahinder, has been especially innovative in the sanctuary area, expanding the basic principles of the meeting room–chancel design. In general, European churches have created admirable spaces with simple materials, but in most the pew arrangement and chancel furnishings are rigid, reflecting a more historic theological orientation. The Vettelschoss church is one of the first of the new European churches to break with the traditional static sanctuary concept. Instead of using just two areas separately, as in the Grace United Methodist Church, it has three areas that can be used in a variety of ways. The large space, or great hall, can be used for all large assemblies, either with the chancel or separated from it for more secular events. The chancel also serves as a chapel and when needed is used for additional seating for worship. The third space is a smaller meeting room and stage that can be used separately for meetings, as expanded seating for worship, or as a platform for programs with interior seating in the great hall or outdoor seating in the amphitheater. The variety of spaces of Vettelschoss opens up many new possibilities in church planning. The dignity of the chancel is preserved, and the total space of the facility becomes a vital and flexible environment for church and community enrichment. The two-part design of Grace United Methodist Church and the three-part design of Vettelschoss are well adapted to contemporary needs and have many possibilities for solving the problems of monumentalism prevalent in the past. The design retains the traditional sanctity of the chancel and still provides a full-functioning environment.

The second solution to more flexible sanctuary design uses a single space for all functions. The space is well designed; it has the dignity necessary for worship and the flexibility of any full-functioning environment. In this design, all the elements of the church can be moved according to the needs of the congregation. The seating, pulpit, communion table, and baptismal font may be relocated, resulting in large numbers of variations and combinations. Some churches may decide to have a standard worship arrangement and maintain that pattern most of the time. Other churches will devise simplified ways of relocating the furnishings, using stacking chairs and specific alternative locations for the communion table and baptismal font. The principal advantage of the single-space design is the variety and flexibility of seating arrangements that are possible within a unified space. Semi-circular seating surrounding the communion table and pulpit, with the choir sitting with the congregation, are particularly well suited to the open plan.

One of the most successful meeting room designs has been achieved at the Hope United Presbyterian Church in Creve Coeur, Missouri, near St. Louis. The church, which has approximately 330 members, is located in a rapidly growing suburban area. The congregation began to meet in rented quarters and was characterized in its early stages by its active participation in the improvement of the area. Before building, the congregation made an extensive evaluation and statement of its beliefs and direction. A church that intended to serve the community, it wanted to be sure that the building would not dominate its primary mission. The members wanted to express their sense of participation within the context of their religious life. The following statement, made in 1965, is from the introduction of "The Report to the Architect on the Future Programming for Hope United Presbyterian Church":

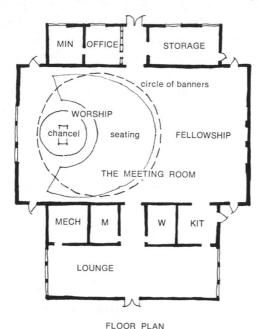

FLOOR PLAN

*Floor plan, Hope Presbyterian Church*

Since in the reformed tradition there is no valid distinction between sacred and secular—this being true also in the spaces of the church building—all facilities should serve the total life of the church through diversified uses. With regard to the question of providing a space designed exclusively for worship it is recognized that while this is desirable it is not essential. In our changing urban culture, buildings ought to plan for the use of a "pilgrim people" with the understanding that needs change and that since our worship is of God rather than of building, the buildings themselves are expendable. In the wisest stewardship of resources, the building should serve all the people of the community as appropriate to the mission of the church and the church should not, through self-concern, use its resources at the expense of the church-at-large. Furthermore, the purpose of the church in the Reformed tradition is fulfilled not through a building elaborately built or sentimentally retained but in worship, witness, and mission in the community and in the world. In the wisest stewardship within the Reformed tradition of the centrality of the word, the church should seek good design through simplicity rather than through lavish decoration.

The congregation not only stated its determination in general terms but listed under separate headings the specific details of its goals. On the topic of congregational seating the members stated:

> Congregational seating: Reformed worship requires the active participation of the people. Number One, any architecture which seduces the congregation into spectator worship is false. Therefore, the theater effect or Gothic tunnel effect is inappropriate. Number Two, since the choir is part of the congregation, its seating should be identifiable with the congregation. Number Three, the congregation should be seated so as to convey the impression of the people of God gathered to receive the word of God as spoken and visualized. Since congregation, pastor, and choir are one, this is best expressed by a single space with no appendages. There should be no barriers between people, pulpit, font, and table.

The resulting design is a large, unencumbered space with beige decorative block walls and a steel truss and wood-deck ceiling. The under floor is vinyl tile covered with a heavy-duty carpet that can be rolled back to the walls. The roll-up carpeting is an indispensable part of the success of a large flexible space because it provides the needed sound-absorbent floor necessary for large gatherings and the sound control necessary for varied use within the larger space.

It would be naïve to assume that the single space does not present problems. The need to move furnishings to provide space for the variety of activities can be annoying. However, as church members become aware of their financial limitations, many would rather move a few chairs from time to time than be continually faced with the overwhelming burden of a mortgage and maintenance budget that dominates every aspect of church life. A specific problem at the Hope United Presbyterian Church is the large size of the main space, and it has been difficult for the members to effectively use the entire area. Another church with the same size congregation and attendance, building in the meeting room concept, could easily build a smaller single room. At Hope, the worship focus requires only a portion of the space, and the remaining area has not been used effectively during the peak period on Sunday mornings. At present, it is used as a fellowship area before and after services. The total value of the space would be more efficiently used if it could be separated in some way, allowing classes to be held during the church service. Another possibility suggested by the present minister is to restructure the Sunday morning program to allow more varied activity by children and adults and thus lessen the need

*Hope Presbyterian Church*

for rigid separations of function. But even if the functions are not expanded at this time, using the total space for worship and fellowship is an important step forward in a better integration of church functions. The real advantage of the space is that it can readily be adjusted to new worship and church school patterns because of the freedom and flexibility of the unencumbered area.

The stroke of genius that makes the Hope United Presbyterian Church different from other churches that have attempted to design all-purpose spaces is the addition of decorative banners. The main room happens to be approximately the size of a small basketball court. If the space were left without some extra decoration, it would appear empty and uninspiring. At Hope, banners shape the space, lend interest to the room, and add a focus of inspirational design and color to the religious setting. The twenty-eight banners were designed by Carl Ritchie, a commercial artist who is a member of the congregation and they were sewn by the women of the church. The designs represent church festivals and the occupations of the church members. The banners measuring 12 by 4½ feet, are made of felt and hung from hooks in the wooddeck ceiling. They may be used to define spaces; they can be arranged in a circle, hung in rows, or placed in a semi-circle, depending upon the needs of the congregation. They are used to create an intimate and personal setting for weddings by using banners especially suited to the couple and the ceremony. The banners have been such a successful part of the church that it is known nationally as the "Banner Church."

Hope United Presbyterian Church uses the large central space for Sunday services, fellowship suppers, and all forms of church gathering. The main room has also been used by a variety of community organizations, and special events such as concerts, from classical music to rock. The combination of the banners, chairs, and total furnishings makes the room suitable for a great variety of programs. The flooring has also been a factor of flexibility, using carpet for more intimate gatherings and the vinyl flooring for more active programs. The meeting room truly serves as a gathering place for the entire congregation of the church and as a major instrument of service to the entire community. Rev. Robert Cuthill, pastor of the congregation when the church was built, said of the total project, "The purpose is to show that worship and the building itself are part of the totality of life."

The adaptability of a single space for worship has been applied to a larger congregation in the First Congregational Church in Melrose, Massachusetts.

This church has been able to combine many of the elements of a full-functioning sanctuary. It satisfies the basic considerations of communication, participation, and celebration in worship. The congregation used to meet in a very old traditional stone structure, which was devastated by fire in 1967. Rather than immediately building a duplicate of the previous building, the church leadership and the congregation elected to thoroughly study the environmental needs of a religious center before constructing a new structure. They interviewed a number of architects and finally selected the firm of Sinclair Associates of West Hartford, Connecticut. Rev. Fuller, senior minister of the church, indicated that Mr. Sinclair was the architect most sympathetic to the church's desires for a thorough evaluation of the church environment in contemporary society.

Not until after a year of thorough study and discussion by the entire congregation were plans for the new building begun. The architect was an important part of these deliberations, translating the feelings and thoughts of the members into environmental and structural realities. One of the most important decisions of the planners was to remain in the center of Melrose, one of the older outlying cities in metropolitan Boston with an active downtown area. The keynote of the year-long investigation was the realization that flexibility throughout the church was an absolute necessity. They also desired and achieved a harmonious blending of traditional New England dignity with contemporary design and adaptability. The sanctuary was placed in the center of the church to serve both symbolically and functionally as the focus of the religious community. The church could have fallen into the easy answer of providing a 700-seat sanctuary based on its projected attendance figures but instead wisely decided to build a space for 300 seats and overflow spaces for another 100. The sanctuary was designed on the premise that additional morning services would be added for special religious occasions. In this way much of the intimacy and involvement of the service could be preserved for a large congregation. The smaller sanctuary, or meeting room, also produced considerable savings in construction and maintenance.

The sanctuary is octagonal and has a flat, carpeted floor. There is no formal separation between the chancel and the congregation. Natural lighting in the room is provided by clerestory windows surrounding the entire sanctuary. The exterior windows are clear glass, but separately framed free-form stained-glass windows hang in front of them. Clear natural light is admitted, but the window areas have the vibrant, translucent colors of stained glass. The windows were designed for the new building but follow the subject matter and figures of the windows of the former church.

In terms of the basic elements of the sanctuary, the congregation clearly stated its direction in the final Building Program:

> Particular care should be taken in arranging the seating to emphasize the role of the congregation as participants rather than spectators. The choir must be accommodated as part of the worshiping congregation, not as performers. Just as the sanctuary is the focus of the entire building complex, so are the three basic elements—Pulpit, Table and Font—the focus of the sanctuary. They should be designed as a unified group so that none is dominant except as the worship service dictates. The emphasis must be clearly on the actions—the reading of scripture and preaching, the administration of the sacraments—and not on the objects or individuals. The relation of these three elements to the gathered congregation must express the meaning and importance of worship.

The architect and the congregation solved the problem of seating by compromising between formal fastened pews and individual chairs. They elected to use white painted benches approximately six feet long, which can seat four people. These are very much like the traditional deacon's benches of many old meeting houses. They are dignified, comfortable, and easily adapted to a variety of seating arrangements. The only disadvantage of the benches is their size, which prohibits convenient storage. Speaking and improved communication were solved by the placement of a pulpit that appears to be permanent but can be moved. The modest size of the room, combined with seating in a semicircular arrangement, gives each person a sense of involvement in the service. The free-flowing spaces of the chancel area will allow varied forms of worship.

The church indicated its basic health by avoiding the maladies of choir virus and organ fever. The congregation could easily have purchased a gigantic organ, which probably would have been used only on Sunday morning and would have been permanently fixed into the sanctuary. Instead, the church placed a small organ slightly to the rear of the center of the seating area. The choir sits around the console, allowing the choir to fully participate in the service and provide leadership for congregational singing. The choir sits on the benches, which are placed on movable risers.

*Melrose Congregational Church*

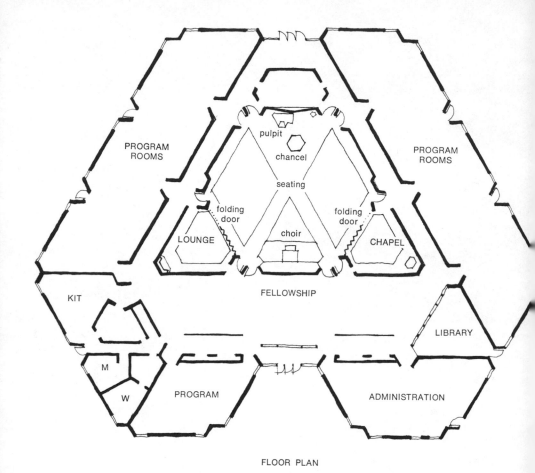

FLOOR PLAN

*Floor plan, Melrose Congregational Church*

The position of the symbolic elements of the sacraments is also successfully accomplished within the sanctuary. The church is a member of the United Church of Christ. The traditional liturgical elements are more modestly represented than in more formal churches. The communion table is a simple movable table, designed in the style of the chancel furniture and the benches. The table is in the front of the chancel space. The baptismal font, also portable, is to the right of the chancel, balancing the pulpit on the loft. The baptismal font is also designed to compliment the other elements in the room.

The sanctuary and fellowship hall of the Melrose church achieve a balance between the two- and one-part meeting room plans. The sanctuary meets all the provisions of the meeting room concept, with only one limitation, the storage of the benches. Active schedules preclude the continual rearrangement of furniture, and some form of adjacent fellowship hall may be necessary. The Melrose church, by designing the fellowship area as a functional extension of the sanctuary, is able to provide the flexibility necessary for a full-functioning program.

The designs of Hope United Presbyterian Church and Melrose Congregational Church at first seem very different, yet they are quite similar. If Hope added a folding door to divide its large room into two areas and if the Melrose church had folding doors between the sanctuary and the fellowship area, the total combination of the meeting and worship areas in the two churches would be similar. Both have provided ample versatility in the worship area, opportunities for fellowship, and the flexibility to provide space for a wide range of programs.

In every dimension of its design, the Melrose Congregational Church has retained the dignity of its past traditions while at the same time creating a delightful, innovative church with all the elements of a full-functioning design. The seating of the worship space is flexible and arranged to encourage a sense of participation within the congregation. Communication is effective because of the small sanctuary area and the increased flexibility of the pulpit and the chancel. The organ and the choir are located to provide their full participation in the worship of the church. The chancel furnishings are an integral part of the total quality of the sanctuary design. The sanctuary and fellowship area together provide a modified form of the meeting room, giving ideal space combination for all forms of church and community activities.

Most of the examples just described are a considerable distance from the pseudo-Gothic or rigid modern designs of the past twenty-five years. In existing churches and new structures, increased flexibility can be achieved. The basic elements of the traditional sanctuary have been modified to make them more compatible with contemporary standards, and this has influenced the shapes and uses of church spaces. In the future, worship spaces will have to become more flexible and more readily adapted to a wider range of uses. There are a number of possible solutions to this challenge. Whether it be the two-part plan of Grace United Methodist Church and the Vettelschoss Catholic

Church or the single spaces of Hope United Presbyterian and Melrose Congregational, each church within its own tradition is striving to find new ways of providing places of worship in settings of beauty—religious environments that can be used throughout the week in the service of the church and the community.

# T

## STRETCHING

## POTENTIAL

he materials in older churches are often elegant, detailed, and impossible to duplicate at the present time because of high construction and labor costs. Even the most expensive new construction cannot match the inherent richness of some older buildings. Part of their beauty is the process of aging itself, which mellows and mutes the materials, blending them into a whole. This mellowness has long been recognized in the visual traditions of both Western and Eastern cultures. Ancient works of art are not just historical curiosities or valuable pieces of property. With the passage of time they have acquired a character that is unique. Capturing materials in their fullness before they become decayed is difficult, and many churches that had the potential for ripeness have been allowed to become bruised and broken.

The special quality of age attracts many people to historical cities and towns. Even those who are not especially interested in architecture appreciate a sense of charm. People visit New York City to be impressed by the grandiose, but they visit San Francisco and Boston to enjoy spacious public gardens, dignified public structures, and graceful homes. Older buildings have a scale and detailing designed during a time of horse-drawn carriages and strolling individuals. Doors, chimneys, railings, stairs, and windows were treated with special attention and decoration. These details encourage us to slow down in order to fully enjoy the richness of the environment.

The desire for "forward-looking preservation" is expressed in efforts to rehabilitate some of the older urban areas, as well as build new structures. Harvey Cox cites Boston as one of the first cities to initiate a significant renewal program for preservation as well as development:

> In the so-called gray areas of the city, a program called neighborhood conservation has begun to replace the bulldozer as the pathway to new

metropolitan life. Most significantly, however, the master plan for Boston's redevelopment envisions the preservation of the distinctive character of such sections as Beacon Hill, Back Bay, and North End. This is important. The nourishment of the local color accumulated in such diverse quarters within a city is just as important as safeguarding variety among cities.[1]

The point here is not to encourage tourism but to show that total urban environments as well as individual buildings can be rehabilitated by combining the best of the past and the present. The challenge for religious institutions is to follow the example set by the cities. San Francisco and Boston have not tried to preserve the past by avoiding the future but have engaged in significant revitalization programs. If they had tried only to preserve their heritage, then they would have died. Their success is in their ability to preserve the traditional, imaginatively create the new, and blend them into a beautiful, united urban environment.

In all types of individual buildings, contemporary remodeling can create unique and satisfying architectural solutions. A recent study of merchandising developments for *Architectural Record* magazine indicated:

> Recent economic trends have made many commercial clients re-examine their existing space and resolve to redevelop it for more intensive use. Furthermore, many marginal or abandoned structures are being thoroughly revitalized by careful renovations. The complexities which such projects present can seem insurmountable to the client's eye. But it is here, more clearly than in most construction, that the architect's ability to seize spatial opportunities, as well as to deal with structural anachronisms and functional problems, pays off.[2]

Urban town houses are being renovated to provide elegant city homes. Warehouse and factory buildings are being remodeled, creating shopping facilities with special charm not found in glass and steel shopping centers. The older settings provide, through their materials, an atmosphere of calm and relaxation, which induces leisurely and enjoyable shopping. The potential of these older structures was largely unrecognized until professional designers and architects produced the first successful solutions. To create a new environment blending the old and the new requires an imagination that is able to see the potential in the existing, and a sensitivity that can balance the special qualities of the old with the functional demands of the new.

It is important that a church planning to remodel bring in an architect or design consultant to help evaluate the physical potential of the existing facility. Churches are one of the few places where people assume they can do everything themselves. Remodeling a church is not a home-decorating game, trying out this curtain or moving that chair. The remodeling of any institutional or public structure requires a delicate balance of skills. It is imperative that professional advice is sought early so that the unique potentials of the old can be evaluated in terms of creating new vital environments.

## ARCHITECT

Extensive denominational and architectural guides have been written about the selection of architects. The recommended criteria always assume the architect is being hired to design a new building. We need to also think of the architect as a consultant for existing church facilities. Architects not only create new churches, they also must help cure the malaise of middle-aged and elderly structures.

The procedure for selecting an architect is too often confusing and inadequate. The experience of a small church in Livermore, California, is typical. The committee attempted to make the selection after conducting a series of interviews with five architects. They began by using a chart similar to those recommended by denominational agencies. The chart was placed on a large blackboard. Across the top were listed the names of the architects. Down the left side were the usual criteria, including design ability, construction competence, personality, schooling, professional memberships, size of firm, church affiliation, total experience, office location, fee range, administrative ability, cost accounting, engineering, and supervision arrangements. After lengthy discussion, the committee decided to place a check next to the requirements satisfactorily met by the architects. As they went through each architect and the criteria, the committee members checked off as adequate most of the items on the chart. With great seriousness the committee proceeded through all five architects before realizing what was happening. Every architect had twelve of fourteen criteria checked. After a long evening of chart-making and discussion, the committee was where it had begun, with five possible architects and no selection. In desperation as the night wore on, the committee threw out all its elaborate criteria and decided to select the architect with the lowest fee. The schemes the selected architect proposed were so poorly done that the church voted the proposal down and waited several years before resuming consideration of its much-needed building program.

If there is a moral to the story, it is to beware of selecting an architect by lengthy charts of endless criteria. Even the manuals that suggest the charts state that they should be used only as a guide. The chart approach fails because inexperienced laymen cannot adequately judge levels of technical competence. Every written work on selecting an architect suggests he should have administrative ability. There is no question an architect needs this ability. If he does not have it, he will not stay in business long. However, administrative ability is not visible during an interview. Administrative ability is strictly a means to the end, which is a completed successful building, and can be judged by laymen only in these terms. Another failing of the chart approach is the inconsistency of the criteria. Unimportant details are listed equally with basic requirements. Schools attended is listed as equal to design ability. Too often officially suggested procedures are written under the auspices of established agencies that are afraid to offend anyone. This leads to vague criteria more suitable for selecting a candidate for Eagle Scout than for selecting a professional architect.

The essential element for selecting an architect is his ability to design or remodel an aesthetically pleasing, successfully functioning building within the limits of available funds. To do this an architect needs certain basic skills, which are difficult to judge but can be evaluated from finished buildings and satisfied clients. There are four essential elements in selecting the architect. First is the architect's design ability; second, his record of keeping within budget limitations; third, his technical competence; and fourth, his desire and willingness to participate in the church's building program.

Design ability is the most important consideration. Beauty is an important part of the religious quest, and all religious structures should consider the qualities of delight and inspiration. The aesthetic quality of a building is an intangible sense of character and distinction. This does not mean the building should have a bizarre design or a weird roof, but rather a certain unified simplicity. The relationship between beauty and simplicity was described in 1963 by the noted architect Pietro Belluschi in a speech before a National Conference on Church Architecture:

The theme assumes that true, eloquent simplicity will enhance the central drama of worship. But simplicity which avoids dullness is a very difficult quality to achieve, and I find it now even more difficult to define. I am sure though that the simplicity we speak about is not that of the fool but rather that of the saint: the result of deep understanding and purification, or, if you will, of an act which has gone through the fires of passion and reason.[3]

The best way of describing the ability of the design architect and his work is not with written words but with examples of completed projects.

Many books and pamphlets on the subject of religious architecture warn against being fooled by elaborate preliminary sketches of the building. They also stress the layout of the plan as the major consideration in the design of the church. One denomination guidebook stated, "Remember that a church is not all aesthetic beauty. A well-conceived plan is first in importance; upon it any good architect can construct a pleasing exterior." [4] On the surface the first sentence seems plausible enough, but it implies that design is really secondary. The second sentence would give many architects nightmares, for it implies that all an architect needs to do is place a few pretty lines here and there and the building will be pleasing. This is a completely inadequate concept of architectural design.

Contemporary architecture is a three-dimensional expression in which it is increasingly difficult to separate plan layout and space formation. The continual warnings against fancy sketches and the emphasis on the importance of plans have weighted the case too heavily against the considerations of appearance and beauty. Planning is important as a major consideration in the development of a significant building to serve the needs and concerns of the church community; however, the planning process must not be considered only as a two-dimensional layout but must be developed in conjunction with the total concept of the building. Facades and walls are not attached to the building after it is planned. They are an integral aspect of any well-designed facility. The church should not be overly impressed with elaborate renderings, but it should not underestimate the importance of beauty.

In selecting an architect for a church, design ability is not just one of many criteria; it should be the basic requirement. If an architect does not have design ability, he should not be considered. Design ability is particularly important in remodeling and redecorating. An architect who is good at economy structures or technical buildings can lack the imagination to see the potential of existing structures. Too often imagination is considered to be the creation of spectacular new structures. Imagination is even more critical in existing buildings, for the limits of the problem, the confines of the building, require particular skills to bring new life to the old structure. A good architect or designer can see the potential of the most depressing room. In addition, his technical training has given him the ability to translate his vision of the room into reality. He knows what can be moved and what cannot, what color can do when it is effective, where decoration is adequate, and where complete alterations are necessary.

Some clients want the most impressive building, regardless of cost; some the cheapest building, regardless of appearance. Others want the perfectly engineered building. In each case the criteria are different, and different types of architects can best satisfy the clients' needs. A church needs an architect who has the imagination to provide a design-oriented solution within a reasonable budget. There are a variety of approaches to finding such an architect. The most obvious is to seek out buildings that are outstanding and find out the names of the architectural firms that designed them. Another method is to speak with junior architects or draftsmen in local firms. They can usually be more candid about the design abilities of local architects than official professional agencies or competing offices. It is also advisable to find which firms have won regional design awards and to have the artistic and architecturally oriented lay people in the church make suggestions based on their own knowledge of local architects. The challenge to the church membership is to develop a list of design-oriented architects; then the other criteria should be used to select the architect most appropriate.

The second criterion is an architect's ability to stay within the available budget. This consideration is particularly important now, when church funds are limited. A church needs to know the total cost of the project. Unfortunately, one of the difficulties with some design-oriented architects is their lack of care about budget limitations. This difficulty can arise regardless of the best of intentions and, in some cases, because of the client's insistence upon building certain features. However, projects exceeding budgets are too common and have created a problem for architects and clients. There is a need for much closer estimation of costs if architects are to remain reliable building guides. It is important that the church find a number of design architects and investigate through direct questions and by contacting former clients the architect's ability to stay within projected budgets. Nothing is more destructive to a project than construction bids that come in 20 percent over the estimated costs. The tendency is to desperately remove basic items, leaving the building gutted and inconsistent, or, even worse, scrap the entire project and begin the long process of design again. Neither solution is satisfactory. Cost control, a prime responsibility of the architect, is a necessity.

The third criterion for selecting an architect is basic and one that most architects can satisfy. The firm must be able to erect buildings of sound construction and mechanical adequacy. It is difficult for a committee of laymen to evaluate the technical competence of any professional, for the field is usually too complex. Many people do not realize that architects hire consultants to design the building's structural frame, electrical system, and heating, with many of their determinations required by legal and code restrictions. The architect maintains the responsibility for selecting suitable engineers, coordinating the structural elements, and assuring their proper functioning, but the actual work is performed by specialized engineering firms whose services are paid from the architect's overall fee. Almost all architects can build reliable buildings; extensive failures or repeated construction problems would have forced them out of business. The criterion of technical competence is mostly a way of eliminating architects who have been extremely negligent. This may be determined by contacting former clients to see if they have complaints about inadequate heating systems, extensive roof problems, and other difficulties. There needs to be one note of caution in this process. Every building has difficulties, particularly in the first year or two, and a period of adjustment is required. Many heating systems that initially seem inadequate have been modified and have proven satisfactory. Lighting is seldom a problem, and complete structural failures are almost unknown. The two main areas of client complaint tend to be roof leaks and poorly functioning air-conditioning and heating systems. Many of the best architects have buildings with a problem, but the overwhelming amount of their work is satisfactory. The most the committee can do in evaluating this aspect of the architect's work is to eliminate the architect from consideration if there is a repeated pattern of technical difficulties.

The fourth criterion is seldom listed during the typical selection process. It is the ability and willingness of the architect to participate in the development of the architectural program. The program phase is of crucial importance in the remodeling and building of church structures. Churches need to define for themselves as well as for the architect the type of environment most suitable for their present and future needs. Industry, business, and public institutions increasingly realize the benefits of having environmental specialists as part of their programing teams. In the past the client created the program before calling the architect. This method was the standard operating procedure, encouraged by all publications and pamphlets discussing architect and client relationships. Architects did not want to waste their time developing programs and clients did not want the architects meddling in their affairs. Programs were easy to devise and in any particular field, such as religion or education, there were many guides detailing step by step, square foot by square foot, the building program. With the rapid rate of change and increasing complexity of design requirements, however, this situation has altered considerably. In most fields, the old programs are out of date, particularly in terms of future needs. Although business and industry have learned the importance of environments, churches have been slow to recognize the relationships between values, functioning, and physical settings.

Site selection was one of the first areas in which the importance of architectural consultation early in the program development was recognized. Typical procedures of the past included presenting the architect not only with a completely detailed program but also with a purchased site. In many cases the land purchased was incompatible with the building needed. The program might require a long, low building, but the site already purchased was often small and hilly. A basement would be a practical solution to portions of the program, but a site already acquired had rock formations limiting excavation. Rising costs have made land one of the most important expenses of any building. Real estate brokers provide guidance in site selection, but their evaluations are often superficial and not necessarily impartial. A building site is not just a piece of ground; it has many qualities important to consider, such as the nature of the soil for drainage and the strength of the substrata for structural foundations. Professional judgments and consultation are required to evaluate both the seen and the unseen factors of the site.

The church needs to evaluate its religious goals, think through the basic elements and expressions of its faith, and work with the architect to translate these redefined goals into a supportive environment. Architects are an indispensable part of this process; they are experts in translating programs into structures. The architect can serve as objective analyzer of the church's stated functions and provide the expertise for their implementation into three-dimensional space. One of the architect's major functions is to coordinate into a whole the diverse needs of the church community. He can facilitate programing by asking the right kinds of questions to help the group develop a meaningful environment for religious life. To every one of the church projects described here architects made an important contribution. Kurt Landberg spent a number of months in church meetings that led to the renovation of Christ Church Cathedral in St. Louis. John Sinclair spent a year working with the Melrose Congregational Church in developing a program.

The church must be prepared to pay the architect for these services. From the architect's point of view, one of the principal difficulties in working with churches is their disregard for professional compensation. Because the members of the church committee are serving as volunteers, they assume the architect should also serve at no cost. As one architect put it, a businessman can operate perfectly normally five days a week, fully expecting to pay for professional services rendered, but this same person on a church building committee suddenly changes all his attitudes and wants everything for nothing. The architect is a professional and is dedicated to doing a good job, particularly in the case of religious structures. He should not be expected to work for a minimal fee, and the church should be prepared to compensate him for the additional travel and time spent in consultation. This fee would be in addition to what is normally expected for architectural services because fee schedules do not include extensive programing. The design and planning phase comes after the church's goals have been evaluated. A number of financial arrangements can be made with the architect. Some architects have applied a portion of their programing charges toward the normal fees and others have made a separate fee arrangement for the programing phase of the building.

Programing allows the architect to become fully aware of the attitudes and values within the congregation so that he may interpret them into an appropriate religious environment. The architect needs to attend committee meetings only from time to time to get a sense of the group's progress and direction and to be of assistance in correlating its thoughts into building development. By participating in this manner, the architect will know the reality and meaning behind the stated program and goals. Anyone who has worked on committee projects, especially in the area of goals formation, knows the real ideas and excitement are in the process of development rather than in the final statement, which is often dry and formal. This is particularly true of a church architectural program. Religion is more than a listing of rooms and their square-footage requirements. The living reality of the religious community is expressed most clearly in the process of developing goals rather than in formal, printed statements.

The architect's role in programing is particularly important when the job will be to renovate existing facilities. The architect can see the potential of existing buildings and has the experience and the knowledge to compare costs of adapting and improving with the cost of constructing new facilities. The present location of the church may have more potential than the building committee realizes, in which case the committee should develop a long-range program with architectural consultation before it decides to construct a new building.

In each of the examples presented here, an architect was involved in programing from the beginning. This involvement helped each group make the decisions that led to outstanding and innovative religious environments. The experience of successful churches using architectural consultants is strong evidence that the architect's willingness to participate in programing is an important consideration in the selection of an architect. It may not have been crucial in the past, but in the present time of flux in all areas of human activity, clear thinking and program definition are crucial to a successful remodeling or building project.

Implied in the programing criteria is the architect's attitude. Most clients assume that any architect would want to design their building. If an architect really is enthusiastic, he will utilize his best staff and resources to meet the client's needs, but if an architect takes the job out of courtesy or obligation, the solution may be quite mediocre. Some would suggest that the architect should have previous church experience. This can work against, as well as for, a successful solution. While some of the operating procedures may be simpler with an experienced church architect, many specialized firms become jaded and lose enthusiasm for new solutions. Their imaginations and energies were used up on their initial projects, and now they are coasting on their reputation. The church specialist may want to give the client only old formulas that are no longer adequate. A firm that has designed quality buildings other than churches is as capable of designing or remodeling a church as a church specialist. This is particularly true because of changing religious needs and the desire for new and innovative approaches. The main reflection of attitude may end up being personality, but the committee will have to judge in some way whether the architect is genuinely interested in the challenge of remodeling or designing a religious facility.

Compared to the four requirements, other criteria for selecting architects are not too important. These include the schooling of the architect, which is only a point of information. All practicing architects are licensed by the state in which they reside and need to pass extensive qualifying tests to be registered. Some of the finest architects have graduated from the most obscure and unlikely schools. Because architecture is related to the arts, there is involved a strong element of personality. Therefore in architecture schooling is only one of many developmental influences. Another factor considered important by some lay people is membership in the American Institute of Architects, the professional organization of architects. The A.I.A. has no official or legal standing and is unrelated to licensing and registration. Some people have the mistaken notion that the letters A.I.A. after the name of the architect signify that he is licensed. Like all professional organizations, the A.I.A. establishes standards for the profession, fosters its interests, and provides services to the community. Although A.I.A. affiliation would most likely signify a reputable professional, the lack of A.I.A. membership should not eliminate an architect who meets other criteria.

In selecting an architect another factor is the proposed fee. The American Institute of Architects provides some guidelines to architectural professional charges, which vary according to the type, size, and scope of the project. These fees are reasonable and variable enough to suit individual needs. Some architects will attempt to get work by reducing fees, but in general lower fees mean reduced performance. If the fee is determined on a percentage basis, a point or two lower will not be a significant factor in the overall cost of the building. It is important that this be understood, for churches often initiate building projects with limited funds and are tempted to save money in the initial planning. A good architect will be able to save money through proper space programing within the building that will more than compensate for minor variations in professional fees. It must be further realized that the scope of the architect's work justifies the fee schedule. Some people complain about the architect's fee even though he designs, provides construction drawings, writes legal specifications, and supervises the construction of a building, yet they never complain about similar fees collected by the real estate broker when they purchased the land, even though all he does is set up the transaction.

In an attempt to avoid the costs of an architect some churches will investigate either prefabricated or total package structures. The prefabricated building company provides the basic components of the building at a fixed fee; these buildings are usually steel structures. The principal difficulty is that the prefabricated parts often rigidly determine space needs, and to date have not been very pleasing in design. The package building concept is more popular. The company provides full building services, from planning to the construction of new structures. The package companies aggressively advertise in religious publications and appeal to the desire to simplify the building process. They attempt to apply some of the principles of industrial production to construction, but in many cases these procedures are more appropriate for large repetitive projects than for individual church buildings. The package companies provide a form of architectural service, but like architects, they vary considerably in quality. A few produce good designs, but most do not. In addition, the companies tend to place all their emphasis on new structures. In general, the space requirements of a church need more time and care than most of the proposals offered by these companies can give.

The principal consideration for the remodeling, redecorating, or building of a religious facility is the selection of a design-oriented architect. It is the church building committee's function to find him; it is their most important task. Design ability is not just one criterion in the selection of a church architect; it is the most essential. The other criteria support the first. The architect should be able to keep costs within the budget, solve technical problems, and be willing to participate in the development of the church's program.

## EVALUATION

A church with a clear concept of its goals and program priorities is able to live fully in the present and work constructively into the future. The existing church environment must be analyzed and evaluated to determine its potentialities. Every church, whether it is presently meeting in a rented schoolroom, an old traditional structure, or a relatively new building, should conduct a building survey in conjunction with its survey of goals and programs. The building survey need not involve the entire membership. A special group or a strengthened property committee could conduct the environmental evaluation. A church should be cautious of entrusting the entire survey to a typical property committee. Too often the property committee is composed of those conscientious and dedicated individuals, necessary to all churches, who are willing to pick up a paint brush. The difficulty is that these people are often not the ones best able to select the colors that they will be using. In most churches, the property committee is extended beyond its ability, for it is usually responsible for the total painting process from color selection to its application. Selecting colors for a home is difficult enough. The selection of colors for the large and varied spaces of a religious environment is even more complex.

To solve this problem, the property committee should be composed not only of willing workers but also of individuals with experience or skill in decoration and color selection. The aesthetic judgment of the committee could be strengthened in a variety of ways. A subcommittee could be formed, charged with the responsibility of making color and decoration judgments, or an existing committee such as an arts group could expand its concerns to include the total church environment. Most property committee members would willingly accept assistance.

A consulting architect can be helpful during the process of evaluation. The committee members can list the rooms and their functions; the architect can help the group articulate the mood of the room and provide expert counsel in some areas of maintenance. He can view the building's environment objectively. This need not be expensive. Depending upon the size of the building, the architect could probably meet with the committee several evenings for a modest fee. He could also help with suggestions to change in simple ways the depressing characteristics of some rooms. The essential point is that the church does not have to build new structures in order to justify acquiring expert assistance. An architect is more than a person who draws blueprints; he is a professional with training and experience in environmental development. He can quickly visualize and articulate needs and solutions for existing rooms even when elaborate construction is not required.

The best procedure in evaluating the religious environment of the church is to begin with the specifics of the building. Rhetorical phrases and glowing words should be avoided. It is not helpful to begin a building survey with long statements about the history and symbolism of the church, "located majestically on the hill." It is equally invalid to use the opposite sort of rhetoric, which says in effect, "We are meeting together in the purity of the early Christians because we gather each week in the dingy basement of the local school."

The simplest way to begin the survey is to list all the rooms in the building and, in order of importance, their present functions. To have any value, the list of functions should include those that are official and unofficial, planned and unplanned. If a room is designated on the master plan as a classroom but is now used for storage, its present function should be indicated. The intention of the survey is to get as clear and accurate a picture as possible of the existing spaces and their use. In many cases the complete list of room functions will be very revealing. If publicized, the list can help others see the total building in better perspective. The listing of room functions is the easiest part of the building diagnosis.

The second consideration in the evaluation of any building is the level of maintenance; this means a simple, mechanical appraisal of the physical condition of the building. One approach is to make a maintenance chart for each room. This should be done only if there is some likelihood that it will be read. There is a tendency in all organizations to initiate paperwork that is conscientiously completed and then filed to gather dust in the inner recesses of the office cabinets. To have any meaning, the compiling of the chart assumes an active property committee with a genuine awareness of the importance of the environment in the life of the church. The detailed appraisal combined with a tangible record of improvement can be useful in developing a successful church environment. In many property committee appraisals, the rooms are considered adequate as long as the doorknob does not come off in one's hand. Obviously more extensive analysis is needed. The chart might also be one way of avoiding the annual property committee ritual, which occurs with the formation of the committee. On an appointed evening the committee walks step by step through the building, checking each room and evaluating possible projects for the coming year. The next step occurs exactly one year later. The new property committee takes the same tour, feels the same curtains, checks the same floorboards, and looks at the same ceilings. Each year the tour is the same; each year the projects are the same; and each year there is no action. Regardless of the good intentions of the property committee, the projects that tend to get completed are those that are the most critical. Leaky pipes and other emergencies will always come before improvements. A maintenance chart would help emphasize the need for a more organized process of development and be a better means of evaluating the present condition of the building.

The third consideration in a building survey is the quality or mood of the rooms and the total impression or feeling one has in the environment. Is it depressing or stimulating, ugly or beautiful? Most people are not accustomed to thinking of the mood of rooms. The typical reaction to a room is probably one of acceptance; it just exists. If the light bulb went out, people would notice the lighting; but if the lighting is adequate, no one pays particular attention.

It seems the bigger the problem, the more likely people are to accept it. The little problems are comprehended and attacked with full fury; a minor noise is considered more annoying than a depressing environment. Most people, including the typical property committee, think of the building and its rooms only in terms of function and maintenance. However, a depressing environment can be as limiting to the full use of the building as a poorly devised plan or a noisy air-conditioning register.

A room's function can be easily listed and evaluated; its maintenance requirements can be seen and repairs made; but the mood of a room is a subjective matter, difficult for most people to articulate. The building survey may for the first time make some church members think of environments as spaces of shape and color that can evoke emotional responses. If possible, it is best if the rooms can be evaluated both during the day and in the evening, as environments can be quite different at different times. As a simple beginning the following descriptive terms are listed. A room can be described as depressing, ugly, strange, dark, stale, uncomfortable, confusing, barren, cluttered, adequate, satisfying, warm, comfortable, cheerful, invigorating, pleasant, beautiful, inspiring. These terms describe an individual's total response to a particular setting. In some cases one word is enough; in others several words may be necessary. There are of course many more words to describe reactions to rooms.

Considerations of the mood can sensitize individuals to the quality of religious environment. Stop reading for a moment and look up. What kind of room are you in? What is its mood? What is your evaluation of the room? Can you list its functions? How could the room be improved? What other purposes could it serve? Just reading questions will be no help. In translating the printed page into the three-dimensional reality of architectural space, it is necessary to stop and think about the environment. Why are some rooms in the church more pleasing than others? How can the mood of every room become more conducive to its function as a setting for church and community activities?

A thorough evaluation of the existing facility using the criteria of function, maintenance, and mood will provide an understanding of the church's assets and liabilities.

The exterior environment of the building also needs to be evaluated. Too many church members feel the exterior is only a covering and setting for the interior and is not an important consideration. The exterior, however, is not merely attached to the rooms inside; it is part of their expression in three-dimensional space. A room with a high ceiling will influence the shape of the roof, and it is obvious the windows affect both the outside and the inside of any building.

The criteria of function, maintenance, and mood apply to the exterior environment. Its functions in some ways seem more obvious than the functions of the interior of the building. Driveways and parking lots are for cars and landscaping for appearance, but even this is an oversimplification. Perhaps the parking lot is used or could be used as a weekday community nursery play area or the grounds for outdoor worship services. The question is, Can these elements be improved to provide better accommodations for various purposes?

Another aspect of the church's exterior design is the total pattern of approach to the building. Can a visitor easily follow the driveway to the parking area and from there to the entrance? Is the approach clear and is it pleasant? It would be helpful for members of the building survey committee to approach the church as if they were visitors and ask themselves if the driveway and parking areas are suitable. It is important to evaluate the building both during the day and at night. Some driveways and parking areas that are clearly indicated and marked for daytime use are difficult to find and use in the evening.

The basic functional elements of the exterior should be evaluated in terms of maintenance. The roof, walls, and windows are generally adequately maintained. If they were not, the church would be faced with considerable interior destruction from water leaks or excessive heating costs from improper weatherproofing. For these reasons, most churches have learned, some through bitter experience, that maintenance of the exterior is an absolute necessity. But many allow the grounds and paving to deteriorate even though they are important aspects of the church's visual appearance.

The mood or the total impression of the exterior is usually neglected. Many dignified older churches placidly assume that this criticism would not apply to them, yet are guilty of neglect. They assume that all they need to do is maintain and care for the historic grounds and building, and they have fulfilled their function. This attitude becomes a part of the problem because their only criteria for exterior development is preservation and historical accuracy. As a result, these churches are distinctive historic landmarks but often prove inadequate for contemporary needs. Increased consideration should be given to current needs, such as parking and building identification.

Many new churches show a similar neglect for the exterior of the building, but for different reasons. New churches often elect to save money by doing their own landscaping, and five years later the shrubs are still not planted and the grass grows only in spots. Ironically, this neglect may be caused by the financial burden imposed by the construction of the new building. In their attempt to provide a more attractive church, the members often end up with a shiny new building surrounded by a moat of mud.

The exterior mood or appearance does not have to be considered in terms of intellectual or aesthetic critiques of style, proportion, or scale, but only in terms of people's general response to the church building. The architect can later provide the aesthetic articulation and the design solutions to the problems that exist. The building might be depressing, deteriorating, foreboding, stark, plain, adequate, dignified, pleasant, or beautiful. Many buildings cannot be completely described in simple terms and need some amplification. Thus, the tower of the structure may be pleasing, but the basic building unpleasant. If the building is an expression of a historic style, the church will need to decide if it is satisfied with this visual orientation. Are there ways in which the present vitality of the membership can be expressed in some manner that still preserves the integrity of the building? If a new building is too stark, will detailing and additional features provide warmth and interest?

The evaluation of the exterior is more general than the evaluation of the interior, but it should not be neglected. It is not appropriate, however, to devote all the resources and energies of the church to the maintenance of impressive grounds and facade. What is necessary is a pleasing, clearly marked, conveniently functioning grounds and building that can be an important asset in the life of the church and the community.

Some will contend that a thorough evaluation of the interior and exterior of the building is too time consuming. They will contend the price of land and construction are rising so rapidly that the church cannot afford to take time thinking and talking. While this attitude has predominated in recent years, the forces of limitations are upon us so strongly that we can no longer assume more building is the desirable solution to a church's problems. There may be a large long-range savings in not building. The evaluation of the church and the resultant construction are not only necessary for the present but will have an influence far into the future.

The advantage of evaluation might take on more meaning if it is applied to a hypothetical situation, that of a medium-sized, older church, facing the growing pains of an expanding population. We can assume the church consists of a typical sanctuary, fellowship hall, church office, minister's office, kitchen, ladies' parlor, nursery, five small classrooms, and auxiliary rooms such as toilet and storage rooms. The seating capacity of the present sanctuary will probably not be affected by the population expansion, for the sanctuary as in most older churches was overbuilt by present standards. The problem is usually too much rather than not enough space. The principal strains of growth occur in the religious education facilities. This church has already attempted a number of solutions to the problem of expanding church school rolls. It has divided its fellowship hall in half to provide space for two classes, but because the room was initially designed with inadequate sound-absorbing surfaces, the noise from each class is a distraction to the other. Another class meets in a large room that was used for the storage of maintenance supplies, but the room is still in bad condition because everyone considered the arrangement temporary.

Characteristically, the church turned the problem of expansion over to the religious education committee. After a brief series of discussions, the committee recommended the optimum solution, typical of past procedures. It decided only one class could continue to meet in the fellowship hall, and the class presently meeting in the storage area needed a new room. In the past few years, the church school program has expanded one class per year, and the committee assumed this trend would continue and planned for a minimum of two new classrooms for immediate expansion and another two classrooms for future expansion. The committee therefore recommended the building of two classrooms for classes presently meeting in inadequate locations, two classrooms to relieve crowding, and two classrooms for future expansion—a total of six new classrooms. The recommendations were approved by the board of the church, and the finance committee began a survey of financial giving based on formulas of present budget allocations and an analysis of current financial obligations. A building committee was organized and diligently did its homework looking up space requirements and compiling square-footage totals. The building committee then interviewed architects, selected one, and gave him the completed building program.

This approach is wrong in every way. The only goals established for the church were those of the religious education committee. There was no evaluation of the potential of the existing facility. There was no consultation with an architect during programing, and the financing was considered in terms of potential giving rather than of financial priorities. A church following more thoughtful procedures could find an appropriate and much less expensive solution.

Before any major change is made in the church facility, there should be a thorough evaluation of goals. The total building needs to be evaluated, preferably by professional consultants, to determine the potential of the existing spaces. It may turn out that the requirements of the religious education program need to be balanced by other priorities. Some churches might decide that the development of an improved worship area or the expansion of the program of community service is as important as space for religious education.

If the hypothetical church had followed the procedures for goals development and evaluation of facilities, a very different solution than the proposed six classrooms could have emerged. With the establishment of a goal to develop worship services with a greater sense of congregational participation, the church could decide to make modest alterations in the sanctuary to make it more appropriate and pleasing.

In terms of a goal of improving services to the community, the church could elect to convert an existing classroom near a church entrance into a community service room. This would require almost no money, only a change of attitude. Another simple step toward increased community service could be the development of the present church school nursery into a community nursery. A few minor interior alterations, the addition of an exterior door, and some protective fencing in the outdoor play area might be all that is needed to inexpensively make this transition. To implement a goal of expanding adult programs and small group activities, one of the existing classrooms could be inexpensively converted into a study library by the addition of carpeting and book shelves. Again, this would require little more than a change in attitude on the part of the membership. A total evaluation of the church facilities might indicate the need for expanding the parking area or providing a new sign so that the church can be more easily identified, or it may turn out the windows or the roof are in bad condition and a major program of repair is required. Each of these building factors needs to be considered in the overall development of the church facilities.

In view of the financial realities of other program priorities and building improvements, the proposed six-classroom addition can be seen in a new perspective and becomes questionable. It is conceivable that the entire religious education problem could be solved without any additional construction and, at the same time, the church could become a more vital center of religious life through the development of a full-functioning program. The ladies' auxiliary area converted to an adult program lounge could provide one of the needed classroom spaces. The church office or the minister's study could be used on Sunday mornings for one of the smaller, less-active classes. If the acoustics of the fellowship hall were improved with ceiling tile and carpeting, the area would be available for two classes again and would have the added advantage of a large, open classroom space. Three other spaces could be developed as full-functioning areas to be used as classrooms when needed. The church could improve the present storage area to make it suitable as a small projects room. Another room could be created in an undeveloped area of the basement now used for the storage of rummage-sale items. This would be the ideal location of the unfinished room and could be inexpensively constructed with simple materials and volunteer labor. Another potential classroom is the existing kitchen. Many older churches have kitchens that are twice the size needed and have large areas of unused floor space. They require only a few modifications to be suitable as a lower grade classroom and provide the added advantage of sinks and protected floors for various activities. The utilization of the present ladies' parlor, minister's office, and kitchen could provide three of the needed classrooms immediately. The next phase could be the improvement of the fellowship hall and the storage area to provide the remaining three classrooms.

In addition to remodeling the existing building for expanding space requirements, other possible solutions include altering class schedules to provide weekday classes or dual church school sessions on Sunday. These solutions are not always popular, but they are a means of solving space problems without additional building.

This case study emphasizes the necessity of evaluating church goals and the necessity of a building survey. Careful study combined with imaginative use of existing facilities can lead to the creation of a full-functioning environment with a minimum of expense.

## SPACE

A major consideration in the evaluation of any building is the functional and aesthetic satisfaction of the space enclosed. Walls, floors, and ceilings are merely the means of providing areas for human activity. They enclose the spaces of rooms, their functional areas. In the words of the architect Bruno Zevi:

> The facade and walls of a house, church or palace, no matter how beautiful they may be, are only the container, the box formed by the walls; *the content is the internal space.* In America, schools of industrial design teach the art and craft of designing packages, but none of them has ever thought of confusing the value of the box with the value of what it contains.[5]

The essence of architectural design should go beyond functional considerations to the development of spatial concepts. The most accomplished buildings are those in which the basic elements, the floors and ceilings, are designed as an integral part of the total three-dimensional reality. As in any work of art, both the means and the ends need to be unified.

To think of a building in terms of space is difficult for most people. They conceive of architecture in terms of its material attributes of doors, windows, walls, floors, and ceilings. Some fifty years ago Geoffrey Scott eloquently expressed the need for greater emphasis on space in architecture, but his words went largely unheeded until our own time:

> Criticism has singularly failed to recognise this supremacy in architecture of spatial values. The tradition of criticism is practical. The habits of our

mind are fixed on matter. We talk of what occupies our tools and arrests our eyes. Matter is fashioned; space comes. Space is "nothing"—a mere negation of the solid. And thus we come to overlook it.

*    *    *

But though we may overlook it, space affects us and can control our spirit; and a large part of the pleasure we obtain from architecture— pleasure which seems unaccountable, or for which we do not trouble to account—springs in reality from space. Even from a utilitarian point of view, space is logically our end. To enclose a space is the object of building; when we build we do but detach a convenient quantity of space, seclude it and protect it, and all architecture springs from that necessity.[6]

Space is the unified result of the three separate dimensions of width, length, and height. It is the area in which human beings function. This human space distinguishes architecture from sculpture. Geoffrey Scott points out:

The functions of the arts, at many points, overlap; architecture has much that it holds in common with sculpture, and more that it shares with music. But it has also its peculiar province and a pleasure which is typically its own. It has the monopoly of space. Architecture alone of the Arts can give space its full value. It can surround us with a void of three dimensions; and whatever delight may be derived from that is the gift of architecture alone. Painting can depict space; poetry, like Shelley's, can recall its image; music can give us its analogy; but architecture deals with space directly; it uses space as a material and sets us in the midst.[7]

These concepts of space have been expressed in the works of Frank Lloyd Wright and Le Corbusier, the architectural masters of the century. Their structures, although different in outward appearance, are similar in their exciting solutions to the use of space. Frank Lloyd Wright's Annunciation Greek Orthodox Church in suburban Milwaukee skillfully combines intimate seating with a sense of lofty, floating space by the use of a circular design and a domed ceiling that seems suspended in air. The chancel, seating, decoration, and exterior are all expressions of the unity of the initial spatial concept and circular theme. Le Corbusier, in what may be the most famous twentieth-century building, the chapel of Notre-Dame-du-Haut at Ronchamp, France, created a similar spatial unity. The interior and exterior spaces flow together in a work of unequaled sculptural grace. Spaces open outward for pilgrimage gatherings and are drawn inward for daily services. Like the domed ceiling of Wright's Annunciation Church, the roof of Notre-Dame-du-Haut hovers, almost independent of the structure, yet providing a unifying element between the exterior and interior spaces. The graceful lines of roof correspond with the curves and towers of the total structure and are a direct expression of the variations and drama of the interior spaces.

In previous eras, religious structures were the dominant expressions of cultural and spatial concepts. Bruno Zevi documents these changes in his *Architecture and Space* and shows how the gradual development of expanding space led to the soaring heights of the Gothic cathedrals. Many contemporary churches have attempted to deal with the spatial quality of religious architecture by designing dramatic and often exaggerated roof structures. This approach has been inadequate and expensive. Starting with the roof and adding a plan is as difficult as starting with the plan and adding the roof. The roof copiers fail because their designs are not integral to the total structure. In Wright's Annunciation Church and Le Corbusier's chapel at Ronchamp the roof and walls and spaces are an expression of the total design concept. The roofs are not separate from the plans but are a natural continuation of their function and spatial relationships. In the words of Frank Lloyd Wright:

> In integral architecture, the *room space itself must come through.* The *room* must be seen as architecture, or we have no architecture. We have no longer an outside as outside. We have no longer an outside and an inside as two separate things. Now the outside may come inside, and the inside may and does go outside. They are *of* each other. Form and function thus become one in design and execution if the nature of materials and method and purpose are all in unison.
>
> This interior-space concept, the first broad integrity, is the first great resource.[8]

The concept of space is important to both new and existing religious facilities. Successful buildings cannot be conceived as two-dimensional plans of length and width, with the dimension of height added on at a later date. More unsatisfactory buildings have resulted from considering the plan as a separate entity from the facade than have ever resulted from too much concern for the exterior appearance. However, a good building is not designed by either of these methods, but by consideration of a total three-dimensional concept from the beginning. Bruno Zevi explains it this way.

The plan of a building, being nothing more than an abstract projection on a horizontal plane of all its walls, has reality only on paper and is justified only by the necessity of measuring the distances between the various elements of the construction for the practical execution of the work. The facades and cross-sections of the exteriors and interiors serve to measure height. Architecture, however, does not consist in the sum of the width, length and height of the structural elements which enclose space, but in the void itself, the enclosed space in which man lives and moves. What we are doing, then, is to consider as a complete representation of architecture what is nothing more than a practical device used by the architect to put on paper specific measurements for the use of the builder. For the purpose of learning how to look at architecture, this would be more or less equivalent to a method which described a painting by giving the dimensions of its frame, calculating the areas covered by the various colors and then reproducing each color separately.[9]

To the layman this means that both the architect and the church building committee need to think of the building in its reality of three-dimensional space.

In the planning of new churches, functional relationships should be considered within the context of spatial possibilities. For the layman, simple cardboard working models can translate words and two-dimensional drawings into the three dimensions of space. Models are now used by architects for design studies and should increasingly be used for describing projects to clients.

The members of the committee need to avoid limiting their thinking to an architectural solution or a series of rooms meeting their square-footage requirements. The church is a living space for people. To help the committee understand these spaces, the architect should conduct imaginary trips through the building. A design model would be particularly helpful. With such an approach, the church entrance, for example, would not be conceived of as a square on a piece of paper, with dimensions that multiply to the square-footage requirements. The committee would begin to see the entrance as the first space that everyone, visitors and church members alike, experiences upon entering the building. The architect should try to describe the three-dimensional setting, indicating what a person would see as he enters the building, so that the drawings take on the three dimensions of the reality of architecture.

One word of caution: the architect and clergy should avoid excessive symbolic language in describing spatial experiences. Entering a lobby is not "entering into the hands of God" or "walking into a clearing in a dense forest." These analogies usually lead to false expectations.

In existing churches, the basic space is of course already there, and the challenge is to use it effectively. The most dramatic element of space in existing churches is the sanctuary. Most older churches were built when theology and the congregation demanded lofty naves similar to those in European cathedrals; it was felt the space should be large enough and grand enough to be worthy of God's presence. These spaces encouraged feelings of awe and reverence. Today, needs and beliefs are different. Most people do not want to feel small in the presence of overwhelming power. They want to feel that they as individuals are significant in relation to other human beings in the context of the gathered religious community.

In our society, the giant corporate conglomerates, extensive metropolitan populations, and the remoteness of government have already made people wonder about their personal worth. They seek in religion an affirmation of their humanness rather than their "numberness." This desire needs to be reflected in the spatial concepts of the church.

Soaring spaces are considerable liabilities at the end of the month when it is time to pay the bills. The vaulted spaces create excessive maintenance and utility costs. In northern climates, the heating bill is often the most expensive item in the budget. High overhead costs begin the destructive cycle of limiting the use of the total church facility to save on overhead, which in turn tends to decrease church activity and eventually membership, leading to stagnation.

All types of buildings are facing similar problems of adapting space to current needs. Through the experimental work of the Educational Facilities Laboratories, school auditoriums, often unused, are being divided into smaller units for classes when the large auditorium area is not needed. Film theaters are another example of adapted spatial environments. Many theaters were built in a time of grand structures. These structures are no longer suitable for the smaller audiences of the present, and the theaters have adapted. Old theaters are being divided into separate smaller theaters, but they share common ticketing, lobby, and refreshment areas. In some remodeling the downstairs seating will form one theater and the balcony seating another theater, with a superstructure built over the space below for the second film screen. These principles of shared service facilities and smaller, more simply decorated seating are also being applied to new theaters.

An existing church has to come to terms with space in a manner different from that of a new building. It has to be especially concerned with the financial problems of maintaining the facility as well as with its theological and utilitarian appropriateness.

Some churches that are supported by active congregations and are centers of denominational religious life may decide after evaluation that the present spacious sanctuary is suitable for their needs. Such a church is the Christ Church Cathedral in St. Louis, but even there, renovation was necessary to make the total sanctuary space more adaptable and appropriate for contemporary use. Flexible seating and liturgical elements have brought a new dynamism to the static pseudo-Gothic interior, and more light has added new dimensions to the sanctuary. Used properly, large spaces can become exciting architectural experiences, enhancing worship.

In most urban centers, several spacious churches are usually within a few blocks of each other. Many of these churches have seating capacities for more than a thousand people. The larger the city, the more likely that the greater part of the supporting congregation has moved to outlying locations and has not been replaced from the population of the immediate area. Therefore on Sunday morning these churches are used for services for fewer than a hundred people and in some cases for as few as twenty-five. Some churches through good fortune, excellent leadership, or favorable population trends have been able to flourish in an urban setting. However, this makes the contrast even more vivid.

If the unattended churches are tired on Sunday, they are exhausted throughout the remainder of the week. They struggle from day to day trying to hold on to their building by maintaining the facility at the lowest possible level. No one is allowed to use the building for fear the heating bill might rise a few dollars. The thousand-seat sanctuary is idle throughout the week, waiting for the big moment on Sunday morning when twenty-five or one hundred loyal souls may attend the services. All this tax free, unused space is wasted at a time when city governments are financially limited because of a diminishing tax base, even though the demand for space within the city is considerable.

The viable churches such as Christ Church Cathedral should be encouraged to remain as important religious and community landmarks and with reasonable modifications can become vital religious and community centers. However, other churches with limited congregations and inadequate financial resources should face the reality of their situation and not try to maintain giant sanctuaries; they should consider other alternatives. There are many possibilities of consolidation or cooperation among local churches or those within the same denomination, through mergers or sharing of facilities.

One possible solution to the problems of an oversized sanctuary is the development of an existing chapel or other smaller meeting area within the building as the worship center. Then the existing sanctuary could be rented or sold to relieve the church of unnecessary expenses and provide additional funds for the full utilization of the remaining facilities. This approach has been successful at Emmanuel Church in Boston, an Episcopal church located in the midst of an exclusive business section near the Public Garden and the prestigious Ritz Carlton Hotel. The church has a main sanctuary with a seating capacity for sixteen hundred. Because of population shifts and the general success of Trinity Church, the famous Episcopal church in Copley Square just four blocks away, membership and attendance at Emmanuel have dwindled. Average attendance at the Thursday evening and Sunday morning services is less than one hundred. The church, however, is fortunate to have a delightful memorial chapel, which it uses for these services. The chapel has convenient access and comfortably provides seating for the congregation. It is adorned with beautiful stained-glass windows and elegant oak decorative detail and has movable chairs. Both in beauty and in space the chapel provides an appropriate setting for the smaller congregation.

Church and community organizations—such as a nursery, a retirement club, and an Alcoholics Anonymous group—fully utilize the remaining meeting and administration areas. The large sanctuary is still intact and is used for special services at Christmas and Easter. This is probably a transitional arrangement, the long-range consideration being the eventual sale of the extremely valuable sanctuary property, which would give the church considerable additional funds to improve its existing facilities and make them even more serviceable to the members and the community. The church could then afford a staff that allows the much-needed community services that have characterized Emmanuel Church in recent years. By having less building, a church can provide more programs for the membership and the community.

Where it is reasonable to maintain the existing church structure, multiple levels might be developed in oversized sanctuaries. Many institutions and commercial establishments have been able to remodel excessive spaces into multiple-level facilities of exceptional merit. Stores have renovated town houses and old warehouses to provide shopping centers that are visually stimulating. Floors have been added or removed to form dynamic spaces. One store in Boston removed the front section of all five floors of a town house, creating a multilevel entrance and staircase, which form private display balconies with exciting views of the various floor levels. Other stores have removed entire floors from old structures for greater ceiling heights or have opened up partial floors to allow a spatial contrast between the one- and two-story elements. In these older buildings, new balconies have been created and old ones enclosed. Another successful technique is the development of free-standing balcony spaces. This could be particularly appropriate for churches. The large sanctuaries could be modified by developing different spaces for a variety of functions. One level could be developed for exhibits or coffee gatherings and another as an adult program lounge. The worship area could be appropriately reduced to a manageable size, and the total worship space would be more efficiently used. The creation of such areas could develop varied spaces with walkways and overlooking balconies to add new excitement. There is no one easy solution to the problems of excessive space. Other institutions and commercial organizations have used considerable imagination in remodeling and renovating existing structures, but churches have not begun to use the available talent and resources in bringing problem facilities to life again.

Space is the essential quality of all architecture; the walls, floors, and ceiling are merely containers for the interior space. Space is the usable portion of any building. Dramatic interiors and roofs with no purpose or relationship to function are as bad as plans with facades tacked on. Any successful building needs to be considered as a spatial entity with the interior and exterior as mutual and integral extensions of each other.

In the design of new church buildings, the membership needs to become sensitive to the possibilities of space and, with the help of the architect, to visualize the project three dimensionally as it develops. In some existing churches, modest renovations will enlarge the spaces and improve their use and flexibility. Other churches may need to use smaller areas of the building that are compatible with their present situation and congregation. In some of these, selling the oversized sanctuary is the simplest and most economical solution. Other churches may find the best solution in the modification of the existing sanctuary space by providing supplementary balconies and other separations that allow more exciting spatial experiences and a better-utilized interior. In both new and existing churches, the three dimensions of space are an important consideration in the creation of a pleasing full-functioning environment.

## MATERIALS

Successful architectural projects enclose pleasant and useful spaces through the skillful use of materials. The selection of materials for the structure to the finish surfaces is basic to any building.

Materials are often a reflection of regional location. Until recent times builders have used local materials for their constructions. The Babylonians built of adobe, the Greeks of marble, and the early American settlers of wood. Although we are less limited by location because of modern technology and transportation, regional location can still influence the selection of materials. If wood is readily available and inexpensive, as it is in the Northwest, it is more likely to be used than some other material imported into the area at higher cost. Building codes with requirements for fireproofing structural elements and fire protection for many parts of the building can also be a factor in materials selection.

Maintenance is another important criterion. Some buildings—such as airline terminals, which are used twenty-four hours a day, seven days a week—require durable and easily maintained materials. As a result, hard floor surfaces such as terrazzo and tile are common, and most of the equipment and wall surfaces are made of long-lasting washable plastics. Unfortunately, these materials create hard, often uninteresting surfaces that seem more appropriate for airplanes than for humans, but they do satisfy the criterion of maintenance and seem to satisfy most people's concept of an airport environment.

In the selection of materials for churches, special emphasis should be placed on aesthetic qualities. A church should have an environment where spiritual and human experience are enhanced. No one material can provide this atmosphere; the essential ingredient is the skill with which individual materials are used in relationship to other aspects of the building.

The proliferation of new materials is one of the problems of contemporary architecture. Many architects are creating structures that seem more like showcases of available products than integrally designed structures. Frank Lloyd Wright warned of this danger:

In this land of ours, richest on earth of all in old and new materials, architects must exercise well-trained imagination to see in each material, either natural or compounded plastics, their own *inherent style*. All materials may be beautiful, their beauty much or entirely depending upon how well they are used by the architect.

In our modern building we have the stick. Stone. Steel. Pottery. Concrete. Glass. Yes, pulp, too, as well as plastics. And since this dawning sense of the "within" is the new reality, these will all give the main motif for any real building made from them. The materials of which the building is built will go far to determine its appropriate mass, its outline and, especially, proportion.[10]

Integrity in the use of materials has led many architects in this country to once again look to Europe for inspiration in church design. This should, however be done with caution. Judgment is needed to learn the imaginative use of materials without being limited by unimaginative functional arrangements.

Many European architects have been successful with concrete, a material particularly appropriate for religious structures because of its modest cost, durability, and design possibilities. Concrete has innate structural as well as sculptural possibilities, an ideal combination for creating spaces for worship. However, much of the admired drama of concrete structures will need to be modified as churches become more budget conscious.

In keeping with the general concepts of the full-functioning environment, concrete will be used not only for the development of spectacular structural displays but for the creation of simple, unified spaces for worship. Instead of devoting all energies to an overpowering sanctuary, the total facility should be conceived as a spatial experience. Pietro Belluschi eloquently expressed the need for honest discipline in design:

It is all too easy to delude oneself into thinking of architecture as an exercise in cleverness. There is real danger that any minor architect may claim the right to innovate without depth or reason. It is essential that our efforts be honest, that innovation be a reflection of inner longings, the result of having found what is central and lasting. Unfortunately, the ways leading to abuse have multiplied with the means placed at our disposal by technology. It is essential for an architect to discriminate and to choose until his work sings with purpose and unity. In the mass of forms and details and techniques at his disposal he must train himself to eliminate, to refine, to integrate—a discipline which requires long and watchful efforts.[11]

Many concrete buildings are dramatic and exciting in their drawing presentations and black and white photographs, but in the three-dimensional reality of the architectural project, much of the excitement is modified by the crude, dull surfaces of the material. When concrete is used as the basic material, it is important that the church building committee visit buildings with the type of surface recommended by the architect. The committee members are often impressed with the initial design concept only to find the completed structure unsatisfactory. The most successful concrete projects have used specially designed formwork or mechanically treated surfaces, such as bush hammer, which creates more interesting colors and textures.

St. Mark's Church in Kansas City, Missouri, has successfully used concrete as the basic structural and decorative design motif. According to the architect, Charles Steele, concrete was chosen because it provided an inexpensive material that was both appealing and durable. He conceived of the church as a community center and felt the material should provide a bright contrast to the repetition and drabness of the low-cost brick housing that dominated the area. The concrete surfaces were enhanced with the use of exposed aggregate panels and detailed formwork in interesting patterns. Mr. Steele stated:

> The residents could only identify architecturally with their immediate inadequate surroundings, which are brick public housing and decaying tenant slums. The architect felt that contemporary clique or traditionally oriented church institutional architecture of suburbia would not provide the unique identity that was necessary for the community. It was also felt that an economical and traditional material was needed but new in concept, capable of portraying a fresh image to the residents—a material which in its simplest form would impart the spirit of strength, durability and stability to this community filled with weakness and instability. For this reason, concrete was chosen as the design media.

Surrounding greenery, multiple levels, and contrasting materials have given the whole building a desirable, inviting quality.

Brick is another material that has been extensively used in the design of religious buildings. It shares many of the advantages of concrete, being a moderately priced, durable surface material. Brick has none of the plasticity of concrete but has the compensating quality of more pleasing and varied natural coloring. In many areas brick is available in a wide range of colors and textures, which when used creatively can produce unique design solutions. The most successful designs avoid the potential monotony of brick by using it in limited areas with contrasting surfaces. The First Congregational Church of Melrose, Massachusetts, used brick as the basic exterior material and for the interior of its sanctuary. On the outside, the material is effective because the brick surfaces are limited to small areas, one story in height, and divided into interesting patterns and shapes. The white fascia, detail, and tower provide a pleasing contrast to the red brick. The use of brick in the interior of the sanctuary is less successful because the areas are large, almost two stories in height, and in the hexagonal sanctuary create an overly austere setting. Perhaps in time, with the addition of increased detail, the overpowering brick walls can be made more compatible.

The rapid expansion of churches in the 1950's brought wood into prominence. The wood arch-and-deck ceiling has become the overwhelming favorite because it provides an inexpensive solution to varied interior spaces. The laminated arch has become the suburban answer to the vaulted ceilings of cathedrals and country parish churches. The wood creates an atmosphere reminiscent of the traditional church, yet modern enough so that the outward-reaching suburbanite can feel a part of a new era. Many of these wood-tented structures are very successful in accomplishing these aims. Beneath the wood shelter, however, all the basic elements within the church have remained the same. The pews are in rigid conformity, the chancel is separated from the congregation, and the total area is conceived as a sanctuary with no other function than the conduct of worship services for one hour on Sunday morning. These laminated-arch churches are still being built with the same design limitations. They are the favorites of most package-church builders. It is unfortunate that the use of wood in religious architecture has reached such a level of conformity. Wood has a natural warmth and used properly is well suited to worship spaces. The Northwest section of the country has a long tradition of working with unique sensitivity with the special qualities of wood. Dense forests have made wood a natural element in their living patterns, and their West

Coast location has made them aware of the artistic traditions of Japan and China in the development of wood structures. Frank Lloyd Wright wrote:

> Wood is universally beautiful. It is the most humanly intimate of all materials. Man loves his association with it; likes to feel it under his hand, sympathetic to his touch and to his eye.
>
> And yet, passing by the primitive uses of wood, getting to higher civilization, the Japanese have never outraged wood in their art or in their craft. Japan's primitive religion, Shinto, with its "be clean" ideal found in wood ideal material and gave it ideal use in that masterpiece of architecture, the Japanese dwelling, as well as in all that pertained to living in it.
>
> In Japanese architecture may be seen what a sensitive material let alone for its own sake can do for human sensibilities, as beauty, for the human spirit.[12]

This is not the time to reject all laminated-arch structures and begin designing Japanese temples, but it is the time to stop the repetitious construction of standardized wooden A-frames. We need to reevaluate wood as a material and apply imagination to its use in the creation of religious environments.

Along with the basic structural materials of concrete, brick, and wood, a newly improved material is worth consideration because it is revolutionizing the interior design of buildings. The development of commercial-grade, strong, washable carpeting has given an entirely new dimension to floor coverings and sound control. Carpeting has helped revolutionize educational planning. There has long been a desire for more open, flexible spaces in educational design, but the lack of adequate sound control was a major problem. The introduction of truly durable, sound-absorbent, handsome carpeting has helped make open planning a reality. The applications of carpeting are extensive in commercial and institutional facilities. Carpeting is particularly appropriate in churches where there are a variety of activities and a desire to create an atmosphere of quiet warmth. Along with its many functional advantages, carpeting is available in a wide range of colors and a full selection of patterns and textures.

The Melrose Congregational Church has carpeting throughout the building, creating an appealing atmosphere for a wide range of activities. The appearance of the carpeting softens the hardness of the masonry walls and provides a flowing unity between the many building areas. The carpeted fellowship lobby and the classrooms provide a welcome entry into the sanctuary and the administration suite. Of course, carpeting is not the answer for every situation. The basement area at Melrose, which is reserved for youth activities, has an exposed concrete floor that is appropriate for dancing and the other activities of the young people. For many worship centers, the carpeting might be too sound absorbent and might deaden the room for musical presentations. In other areas, wood or vinyl flooring may be preferred for appearance or continuity. The architect and the client must make the decisions of the proper application of the flooring based on the criteria of location and function.

All materials have a special significance in existing buildings. Unlike a new project in which the range of choices is enormous, the task in remodeling is to work within the discipline of the existing building. If existing materials are used appropriately, they can help create unique environments. With all their present functional inadequacies, many existing churches have the advantage of being constructed of elegant materials with distinctive decorative details. By contemporary standards of taste, these decorative features are usually considered excessive and distracting. A skilled architect can use the best of the existing materials and emphasize their unique qualities. It is a constant irony that existing churches do not suffer from too little but are afflicted by too much. The sanctuaries are too big, the materials are too rich, the decorations are too elaborate. The challenge is to skillfully eliminate the existing elements that are unnecessary and to enhance those features that can form an appropriate setting for contemporary worship.

Many existing sanctuaries lack adequate lighting. Most older churches have large poorly lit areas; these churches still use lighting systems that date back to the time of construction or were devised to create a worshipful mood duplicating the dark interiors of medieval cathedrals. People today prefer and expect much higher levels of illumination.

Materials and their surfaces are an important influence on lighting levels because of the reflective qualities of the wall and floor surfaces. Lightly colored walls are more reflective than darkly colored walls. Existing churches have the darkest, least reflective surfaces of any type of building and often have an aura of depression rather than celebration. In most cases, the original churches were never intended to be as dark and foreboding as they are now. A simple cleaning of the walls and ceilings would bring new life to these dark interiors.

One of the architect's most important contributions to any project, new or existing, is his sensitivity to the potentialities of various materials. Whether the choice be concrete, with its economy and sculptural possibilities, or brick, with its warmth and durability, the architect should be able to make the right choices for the church's requirements. Some materials, such as wood, need to be used with care because of repetitious and standardized use in the past. However, such materials still have many inherent qualities for creating inviting areas of worship and human activity. New materials, such as durable carpeting, expand design possibilities in open planning and sound control. The materials in every building, new or old, are the basic elements for the orientation of beautiful, usable space.

## ENTRANCES

One of the fundamental elements of any structure is the entrance. The entrance sets the tone for the entire building. When grandeur is desired, entrances are imposing. An individual passing through the portals of a medieval cathedral can only be in awe of the majesty of the decorative sculpture and magnificence of the entrance, which indicate that entry into the cathedral is no ordinary experience. In contrast the entrances of contemporary churches should imply invitation and acceptance.

Recently, much has been written about baptism as a symbolic entry to the religious community. This has led to renewed interest in placing the baptismal font near the entry of the church. More emphasis has been placed upon the symbols around the entrance than upon the symbolic value of entrance itself. However, the physical entry to the church can have more initial significance as a symbol than the location of the baptismal font. If doors are hard to find, inoperable, or lead to dark, dingy, obscure hallways, entry into the church is a difficult passage in the literal sense. The entrances take on importance through their basic function of providing a transition from exterior space to interior enclosure, a most dramatic change. Passage through the entrance is the transition that all who use the building must experience. The convenience and grace with which entry is accomplished create a mood that is important to an individual's reaction to the building and its habitants.

There are two basic aspects in the experience of entry to any building. The first is clarity of direction, and the second is the creation of an atmosphere compatible with the purposes of the structure. The need for clarity is particularly evident in existing structures, which more often confuse than assist the individual in his attempts to enter the building. Eugene Ruskin, in his *Architecturally Speaking,* gives these words of advice to architects:

> You must also determine, with considerable accuracy, the moment when your observer will want to know where the entrance is. There is nothing so quickly destructive of response to architecture as lack of clarity on this point. If your man feels any doubt at all as to where he is supposed to go in order to get into your building, you have lost the game of sequence, as far as he is concerned, right then and there. His steps hesitate, his brow shows a wrinkle; in short, you have baffled and irritated him. Even though you may have done this in only a very slight degree, you have committed an unforgivable sin, for, leaving out all questions of architectural technique, you have no right to baffle and irritate your fellow man. He has a tough enough time in life without the added burden of your ineptness.[13]

The entrance of an existing church should be reviewed and carefully evaluated. Trying to get into a church during the week can be extremely frustrating. The front doors are usually locked, and there are inevitably three or four side doors. It is possible to spend ten or fifteen minutes walking around the entire building before finding an open door. Every church should have clear signs indicating which doors are open for what purposes and giving directions to their location. Even on Sunday morning there can be confusion about the appropriate entrance. It is often unclear whether the front doors are to be used or are only for decoration. With most parking space in the rear of the church, the visitor does not know whether to look for a special rear entrance or return to the front door. Once inside, it may be equally unclear how to get to the sanctuary and where to bring the children.

Not only the doorway but the entire environment of the entrance should be thoroughly considered. The entrance should provide shelter and protection from the elements, and it should be bright and cheerful inside, with space for clothing and conversation. In the evening, it should be well lighted. Many older churches are dominated by foreboding entrances with long flights of stairs, highly decorative facades, and enormous doors. These designs were adequate for their time, striving to imitate medieval cathedrals. A large, carved door can be very handsome and impressive, but it can also be formidable.

Rather than encouraging entry, a large, poorly maintained door can discourage the newcomer. Older churches need to find dignified ways of improving their entrances without destroying the integrity of the building. Many churches have made improvements by simply paying more attention to the maintenance of the doorways by restaining wooden doors and polishing hardware to bring out the elegant qualities of these materials. Other churches have repainted the doors with lively colors that say to the community, "We are alive."

Older churches often have back doors that formerly were emergency exits or maintenance passageways and now, with the development of parking areas in the back of the church, are major public entrances. These entrances need to be improved to perform their new function. Churches often have rear entries that are so clogged with unrelated accessories such as trash barrels, fire extinguishers, and cleaning equipment that they obstruct convenient passage. It is most important to remove these items, which were acceptable for a service entrance but are now completely out of place. Panels of glass can be added to rear doors to let natural light into what is often a dark back hall; walls can be brightened; and large welcome mats placed on the floor can change an old rear door into a serviceable major entrance of the church.

Along with clarity of direction and function, the mood of the entrance is important. There should be a greater emphasis upon the entrance as a transitional area between the more prosaic secular setting and the religious center. This does not mean making the church a retreat from reality; it means, rather, attempting to provide a dignified environment for human activity. Some of the most effective entrance approaches are those with modest gardens, a reminder of the beauty and amenities of living that should be a part of the religious tradition. Church entrances should not be grand plazas that make the individual feel insignificant. They should have a human scale, enhanced with benches, pools, and plants to provide a receptive atmosphere and areas for pleasant relaxation.

One of the characteristic features of Pietro Belluschi's designs for churches has been the use of courtyards for transitional space. The First Lutheran Church in Boston, located in a busy urban area, has a small garden partially enclosed with brick walls adjacent to the building. The area not only serves as a quiet place of rest in the bustling city but is also an integral part of the approach to the building. Many urban churches have given similar attention to the transitional aspect of the exterior entrance. St. Mark's in Kansas City, Missouri, has a generous terraced plaza. The Augustana Lutheran Church of Hyde Park in Chicago has a small entry courtyard that provides a pleasant garden of greenery and sculpture between the streets, dominated by commercial buildings, and the church facility.

The interior space of the entrance also needs to be designed as an important part of the total sequence in order to provide an entry with clarity and dignity inside as well as outside. Eugene Ruskin says:

> Very well. You have survived this hazard and brought your man to the entrance. Now he enters. A simple enough matter, it would seem. An instant ago he was outdoors; now he is indoors. That's all there is to it.
>
> Yes, that is all there is to it. But how many architects have failed to realize the tremendous psychological concomitants of that transition! With the passage from outdoors to indoors, the man's whole relation with his environment has changed radically and with it . . . his own state of being. A moment ago he was in limitless space, looking at an enclosed volume which he was preparing to penetrate. Of course, he was not feeling it on a conscious level, but he had a sense of free personal choice, mingled with a kind of aggressive purposefulness, which served to condition his responses to the building.[14]

Most churches do not meet the requirements implied in Ruskin's commentary. Church entry spaces, especially in older buildings, are usually cold and uninviting. Whether it be called the narthex, lobby, foyer, vestibule, or entry, the area often repels rather than attracts. There are usually too many doors, the area is dark, the walls and floors are made of hard-surfaced materials. There is an awkward atmosphere of indecision within the entry, for it is too small to be a gathering place and too big to be a corridor. Often churches load the vestibule with clutter. One church in Rhode Island has an entry approximately six feet long by eight feet wide. There is hardly room for two people to take off their coats; yet the space is filled with display racks, tables of brochures, posters, wall decorations, and an offering box. Instead of feeling welcome, the individual is assaulted by a barrage of paper and furniture.

Uninviting entryways can be transformed with modest expense by improving the lighting with supplementary fixtures and painting the walls light colors. Carpeting would be a welcome addition to most entrances. The whole host of pamphlet racks, display tables, memorial plaques, donation boxes, coat stands, and miscellaneous equipment should be carefully evaluated, and the items that distract rather than enhance the area should be eliminated. By presenting their full repertoire of pamphlets and printed materials in the entry hall, some churches give the impression they are afraid the visitor will never return.

Newer churches have used innovative ideas to successfully develop the interior of the entrance. The Melrose Congregational Church has a generous lobby with full carpeting providing a warm, inviting area. The architects of the Interfaith Center in Columbia, Maryland, designed a large foyer as a spacious indoor patio, full of light and plants, as the entrance and gathering place for the members of the various participating congregations. Many churches use the center for worship at different times, in different spaces, and with different rituals, but the foyer is a gathering place for all. According to the architects, the patio serves as the major architectural symbol of the ecumenical spirit of the center.

All churches, old and new, need to pay greater attention to the entrances of their facilities. The grandeur and domination expressed in the doorways of Egyptian temples, medieval cathedrals, and eclectic structures in our own country belong to the past. At the present time, there is a need for entrances with a human scale, entrances that invite rather than overwhelm. In existing churches this often means changing the entries to be more compatible with present needs. In new churches more consideration will need to be given to the experience of passing from the exterior into the interior of the building. The entrance should convey a generous welcome and provide an area in which the religious community can gather. A well-designed entrance represents a significant introduction into the religious environment.

## FEATURES

While many urban churches are burdened with too much space, the typical problem of older smaller churches in growing suburban locations is how to better utilize existing space. Often these churches served small towns quite adequately, but with expanded metropolitan growth, they have been swallowed up. Before the churches and the towns realized what was happening, they had become part of the metropolitan region. With a sizable increase in new members, particularly families with children, church facilities were found to be inadequate. Formerly, this meant constructing a new church building or at least a new religious education wing. Many of these buildings and additions could have been avoided through better utilization of available space within the existing structures.

Often large, neglected areas can be modified to solve many of the churches' space problems. One of the most frequently neglected areas is the basement. In many churches, large portions of the basement are filled with storage from the past century. The difficulty in the past, which is still a problem in the present, is that no one is willing to take the responsibility to throw out items that should have been thrown out twenty-five years ago. The minister is not interested in cleaning out the basement, the custodian is afraid to touch it, and the church women cannot agree on what is valuable. To avoid grief and problems, the stuff is left to accumulate in the hope that it will be sold at the next rummage sale. The situation grows critical as the cost of building and maintenance increases. If new space has to be built to meet the needs of the church because existing space is cluttered with junk, the time has come to take stock. If all the items for the rummage sale were realistically evaluated, the total worth would probably not exceed $200. Since new space costs $30 a square foot to build and is a continuous expense to maintain, the modest profits from the rummage sale can be seen in a new perspective. If the rummage-sale goods tie up large areas of the building when space is needed for other functions, they are an expensive method of saving money.

The issue is not rummage sales but all unnecessary storage within the church. The potential use of storage areas is not limited to the uncovering of dark recesses in the basement. In many older buildings, there are rooms designed or converted into storage areas during the days when the churches were serving sleepy little towns and had no thoughts of providing anything more than Sunday services for faithful members. With new functions and new space demands, these storage areas need to be revitalized. Many could be converted into peak-period classrooms with a modest amount of effort on the part of the church membership. Many items that are stored in these areas are used infrequently and should be moved to less critical locations. Others, such as folding chairs or tables, could be placed on racks, moved out of the room during peak time periods, and returned to the room for out-of-the-way storage during the week. In the past, churches have thought it easier to build new space than to get involved in efficient space utilization. However, the financial realities of the present have shown that in the long run it is easier to move a chair rack each Sunday than to continuously try to raise money for mortgage and maintenance costs for rooms that are seldom used.

An example of these difficulties is the experience of a church in Cherry Hill, New Jersey, which met for many years in a rented hall. The members grew tired of cleaning up clutter on Sunday mornings left over from the previous renters' Saturday night parties. After building their own structure, the members assumed that the days of annoying custodial duties would be gone forever. Then the church began to have difficulty meeting rising overhead costs and began renting the building to other groups, including one that paid a substantial rent to meet on Saturday evening. In their revelry, these renters left a trail of discards, and the church was right back where it had started, picking up clutter on Sunday morning.

Most building programs have happier endings, but there is an element of truth in the Cherry Hill experience. In many cases, building does not eliminate difficulties but exchanges one set of problems for another.

In addition to basement and storage areas, many older churches have tower rooms or their equivalent, which most members do not even know exist. For one reason or another, these rooms have been unused, but many of these spaces are potentially usable areas. Sometimes one new lighting fixture, an emergency exit, a carpet on the floor, paint, or perhaps a supplemental heater can make the room into a serviceable conference and classroom area during the peak time periods. Most of these hidden areas would require too much expense to develop into continuously used spaces, but they can at modest expense be made into auxiliary areas for use during periods of heavy activity.

Older churches often have small stages that are used only a couple of times a year but that could become a more functional part of the church environment. Many churches have made the mistake of assuming they no longer will use their stage and have permanently remodeled it into a classroom, losing the advantage of the stage area. If classroom space is an immediate need, the stage can be transformed into a temporary classroom by the simple addition of sound-absorbing draperies or even a folding door behind the stage curtain. In this way, the stage is still usable and the total expense to the church is minimized. The stage can be further developed into a small art exhibit area that would be appropriate for intimate showings of the works of individual church members and local artists. Because of its layout as a stage, the area could be conveniently closed off when not in use, and the exhibit in no way would interfere with scheduled activities in an adjacent large meeting room. Whether modified for peak-period classroom space or as an exhibit area, the stage can become an important part of the religious environment.

The kitchen is another potential area for development for peak-period use. Many older church kitchens were designed to provide large spaces for a cadre of volunteers to prepare a church supper. With the decline of church suppers and the popularity of the pot luck supper or buffet, these large kitchens now look like deserted battlefields. The kitchens are usually filled with unnecessary tables and furnishings. They end up as dumping grounds for everyone's donated discards, extra stoves and refrigerators that do not work. In time, these pollute the kitchen with ragamuffin, inoperative, and generally ugly accessories.

Some churches have successfully converted their kitchen into dual-functioning areas. The appliances have been positioned into one portion of the room, and the paper goods, staples, and pots and pans have been placed in cupboards and cabinets with doors so that they are out of the way and out of sight. Inoperable and unnecessary equipment has been removed and auxiliary tables relocated to areas where they are needed. Such changes, which will be different for every church, leave a substantial area within the room that can be developed for other purposes. This newly found area can be converted into classroom space for young children. It has desirable features such as durable floors, good lighting, and, most important, sinks and other facilities ideal for both art and kitchen projects. In some cases, the new area can be separated from the now smaller kitchen with a divider or wall, or it may be enough to repaint a corner or the entire room to make it brighter.

In the search for space within existing structures, it is important to remember that all walls are not necessarily permanent. With the help of an engineer or an architect, it may be determined that entire areas can be opened up or closed in, depending upon the needs of the church. Even the oldest buildings do not necessarily rely on interior-bearing partitions, with most structural loads supported by exterior walls and interior columns. Not only walls, but ceilings too are flexible. Many churches have sizable interior spaces that look like empty halls, largely because of the inadequate development of the upper spaces. Many of these churches have false ceilings that could be removed to expose more interesting structural systems. Other churches will need to lower their ceilings to provide more intimate spaces. This can be achieved with a variety of suspended systems from simple wood slats to standard grid patterns. In any church structure it is important to look closely at every element, for what may seem entrenched for all time may in fact be altered or moved to create more usable spaces for current needs.

Finding usable spaces, moving walls, and changing ceilings are important steps in fully utilizing the potential of an existing building. Another procedure that is often overlooked is the revitalization of existing features, which not only provide additional floor space but also enhance the life of the church. Such a feature is a fireplace. Many churches have fireplaces that are attractive but are never used to enrich the atmosphere of meetings or events at the church. One of the appeals of meeting in members' houses rather than in the church building for small group activities is the presence of such amenities as a warm fire and an informal home atmosphere. In spite of these acknowledged advantages, no one makes the effort to provide a similar setting for programs at the church. Many older churches have features that show a considerable amount of architectural imagination. One of the most consistent is large overhead and sliding doors that open entire walls to adjacent rooms. These doors make possible the convenient expansion of rooms. A small room with sliding doors can be expanded to provide space for larger groups while still maintaining the atmosphere and intimacy of the smaller area. Many fellowship halls can be expanded for special functions, and in turn sanctuaries can be expanded to seat more people. In many churches, the members and the ministers do not even know the doors function. In a typical situation, at some time in a church's history a door will get jammed. The problem is minor but, because the church members do not see the potential flexibility the door can bring to the environment, they leave it in an inoperable condition. As time goes on, it is considered permanently inoperable; everyone assumes it would cost a large amount of money to repair the door, otherwise it would have been fixed. It may take only a little persistence and a few dollars to have the door operating again.

The furniture of a room is another important part of the environment and has the advantage of being among the easiest and often least expensive improvements that can be made. Many rooms may require no more than the elimination or more careful placement of some of the basic furnishings. In evaluating any building, it is important to note that many of the furnishings are movable. A church also needs to realize that just because it possesses certain furnishings, they need not all be used. Some churches fill every room with all forms of discards merely because they own them, not because they want or need them. The church will increasingly have to take the prerogative of placing an item in storage until it is needed, and if it will not be needed in the foreseeable future it should be sold or given away. Religious environments are for people to use, not to store attic discards given as gifts or to serve as collections of Early Americana. While much church furniture is unsatisfactory, there may be some furnishings in the deep recesses of the basement that can be restored and made into important decorative features. The object is not to replace all the old furnishings with new ones; many of the older pieces, if they are used, are appealing and appropriate. The only danger is that many church members are so protective of the older items that the church turns into a quiet museum instead of a full-functioning environment.

It is important to realize that furnishings are movable on a temporary basis, allowing for a variety of functions in any room. Though accustomed to movable tables and chairs in assembly rooms, most churches do not see the same potential in other rooms. Whether in a library, office, classroom, or media space, furnishings can be moved; office desks can be pushed out of the way, tables can be put in storage, chairs and other accessories can be easily removed. Almost any room can provide clear floor areas or a conversational area by just relocating the furniture.

Furnishings and movable objects can affect the mood of every gathering. The placement of tables, seating, and lighting can influence human relationships; therefore, consideration should be given to these movable objects in the preparation for any meeting. The most obvious example, and the most important, is the arrangement of tables and chairs. An awkward setting can inhibit honest exchange and meaningful discussion. The room should be prepared for the kind and style of meeting to be held there. The projected attendance should be indicated and chairs set up accordingly. Too often the custodian sets up too many chairs. In most situations, no one has the presence of mind to eliminate some of the vacant chairs so that the group can be physically close to encourage communication.

The basic purpose of any meeting of people is communication. In some cases, it is the presentation of specific content; but increasingly it is the mutual exchange of ideas and information. Therefore, it is imperative that the tables and chairs in the meeting room be arranged to allow complete expression and participation. Each person should be able to see the face of every other person and clearly hear their voices. These ideas may seem obvious, yet they are often not carried out at church and community meetings. In the typical meeting of fifteen or twenty people, standard-sized rectangular tables are arranged end to end, so that a person speaking from one corner cannot be seen or heard by those at the other end of his side of the table. Another arrangement is the equally obstructive T-shape, in which the tables are placed perpendicular to each other. When anyone speaks from any end of the T, those at the other end cannot see or hear him. As meetings grow larger, usually the setting becomes more perverse. If a third table is needed, inevitably it takes the extended T-formation, with the head table for leaders and the two long tables for the followers, and the listening gap is even more exaggerated. These designs may be the result of too much emphasis on public speaking and not enough on public listening. Individuals in meetings assume that if they are talking, they are being heard, and that therefore it does not matter where the listeners are sitting. With greater emphasis on the mutuality of exchange, on listening as well as speaking, it is essential to create a more conducive setting.

There are solutions to these problems, and a little care and more explicit directions to the custodian are required. When a small group is meeting and standard-sized tables are used, it is important that they be placed not end to end but side by side. This approximates a square and provides a more intimate setting, which encourages personal exchange. When three tables are involved, the square should be approximated by placing tables corner to corner forming a U-shape, the size depending on the number of people. This shape can easily be expanded with a fourth table to accommodate a much larger group.

Most church meetings should be informal. We often get trapped into formats used by other groups. Many meetings are purposely organized to discourage a personal approach and encourage symbolic participation. Boards of directors notoriously have constructed formal rooms both to impress themselves and to maintain the formality of the meeting. The ultimate of this approach is the formal exchanges between representatives of different nations, in which the placement of the chairs and the arrangement of the tables take on exaggerated symbolic importance. The greater the distance between the participants and the grander the accoutrements, the more separated the individuals and the more limited the possibilities of human communication. A swivel leatherette chair, a pitcher and glass of water, and a microphone inevitably produce speech-making rather than honest mutual exchange.

Circular seating is particularly appropriate for a religious community; it makes an ideal arrangement for the exchange of ideas among equals. If a room were stripped of furniture and people were asked to sit on the floor at a meeting, they would not form a square; they would naturally sit in a circle. Churches would do well to consider purchasing large round tables rather than the standard rectangular ones. Perhaps the ideal would be to have a variety of tables for different functions. Meals at the church would be much more enjoyable at round tables than at the rectangular tables so characteristic of church basements.

Churches should also reconsider the continual use of full-height tables. The concept of tables relates back to schooldays when everyone needed a place to put books and take notes during class. Now most adult groups discourage passive note-taking and desire direct involvement. A group meeting in a home does not expect to use standard meeting tables, yet the same group meeting at church would probably sit around a conference table and then, after the meeting, wonder why the session seemed less enjoyable. As a compromise, churches should acquire low, large coffee tables, preferably round, for informal gatherings. These tables, being lower than average, would encourage informality and also provide a surface for books and other accessories and coffee cups. With this arrangement, the church could provide a setting that approximates the informality of the home, with the added advantages of general convenience of location and adequate parking. The church environment influences not only the total life of the church but also individual events; therefore, the arrangement of the furnishings can be an important factor in creating settings for positive human relationships.

The changes in one room of the First Unitarian Society in Milford, New Hampshire, illustrate some of the diverse ideas related to the utilization of space and the potential features and furnishings within the church environment. The room was initially designed, and for over seventy years served, as the women's parlor, indicating both the influence and importance of women in the life of this small-town New Hampshire church. Then in the early 1960's, when the church decided to come alive as a contemporary institution, the minister went through the struggle of changing the room from the women's parlor to the church office. The parlor furnishings, including vanity tables and large mirrors, were removed. The next significant change came six years later when the office was converted into a full-functioning room. As an office the room had been used largely as an administrative center and occasionally for meetings. A conference table was in a corner and a metal office desk in the center of the room.

The church was growing and faced the need to use the room for more varied activities. The space was of modest size, twenty feet square with a very unusual pitched ceiling about twenty feet high at the peak. The room had such amenities as a fireplace, a Persian rug, and a wall of overhead doors opening to a larger fellowship hall. The fireplace had been covered with a metal sheeting to protect against drafts and as a result had not been used for many years. The rug was so cluttered with office furniture that it was not noticeable. No one in the church had opened the overhead doors, so even the custodian did not realize they were operable. The lighting was so poor that in order to do office work an old lamp, left over from a rummage sale, was brought up from the basement and placed in a corner of the room.

The goal was to change this room from a dull office to a pleasant environment that could be used for a variety of functions. The church was small and the budget for remodeling was limited; therefore almost all changes were a matter of experimentation and placement rather than expenditure. The first change was moving the office desk from the center of the room to a location against the wall facing the window. The conference table was moved from its corner location to the center of the room, directly opposite the fireplace, giving a new focus to the room as a meeting area. With the removal of the metal sheeting from the front of the fireplace, a distinctive feature was added to the room, creating a more pleasing setting. One of the reasons the overhead doors were never used was that a large bulletin board had been placed in front of them. The bulletin board was filled with graphs and charts and gave the room the atmosphere of a sales office rather than a church gathering place. Moving the bulletin board to another room made it more usable to everyone and allowed the use of the overhead doors. These changes involved no expenditure of money. The only alteration that required a modest expense was the addition of supplemental lighting. The leftover rummage-sale lamp was not only inadequate but hideous. The existing overhead lamps, installed in the building many years earlier, were handsome but did not provide an adequate level of illumination. The high pitched ceiling presented problems. Some churches might have taken out the old lights and installed new fluorescent fixtures, but this would have been a grave mistake in terms of preserving the integrated beauty of the room. Instead, two small spotlights were installed on the sides of two cross beams, providing inconspicuous and inexpensive lighting for both office work and evening meetings. A few additional minor changes helped make the room even more pleasant. Old documents, faded and poorly framed, were taken off the walls, for the room already had enough detail with its exposed beams, tiled fireplace, and leaded glass windows. Previously, the fireplace mantel and other spaces had been left bare or had collected papers and forgotten gloves. With the addition of decorative candles and a dry flower arrangement, these areas enhanced the room.

The room is not only better lighted, pleasant, and inviting now, it also serves a variety of functions—as a library, an office, a counseling area, a meeting room during the week, and a classroom on Sunday. The overhead doors open up one side of the room for expanded seating, providing enough space for small winter fireside services. The conference table is on wheels and is easily moved to the adjoining fellowship hall, and the desk can also be moved. Chairs can be brought into the room, with seating extended into the fellowship area, creating a seating capacity for as many as seventy-five people without discomfort. The focus of the small winter services is the now working fireplace. These fireside services have been overwhelmingly successful. Few experiences are more enjoyable than a worship service in an intimate atmosphere around a warm fire on a cold New England Sunday morning.

The most recent experiment with the room was for an evening fireside service. The furniture was removed, leaving only the Persian rug. The congregation was dressed informally and sat on the rug or on pew cushions brought in from the sanctuary. The only lighting was the glow of candles and the fire, which was the visual focus for the service of poetry, meditation, and music. Old and young alike agreed that this was a special evening, which created a genuine sense of community among the members.

The revitalization of the Milford church office was achieved by respecting the basic elements of the original design, the space, and the materials, while at the same time enhancing and improving the existing features of the room. Movable furniture was utilized to make these changes. The result is a room that is appealing and provides for a wide range of functions.

The potential for such change resides throughout existing churches. There are basements, towers, stages, kitchens, and other spaces that are not being properly used. Space requirements need to be evaluated, priorities established, and rooms adapted accordingly. Rooms can serve a variety of functions. The potential is there; the church needs only the willingness to create a full-functioning environment within the existing facility.

## COLOR

In any consideration of environmental development color is an important factor. It is basic to all visual experiences. We see objects because they reflect light, and that light is diffused into color. When light strikes an object it penetrates the surface; the extent of penetration and absorption depends upon the texture of the object. Color is determined by the ability of an object to absorb light rays. Objects do not absorb the same quantity of light rays at each wave length and therefore produce different colors. If an object absorbs all colors except blue, blue rays are reflected to the eye, and we say the object is blue. White surfaces reflect all colors and absorb none. Black surfaces do not reflect but absorb colors; thus black is the absence of light and color.

In architecture color begins with the materials of the building, and therefore in existing structures the original materials will be an important factor in all color decisions. Many existing buildings have suffered from excessive decor dictated by previous design tastes, an abundance of rich materials, and the availability of craftsmen. Now both economy and design preferences encourage simpler settings with greater emphasis upon centers of attention. Wood beams, paneling, or carvings can best be complimented with light, neutral walls that provide background for warmth and texture. In the same manner, a simple chancel setting can provide a suitable background for a strong visual focus on the altar and other liturgical elements.

When feasible, it is generally best to allow materials to retain their original color. Some architects are emphatic about the integrity of the materials, insisting that the colors and textures not be altered with surface coverings. This emphasis upon natural materials usually has the advantage of reducing maintenance. However, some materials have inadequate surfaces for general use; some woods, plaster, and gypsum wallboard require an applied surface.

Paint is an important surface covering and an important source of color. In general, paint is used less to protect materials than to enhance their appearance. The importance of paint is often underestimated because it is applied only to the surface of materials and, compared to other building costs, is relatively inexpensive. However, the wrong choice of color can destroy all the effort and judgments related to the other phases of the building. Paint at its best can bring an unbelievable liveliness to an old structure; at its worst, it can destroy the most beautiful building.

The selection of colors is particularly critical in any building. Because someone has picked colors to repaint his bedroom does not mean he is qualified to select colors for the larger spaces of the church setting. These choices should be given to professional consultants or experienced lay people. It is difficult for most people to visualize a fully painted room from the small paint chip usually provided for color selections; the proper choice of colors requires experience and knowledge of color relationships. This does not imply that aesthetic snobs should make selections, but only that the needs and wishes of the church should be interpreted by experienced people.

A beige wall will have a much different appearance in a room with a dark floor or a dark ceiling than in a room with a light floor or ceiling. The lighting of the room, both natural and artificial, will substantially affect the reflection of the color and, reciprocally, the lighting level and appearance will depend upon the reflective qualities of the walls. Albert O. Halse, in one of the best books on color selection, *The Use of Color in Interiors,* describes the complexity of color relationships:

> There are certain other phenomena which should be kept in mind when selecting colors for an interior space. There must be, for instance, a delicate balance between the several colors used. One color must predominate. A wall painted in a bright color will seem to be larger than it actually is, because a bright color is more stimulating to the retina than a grayed hue. A white area surrounded by a darker area appears to swell in dimension. If the same color is used in several parts of an architectural space, it may appear to be different in hue in different places because of the variation in the amount of light to which it is exposed and also larger than one painted orange, and an orange area will seem larger than one painted red. Invariably, a blue area will seem larger than a black one. A bright yellow pillow will not look the same on a cool gray sofa as it will on a tan one. The fabric of a chair will seem to change if it is moved from one background color to another. In short, colors affect one another. Used by itself, a color will often seem adequate in a given location, but

when used near another color, even one of the same color family, it will suddenly appear to be "dirty." A yellowish green, for instance, can make certain shades of blue look purple when they are used together. A very dark shade of, say, mulberry used on a wainscot will make a very pale shade of the same color used on the upper wall appear white. The fact that colors look different in different surroundings has led to many disappointments when colors have been selected for decoration with no thought of their eventual neighboring colors.[15]

The recession or projection of surface planes is a complex subject often discussed in great detail by color theorists. Cool colors such as blue tend to recede or appear farther away, and conversely, warm colors tend to project or appear closer. Vivid or bright shades of any color will attract the eye and bring a surface into prominence and forward toward the viewer. A pale blue will recede more because it is pale than because it is blue; a bright blue will project.

These principles can be used effectively in remodeling. The impression of the shape of a long, hallway-like room, for example, can be changed through the proper use of color. The application of an intense color on the short walls of the room will draw the viewer's eye, and the long walls will be less noticeable. This will have the effect of lengthening the short wall and shortening the long wall, helping to balance the room's dimensions. Similar effects can be obtained on floors and ceilings. The more vivid the colors, the more noticeable and closer the surface seems. If a ceiling is very high, it can be made to appear lower by painting it a bright color, whereas a light-colored ceiling will appear higher. Most new buildings use white or light ceilings to give the effect of spaciousness. Another effect of color on ceilings that has been used many times in remodeling work is painting the existing ceilings, pipes, and other equipment in the upper recesses of a lofty space black. This black area all but disappears when coordinated with a revised lighting system. Color, when used properly, can be an important source of needed environmental change. Walls can be painted light colors not only to enhance whatever natural materials there may be, but also to raise the level of illumination and impart a sense of liveliness to the room. Painting walls white is only one possibility; there are a whole range of other possible colors, depending upon the total situation. Accent colors or materials on individual walls can be very helpful in giving spark to individual rooms; a brightly painted accent wall, a hanging, or paneling can give an entire area new vitality. Trite, obvious colors should be avoided. There is no reason the nursery area should always be painted pink or the preschool area baby blue. These colors have outlived their usefulness. Moreover, the clichés of pink and blue classify the areas as baby rooms and in a full-functioning environment the rooms may serve a variety of purposes and age groups.

The tendency in most churches when repainting is necessary is to let the religious education or property committee select the colors on the assumption that it really does not matter and the cost is negligible. If we became more aware of the power of color to transform environments, we would be less casual about allocating this responsibility. While the church does not need a consultant to repaint a wall or even a room, it would be appropriate for every church to have consultation in developing a master color plan to give direction to the random, volunteer painting projects that occur throughout the year.

The changes in the parish hall of a church in a small community in New Hampshire are indicative of the power of color to transform a room. The church is typical of many older, modest-sized churches in the midst of suburban growth. The building is over eighty years old, with a fifty-year-old basement addition measuring approximately twenty-five feet by forty feet. The room had been neglected for many years. The tiny basement windows were covered with dark, musty leftover curtains, which even when fully opened covered two-thirds of the window, blocking out the little available natural light. The walls were dull brown, and the floor was unpainted concrete with cracks running across its surface. The room was depressing, but with a simple change of colors and the application of paint by volunteers at almost no expense, the parish hall has been revitalized into an exciting part of the church's total environment. A small aesthetics committee selected off-white for the two long walls of the room to bring needed brightness and spaciousness to the basement location. Persimmon was selected for the end walls to provide color and warmth. The floor was repaired with crack filler and painted with a neutral brown masonry paint; the long-range plan was to cover the surface with burnt-orange indoor-outdoor carpeting. Natural lighting was substantially improved by simply removing the deteriorating curtains. A movable curtain of multicolored fireproof burlap was added within the room to impart a festive appearance and to visually separate the preschool equipment and toys, for the room functions as a preschool area on Sunday mornings. Play equipment and posters were added, and now the room on Sunday morning and throughout the week is a space alive with color and activity.

The refurbishing of this basement room not only created an inviting space for throughout-the-week use, but the transformation was achieved with almost no expenditure of money. A few cans of paint, some pieces of equipment, and a discriminating decorating group created a pleasant environment in a previously depressing area. The room is now used for candlelight church suppers, all forms of gatherings, Boy Scout and Girl Scout meetings, community functions such as Alcoholics Anonymous meetings and preschool care, yoga and exercise classes, and on Sunday morning as a preschool and classroom area.

In the basement room of this church, less turns out to be more. The church can be relatively free with the area for all forms of church activities and community services because the room has limited decorations and accessories. There is little that can go wrong. The walls are plain, the floor is simple, the tables and chairs are durable. This is in contrast to the typical plush director's room used for community meetings where owners become overly concerned that someone might soil their expensive carpeting or mar their walnut-finished table. If the congregation had spent a large amount of money to improve the parish hall, it would probably be less valuable for community service because the church members would tend to become very protective of their investment. But as a result of the modest and inexpensive changes, the area is attractive and pleasing and still available for a wide range of church and community uses.

In new buildings, the task of material and color selection is largely in the hands of the architect, with the church building committee limited to guidance and approval. Most buildings go astray when the committee demands colors unwarranted by the design. If the committee members were more knowledgeable, they might have more confidence in the architect's proposals. Of course, all architects are not color experts; some select unsuitable colors. The committee must be aware of their architect's limitations. A visit to one of the architect's buildings will give an indication of his color sensitivity. Architects, like most people, tend to have favorite colors and color combinations. By seeing these colors in the reality of another building, the committee can best judge their appropriateness for the church project.

During the course of construction, the planning committee will often become engaged in lengthy discussions about such details as the size of a particular closet. As the program goes on, people get tired and, near the end, when it is time to coordinate color selections with the architect, no one seems to care. This is the very time the committee should be particularly involved, for the colors will substantially influence the total appearance of the building much more than will the closets.

Another source of color for both old and new buildings is decorative tapestries. Tapestries are appropriate to a church, especially the sanctuary, and do not require extensive remodeling or excessive cost. They add color to many older churches and provide a sense of drama appropriate to buildings of all ages. If designed properly, tapestries can enhance the space as well as the detail of the sanctuary. They have the further advantage of being portable and can be changed, depending upon the needs of the church. Tapestries have been added to the nave of some churches, and they have been placed as a focus in the chancel areas of others. The new Hope United Presbyterian Church in Creve Coeur, Missouri, has used banners as a way of creating a symbolic expression and a spatial focus in its new building, and St. Mark's Church in Kansas City, Missouri, uses banners as a major decorative element in the sanctuary to provide detail and color and to soften the harsh surfaces of the concrete walls and ceilings.

Whether a church is building, remodeling, or refurbishing, one of the most important considerations is the selection of colors that will express the mood of joyous celebration. Churches, especially those dominated by historical architecture and nostalgic congregations, have too often maintained a dreary and depressing environment. Walls that are musty and spaces that are gloomy speak louder than the nicest welcoming words. In contrast, many commercial establishments pronounce joy with every ounce of energy their merchandising and advertising can muster. Their motivations may be questionable, but the result in the environment of stores is festive. The colors are bright, the decorations gay, the total mood is pleasant. This attitude is not limited to business. Educational institutions at all levels are redecorating and building teaching environments that are pleasant and full of color. Even hospitals, which have prided themselves on the sterility of their surroundings, are beginning to alter their concepts with the increasing realization that pleasing and colorful environments can be a very important factor in aiding recovery. Until recently,

churches also assumed sterility was the best atmosphere. Too many churchmen believed a somber atmosphere indicated dignity and depth of religious
feelings. It may indicate only fear of change and depression.

Churches need to begin realizing the importance of color in developing the
religious environment. Color is a basic element in the visual experience. Its
harmonies and relationships are subtle, and the selection process should be en-
trusted to experienced individuals. Color can be magic, with many tricks to
play; it can enhance or destroy a building. Careful color selection needs to be
an important part of church revitalization and building.

## LIGHT

Light is the essential element in the visual perception of our environment.
Every person is influenced by light. It is a basic ingredient of daily life. The
amateur artist and photographer soon learn the importance of light to the visual portrayal of any object or mood:

> All artists, including sculptors, are children of light. They labor in, with
> and through light, they shape their work to give light back again. Velas-
> quez' light is like transparent golden bees swarming the honeyed shadow,
> while Rogier van der Weyden's is like water over marble. Picasso's light
> seizes, smears and shapes a dark core. An artist's feeling about light is
> central to his creations. So central that a broad stylistic shift in the han-
> dling of light will reflect a shift in the whole culture.[16]

Le Corbusier wrote of architecture and light, "The key is light and light illu-
minates shapes, and shapes have emotional power." [17]

Light has always been, in all cultures, an important factor in the design of
religious buildings because its elemental quality permeates everyday living as
well as transcends earthly reality. Light provides that unique symbolic quality
that most closely represents divine omnipotence and omnipresence. With the
symbolic concepts of light, darkness emerges as a necessary and equal opposite
pole. Whether it be the yin and yang of the Hindus or the concept of good
and evil of Christianity, each religion has created strong symbolic dichotomies
with the concepts of light and darkness. Ancient tribes feared the dark of
night; the Egyptians worshiped the radiance of the sun. The Greeks had their
gods of light on Mount Olympus and their counterparts in Hades, the under-

world of darkness. These symbolic concepts of light and dark have also been important in Christianity, reaching their highest symbolic expression in Dante's *Divine Comedy*.

In three-dimensional visual forms, the interplay of light and shadow reached the apex of their artistic success in the cathedrals of Europe, most notably the Gothic churches of the twelfth century. These structures captured within the physical world the unique tension between light and dark in the contrast of the stained-glass windows. In this country, we have both a conscious and an unconscious attraction to these medieval spiritual resources, hoping to capture the elevation of religious experience, while still having all the advantages of the technological world. However, cathedrals were a unique creation of a time and a place and cannot be duplicated. The eclectism that has plagued our religious architecture for the first half of the century has limited the forward thrust of religious evolution. The intrigue and power of the grand medieval spaces of contrasting light and shadow are not environments suitable for the continuous gathering of the contemporary religious community. We now desire light for clarity as well as mystery. Church buildings need to provide a variety of moods with a much greater economy of resources. Some of the most successful of the eclectic structures need to be maintained, for they provide significant settings for a limited number of congregations and for a variety of special events. However, to maintain large numbers of these vacant spaces at extremely high cost to provide a historic visual experience for a few nostalgic souls is absurd.

In evaluating the eclectic structures more specifically, we have to face the reality that many of them do not have the quality of stained glass and light equal to the masterpieces of medieval Europe. Many church people labor under the illusion that every stained-glass window is in some mystical way related to the artistic triumphs of Chartres and Notre Dame. It is true that the windows of the local church are expensive to insure because of the difficulties of duplication, but their actual value can be negligible. If they were truly works of art, museums and other art patrons would be interested in preserving them, but such is not the situation.

Limited interior light within the church has often been considered a desirable quality. Theologically, it was assumed that the cathedral or its copy was a house for God and that a specially controlled atmosphere was necessary to remove the congregant from the cares, sights, and sounds of the outside world.

Contemporary churches require a greater sense of outward identity. Places of meditation apart from the cares of the world are still needed, but we do not need giant structures dedicated only to this purpose. The importance of light throughout the history of religious architecture shows the need to consider its role in the church environment carefully. Stained-glass windows in existing buildings can no longer be considered sacrosanct. If they are a distraction or create a mood of gloom within, their modification or removal should not be beyond the realm of possibility.

Past approaches to building and financing churches have a way of haunting the present. The grand concept of design made the sanctuary into a monument that became a repository for memorial gifts. Among the most sacred of these objects were the stained-glass windows. They were usually donated by groups or individuals with their names proudly embellished on them. The windows are further protected by endowed maintenance and insurance funds.

Stained-glass windows should be evaluated in terms of their role within the church environment. The best should be retained; others should be adapted to the present. Each sanctuary has its unique aesthetic qualities. In some churches, the windows may be of such good quality that they definitely should be preserved and, if possible, made more prominent through the simplification of the surrounding detail. In other churches, the problem may not be the quality of the light as much as the inadequacy of the art work. Here several experiments could be tried, including the placement of various patterns of opaque glass on the inside of the windows. The glass could be completely removed and relocated in a more desirable location, or the unit could be returned to the same window area with some of the sections removed. The best parts of the glass could be preserved and relocated as decorative features against walls or suspended in front of other windows within the building.

The Hill Area Grace Lutheran Church in Pasadena, California, is a church that had an inadequate, dark sanctuary, with the only exterior light coming through a row of small stained-glass windows along the sanctuary walls. As part of the expansion and remodeling of the interior of the church, the architects created large new glass areas overlooking a garden next to the church. The original windows were preserved in special free-standing, decorative frames within the new glass areas. The total result was the transformation of a dark restricting sanctuary into a beautiful open space full of light.

There is no question that these remodeling suggestions require effort and expense, but some churches have seemingly built new buildings just to avoid the church environment largely created by the windows and the fight to do anything about them. In these cases, the only winners are the wrecking companies. If the members are willing to be more flexible, they can persevere and still provide the setting for an active, growing church.

New buildings provide a better opportunity to reevaluate the entire question of light and the role it should play within a contemporary religious structure. Few cathedrals will be built in the future, and the contemporary congregation will have to deal with a different set of theological and practical assumptions, but many churches still do not question their need for stained-glass windows. Churches will increasingly have to do some serious thinking about the need for stained glass. If the tradition is continued only because it is "churchy," then it should be discontinued. Is natural light refracted into red light any more religious than clear natural light?

Within the category of stained-glass windows, there are many variations, including faceted glass, sculptured forms, laminated glass, and a host of translucent materials. If some form of stained glass is selected, there is still the problem of implementation. The project can be commissioned directly to an artist, with the technical work to be completed by a studio, or the project can be commissioned to the studio as a single package. Some studios have achieved excellent results, but much stained-glass work has been unimaginative and stereotyped.

Stained-glass design in this country has been less than exciting in comparison with the new forms presently being created in Europe. Robert Sowers, a stained-glass designer states:

> What the studios apparently are attempting to do is to perpetuate a design function which, however adequate it may conceivably have been in the heyday of Gothic revivalism, is hopelessly inadequate now. Far from being any longer the highly conventionalized retrospective thing it was fifty years ago, stained glass is now attempting, like contemporary church architecture, to be the kind of deeply searching, confidently realizing, open-ended enterprise that great art always is, must be, and eminently was when the great cathedrals, abbeys and parish churches followed one upon the other in such an exuberantly inventive stream. As the late president of the Guild for Religious Architecture, Mr. William Cooley, once put it: "The art of glass is at the crossroads. If the talented are encour-

aged, a brilliant era awaits. If the banal triumphs the importance of stained glass will decline." [18]

In another approach to church design clear glass is becoming increasingly effective. If the church can control the view, such as an outside garden surrounded by walls, clear glass can provide natural light and a special sense of natural beauty. The garden could serve as an entry court or as a meditation area. Some existing churches could, with small modifications, create areas of glass overlooking small gardens such as that developed at the Hill Area Grace Lutheran Church.

The designers of medieval cathedrals were mostly concerned with the possibilities of natural light. One of the most important design factors in our time is the creative and practical use of artificial light. Each year the lighting possibilities expand, and the lighting level standards for commercial and institutional buildings increase.

Lighting is particularly significant in the creation of environmental moods in churches. With the higher levels of illumination required and the decreased emphasis upon natural light, the contemporary lighting system assumes a function similar to the role of stained-glass windows in the past. The dramatic mood of the Gothic cathedral was influenced by the quality of the windows and the brightness and position of the sun. Contemporary environments are influenced by artificial lighting systems, especially as the church becomes more fully functioning and evening use is as frequent as daytime use. Lighting that is too bright can discourage human interchange by creating an uncomfortable setting; dull lighting can inhibit communication by making people drowsy.

Architects have long recognized the importance of lighting moods and use lighting to create special settings for specific purposes. Restaurants provide the clearest example of the variations that are possible in lighting systems and their influence upon behavior. The downtown cafeteria that builds its business upon low prices, fast service, and volume trade, inevitably has a lighting system of high intensity and brightness. This is in part to encourage night-time customers but, more importantly, it is to provide a setting that discourages people from lingering over their food. The goal is to keep people moving and thereby increase the volume of sales. In contrast, prestigious restaurants encourage the customer to enjoy leisurely meals with cocktails, wines, and desserts. The entire lighting atmosphere is designed to make diners feel relaxed. The lighting is subdued, with individual lamps or even candles on the tables. Both the inexpensive cafeteria and the exclusive restaurant realize the importance of lighting in creating an appropriate atmosphere.

Lighting systems should serve, not dominate, the environment. In the past, churches have been dominated by darkness, but there is no reason for them now to be overwhelmed by light. What is desired is the capability to adjust the lighting according to need. The flexible use of space makes it imperative to design flexible lighting systems.

We can no longer design giant cathedrals for one special spatial or lighting effect. Today, churches need to find new, more practical ways of creating a variety of environmental moods. It is easier to change schedules and lighting than to construct new buildings. Worship services can be enhanced by a sense of drama by holding them in the evening. There are times when the atmosphere for worship is best created with no illumination other than the flicker of candlelight. At other gatherings, such as a business meeting, higher levels of illumination are necessary. Lighting variations can be implemented within the same space; the only problem is learning to effectively install and use new lighting devices and systems.

One of the most popular devices for controlling lighting is the rheostat switch. The rheostat, which can gradually dim or increase lighting, can be installed in both new and existing buildings at a minimal cost. Rheostats have been misused and treated more as a toy than as an important environmental influence. There are churches that try to use them as a dramatic device for raising and lowering the lighting, depending upon the words of the service, but usually people feel that the atmosphere is not genuine and that they are being manipulated. The rheostat is most functional in the sanctuary when variations in lighting are kept to a minimum. The rheostat is not limited to the worship center. The adult program lounge, media room, and unfinished room can all use this variable light control. There are many possibilities for variable lighting in addition to the rheostat. Lighting tracks with fixture locations at any point have superb flexibility. Theater lights and the entire range of available spotlights can provide effective solutions to many lighting problems and create almost any mood. Churches have to avoid the temptation to satisfy the lighting needs of any room with long rows of fluorescent fixtures. In rooms where high levels of illumination are desired, the fluorescent fixture can be suitable, but in other areas, such as the reception area and the adult program lounge, other lighting should be considered.

Areas of special focus need to be evaluated. If exhibits are planned, lighting provisions should be made in advance. In the sanctuary the chancel area requires a higher level of illumination. Proper lighting can enhance the sacredness and preciousness of the sacramental elements and can shape the space. In the North Christian Church in Columbus, Indiana, the chancel is surrounded by seating in the round with a high level of illumination on the chancel and a lower level in the seating area. This has helped focus the congregation's attention on the altar and has modified the awkwardness of opposite seating. Churches should avoid the trap of thinking there is a difference between a so-called religious light fixture and the fixtures used by every other type of institution. The addition of a cross or other symbolic decoration does not make the light religious. Many theologians and clergy are coming to the realization that excessive use of any symbol detracts from its value. This is especially true when a symbol is used repeatedly throughout the religious facility. The cross, for example, has much more meaning when it is used with discretion and dignity rather than being spread throughout the church on radiator covers, pew ends, and lighting fixtures.

Church remodeling requires the updating of the original electrical wiring and fixtures. The work can be expensive but usually does not require altering major portions of the structure. The wiring can almost always be hidden or at least made inconspicuous within the existing building. Unlike some changes, such as heating systems alterations, electrical work usually does not force additional remodeling. One constant in electrical remodeling is the expansion of the lighting panels to provide greater electrical capacity. At the time when many of the older churches were constructed, electrical service was in a primitive state, and buildings were provided with only minimal wiring, outlets, and fixtures. With increased capability and standards, all these elements require expansion.

There are a variety of consultants available for electrical remodeling work. The architect, a consulting electrical engineer, or a competent electrician can be very helpful in working toward improved lighting systems. The architect is probably most concerned with the function and appearance of the system and methods of coordinating changes within the existing structure. However, a good, aesthetically oriented electrical engineer might be the best recourse. If the church can clearly state its requirements for small amounts of work, an electrical contractor may discuss at no charge the general feasibility and cost of the proposed changes. The main concern is to be sure that the contractor is giving enough consideration to the final appearance of the room.

Churches should develop a clear concept of their intent in improving the lighting system. Areas for greater lighting, increased flexibility, special focus, and overall appearance will need to be determined by the church. Churches should be able to clearly state the objectives and let their consultants select the means.

It is important to realize that we are not only raising levels of illumination, we are dealing with the entire question of spatial possibilities. In areas with high ceilings, new fixture levels combined with repainting can have the effect of lowering the ceiling; in areas with low ceilings, recessed fixtures can have the effect of raising the ceiling. Even the most flexible room is not fully usable if the lighting system remains rigid. If all the focus lights are in one area of the room, then the lighting fixtures, more than the architecture, will determine the arrangement of the room. The lighting system must be designed with the same capabilities as the architecture. In the medieval cathedral the lighting was established by the window artist, and the church accepted these glories and limitations. In the contemporary church the members and the clergy are more knowledgeable about the possibilities of lighting variation. The walls and ceilings of an inadequate room can be virtually eliminated by controlling the evening lighting to focus attention on a centrally lighted area. A bright room can stimulate vitality, and controlled darkness can create mystery. A large room can be made smaller and more intimate by using lighting in only one area; the same room can be larger with the full use of all the lighting.

In addition to dramatic changes in interior artificial lighting, the lighting of building exteriors has become increasingly important in recent years. New forms of lighting and new attitudes have developed exterior illumination into an important aspect of any lighting plan. The most obvious concern is the development of functional lighting to provide convenient and safe access to and from buildings. Morality may come from seeing the figurative light, but crime, the power companies tell us, is reduced by literal light, and raising the levels of artificial illumination discourages thievery.

In addition to functional considerations, lighting can be part of the continuing visual identity of the church. With timeclocks to control the hours of use, the cost of night lighting is negligible. Beyond considerations of safety and identification, night lighting can be a source of pleasure. If the church has an outdoor courtyard or pleasant exterior grounds, these can be lighted in the evening, creating delightful vistas outside the church. In this manner the indoor-outdoor relationship is maintained throughout the day and night. With night lighting, trees take on new dimensions of interest as their shapes are outlined against the dark sky.

Whether it be the brilliant light of the sun, muted, shaped, and altered in patterns of glass, or the light from the endless varieties of artificial illumination, light is an essential in our basic response to the religious environment. Colored glass, used in either an old or a new building, should not limit religious life. The lighting of the interior of the sanctuary and every area of the church should be designed to give appropriate levels of illumination and the flexibility to provide lighting for a variety of functions and moods within the same space.

## VISUAL COMMUNICATION

Communication is a necessary function of human relationships. Interrelated disciplines and advanced technology require the coordination of our activities through all forms of efficient and rapid communication. As a result of this need, the language of visual and graphic symbols has returned to a new state of prominence, which is displayed in every element of society from the flashing neon signs of the commercial strip to the integrated and sophisticated graphic language of many corporations. Unfortunately, the church is farther removed from these important changes than any other institution. This is an ironic turn of events considering the church's long heritage of significant influence in the development of visual symbols. In the Middle Ages, the town and cathedral were a graphic artist's delight, with shop signs and church decoration almost entirely in pictorial rather than literal form.

In our own society, we have all become sensitized to a new level of graphic awareness. Exposure to the constantly changing and creative graphics of movies and television have made many people aware of the possibilities of visual expression. The business world has recognized this, and in every aspect of their work, from commercials in magazines and on television to the development of company offices and grounds, businesses have emphasized visual coordination and graphic excellence.

As an integral part of building design, quality graphics are increasingly important. This, unfortunately, has not been realized by the churches. It is quite common to see an elegant new religious facility with a home-workshop, hand-lettered sign, half falling over at the entrance. The sign completely distracts from the visual excellence of the new building. A church does not have to become slick or exaggeratedly avant-garde in its visual communication, and it does not need to compete with giant corporations or their advertising agencies in increasingly outlandish visual gimmicks, but the church does have a responsibility, as part of its artistic and symbolic heritage, to improve the present low level of everyday visual communication within the church.

Visual communication serves two basic functions. It provides specific information in words and numbers, and it creates a visual impression. Churches too often limit themselves to the first function. The emphasis upon the word of the Scriptures within the religious tradition may have enforced a church bias toward literal communication, when much of the rest of society has moved into the changing realm of electronic and visual communication. Many theologians and clergymen write lengthy articles about the role of imagery and symbolic language in the creation of worship and the expression of spiritual values, but no one within the church pays any attention to the simple, practical concerns of everyday visual communication.

There are a variety of levels of visual communication, and it would be foolish to contend that changing a sign inside or outside the church is going to affect the faith or commitment of the members, but a new sign can be a visual expression of the revitalization process. A new church sign can serve both functions of visual communication by providing clearer information and representing or symbolizing the changes taking place within the church.

If exterior signs on new church buildings are graphically amateurish, signs on old buildings are often totally inadequate even as communication. Many churches have retained signs that were placed on the structures over fifty years ago and were designed for people walking by with plenty of time to read them. Some of these signs are attached to the buildings in places almost impossible to find and, when found, they cannot be read because the lettering is so small. The signs list every possible worship service, church function, and staff member. The only way the signs can be read is by walking up and reading them; very few people are that interested in church signs. Many congregations assume they do not need a new sign because they have one of these ancient gems, yet many people, even in the immediate area, probably could not identify the church because the sign fails so completely in communication.

Another favorite sign used by churches is the enclosed bulletin board. These have been used over the years because they can be changed weekly to indicate special events and sermon topics. The assumption again is that people get information by reading the words on signs, and this assumption is totally false. Enclosed bulletin boards have become so overused that they are now a cliché and add to the dull, monotonous image that exists for many churches. A vivid contrast in church life is a pastor trying to add appeal to his services with a catchy sermon title and then posting the title in these tired wayside bulletin boards. To the viewer, the setting says the title has changed but everything else is the same. In a time of graphic revolution, changing words is not enough. The entire visual setting must also be altered.

The solution lies in a concerted effort on the part of the churches to improve their total visual communications. There is no better place to begin than the front of the church. A new sign, which can be an expression of renewed vitality, can be an important design tool. The cost of remodeling the front of many old structures to provide an inviting contemporary exterior may be prohibitive, and in some cases remodeling may be undesirable. Nevertheless, much of the same effect may be obtained by the construction of a handsome, inviting exterior sign.

The church should not skimp in the purchase of a new sign. Almost every church sees it as one of the places to hold back money, yet it is the very place where the money is most effectively used. There are many things the home-workshop craftsman can accomplish, but signs are not one of them. Basement workshop renditions are either too fragile and temporary or are grossly overbuilt. If the error is compounded with amateurish lettering, the result can be disastrous. Exterior signs are complex design problems, and it is well worth the money to have the sign designed by an architect or designer and constructed by a reliable construction firm. In some cases, the architect may recommend a preassembled manufactured sign. The judgment of the architect is invaluable in correlating the sign to the church building; too often the average property committee wrongly assumes that it could just pick any sign found in a manufacturer's catalogue.

The design and selection of an appropriate sign should be approached with considerable care. The sign must convey a message in an economical manner, and it must be attractive and scaled to fit its surroundings. The total amount of information on the sign should be limited; it is enough to indicate the name of the church in easily read, bold letters, and the hours of worship services. Data such as the organizational meeting times and the name of every staff member are generally not necessary. Each design must meet the needs of its particular setting. For example, a massive stone church building will need a large, bold sign to correspond with the monumentality of the structure. It is imperative that a cardboard or paper mock-up of the sign be constructed and held in the intended location to determine the appropriateness of its scale and location before construction begins. It is also desirable to design the sign so that it can be lighted in the evening. In some cases, this could provide an inexpensive alternative to illuminating the entire building.

The visual communication of a church should not be limited to a sign in front of its building. The overall intention is to make the function of the church as convenient and efficient as possible and to develop a visual awareness that indicates a church of vitality. Any church serving the community

will be used by a wide variety of people, and the building should be easy to find and clearly identified. Going in circles on urban or suburban streets trying to find a building, being unable to get a parking place, and then being further aggravated by going to several locked doors trying to get to a meeting on time is frustrating. Small signs directed toward the church at major intersections, a large, easily read sign designating the church, and auxiliary signs indicating parking areas and entrances will go a long way to avoid much of this aggravation.

Improved visual communication should not be limited to the outside; it needs to be continued throughout the building. Newcomers to any facility need assistance and directions to meeting rooms, and the church should maintain high-quality graphics in the interior. It may even be possible to maintain the same lettering style and graphic designation of the outside sign, providing continuity between the interior and exterior of the structure. Many fine buildings lose much of their interior visual effectiveness through hand-scrawled signs scratched on cardboard or paper, generously sprinkled with graffiti. There should be a place for all kinds of posters and temporary notices for special events, but permanent signs should be substantial and can be printed inexpensively on a variety of surfaces that are compatible with the building's interior.

Visual communication has been an important part of the heritage of the church, but in recent times the concern has been limited to the traditional religious symbols. The rapidly changing areas of graphic communications within society have been largely neglected. Cluttered, unreadable signs on old bulletin boards do not present a stirring image of a renewed church. Improved visual communication can not only provide a clear designation of the church facility but can also become a symbol of revitalization.

## CHRIST CHURCH CATHEDRAL

The Christ Church Cathedral in St. Louis serves as an example and an inspiration to churches reluctant to attempt remodeling. Christ Church had many of the characteristics of the tired dragon. It is located in an urban center in a century-old, neo-Gothic building. It is the oldest Episcopal church west of the Mississippi and celebrated its hundred-fiftieth anniversary in 1969. In the words of the Very Reverend Thom W. Blair, Dean of the Cathedral:

> For some time, Christ Church Cathedral had been wrestling with the familiar difficulties which have confronted many churches, difficulties which are magnified in a metropolitan center. Many of those who had made up the population of the city and the membership of the cathedral had moved to the suburbs, leaving behind a shrinking population and a cathedral with a rapidly declining communicant list. Times change. No more did large numbers of faithful worshippers crowd the cathedral for noonday preaching during Lent. The cathedral still stood in the geographical heart of the city, but an ever-widening gap was appearing between the church and the crowds that passed its doors. Now they seldom came in. If this gap was to be closed, if the cathedral was to remain in living contact with the world, some radical action was necessary. No minor modifications in the cathedral's life would be an adequate response to the growing gulf between the church and the world.[19]

Christ Church Cathedral has taken a deep breath of fresh air, has stirred back to life and is now stretching toward a new vitality. A series of seemingly unrelated events led to the initial consideration of changes within the sanctuary. A new organ, built in 1964 to replace the existing instrument, was placed in the rear balcony to assist congregational singing. The large original organ

*Tower, Christ Church Cathedral*

cases, which filled the walls of the north and south transepts in the front of the church were now empty boxes. To remove these nonfunctioning containers required modifications of the transept walls, and the anniversary seemed the appropriate time. The membership also wanted to install air-conditioning in the sanctuary to make the facility more comfortable during the hot and humid summer months.

The full development of the program did not begin until the architectural firm of Burk and Landberg was consulted. Along with improving the transept walls and adding air-conditioning, the architects encouraged a thorough architectural evaluation of the sanctuary area, including a review of past and future functions and of all the elements that composed the architectural and liturgical setting. The architects participated in this initial programing and were consultants throughout the project, meeting with small groups to listen and explain the proposed changes.

The basic church elements were evaluated within the context of the existing sanctuary. It soon became evident that if the church wanted to more effectively use its existing space, a flexible and inviting facility was required. The rigidly fixed pews, pulpit, and altar within dark, towering stone walls created an unappealing atmosphere for worship or any other activity.

The pews, designed over a century ago, were uncomfortable and limited the flexibility of the interior. The possibilities of flexible seating entered into the evaluation and opened up new opportunities of arrangement and use within the sanctuary. Further research showed that the use of chairs was not a radically new concept but in many ways was more historically appropriate than the pews. Coventry Cathedral, the ecclesiastical center of England since the year 597, St. Paul's Cathedral of London, Notre Dame of Paris, and the National Cathedral in Washington all use individual seating. In this sense, a return to individual chairs was more a restoration than a modernization.

The pulpit and sound system were evaluated. The existing pulpit was refurbished to simplify its design, and a portable pulpit was added to be moved closer to the congregation in a variety of locations. A new, more flexible sound system was installed to provide greater adaptability in tone control for various services. To further promote the flexibility of the space, a movable altar was added to supplement the fixed stone altar placed against the rear wall of the chancel under the reredos. The portable altar was designed to the same dimensions as the existing altar to allow the linens to be used interchangeably;

*Canterbury Cathedral*

this exemplifies the endless attention to detail by both the church and the architects. The existing altar is still used for ceremonial occasions, and the new altar is used for Sunday services, placed in the center of the chancel to allow the officiant to face the congregation while celebrating communion. The new altar is also occasionally moved to the center of the sanctuary, when a more intimate setting is desired.

The remodeling of these elements was a prelude to the remodeling of the entire sanctuary. The cathedral has a central nave approximately one hundred feet long by thirty-six feet wide, with side aisles that add another twenty-four feet, making a total width of sixty feet. Though the cathedral is smaller in total dimensions than other structures of comparable style and period, it still encompasses a large space, with a ceiling eighty-five feet high at the peak of its pitched roof. This large space needed remodeling to allow its full utilization for a variety of services and functions. The area was suitable for grand occasions but was overpowering for small religious gatherings. Even where a large space was appropriate, as for conferences, the fixed pew seating did not facilitate communication. The area needed to be made more versatile by balancing the drama of the spatial heights with control of the mood and communication for more intimate occasions.

The evaluation of the building continued with an appraisal of the existing material. The walls were dark and dirty from soot accumulation during the so-called smoke years in St. Louis; they were porous and absorbed sound and limited the acoustics. Stone normally is dense and smooth, providing excellent sound deflection, but close investigation revealed these walls were pocked with miniature holes. The accumulated grime was removed by steam cleaning the walls, creating a new brightness within the building; the acoustical problem was solved with the application of a clear plastic sealer, which created a nonporous, reflective surface for vastly improved sound within the sanctuary.

In addition to the walls, the floor was unsatisfactory and needed to be replaced by a hard-surface material. After considerable deliberation and research, marble was selected as the most appropriate material. At first, this seems like an expensive solution and indicates that the church was right back to creating monuments instead of an active, religious environment. In every respect, however, marble was appropriate. The architects reduced the thickness of the slabs, which substantially lowered the initial costs. In addition floor maintenance costs have been reduced; no major floor cleaning has been required in over two years. The marble surface has proven to be excellent for sound deflection and, most importantly, the Roman travertine marble blends beautifully with the existing materials, enhancing the whole. As a bonus, the floor divisions of the marble are excellent guides for the placement of chairs in the varied arrangements.

The outstanding existing feature of the cathedral is the reredos placed against the end wall of the chancel area. The reredos, which were dedicated in 1911, are thirty-five feet high and thirty feet wide. They were carved from Caen stone by Harry Helms of Exeter, England, and are said to be the most important and largest reredos made in that country since the Middle Ages. A gossamer rood curtain of natural linen was installed from the sixty foot chancel arch to separate the stone altar and reredos from the nave. When the altar is lighted, and the curtain closed, it provides a spectacular view of the altar and the reredos through a gauze-like screen. When the chancel lighting is off, the reredos disappears, and the nave can be used for a variety of community functions. The chancel curtain is an excellent example of the relationship among the basic elements within any structure. The space is shaped by material, the curtain, through the use of lighting to enhance the sculptured feature of the building.

Looking down from the lighting balconies of the cathedral, Karl Landberg, the architect, summed up the alterations of materials and color in the project this way:

> One of the major changes in the nave is that it is now full of light and color where formerly it was dim and gray with dark, heavy-looking walnut woodwork. Now you are conscious of the amber ochre of the soaring Gothic sandstone arches against the gray of the Indiana limestone trim and the warm beige of the new Roman travertine marble floor. All of these colors are the perfect foil for the light, cream-color of the Caen stone altar and reredos, 35 feet high, the crowning glory to the Cathedral.[20]

The architects further developed the chancel with the addition of a movable front area. The existing chancel was too small for the wide variety of events expected, so the area was enlarged. Burk and Landberg developed a portable front portion for the chancel composed of cube-like, movable sections measuring four feet by four feet by two feet nine inches high. They also developed stair sections and outside and inside building units to create a platform area of

*Interior, before, Christ Church Cathedral*

*Interior, after*

*Movable platform*

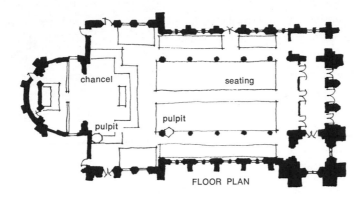

*Christ Church Cathedral*

any size and shape. The fixed sections in the rear of the chancel and the mova-ble front sections are all designed with a common modular pattern of specially designed parquet floors of small, walnut squares edged with strips of contrast-ing birch and oak. The units are both handsome and large enough to appear as a permanent installation, regardless of their arrangement. To provide for sim-ple maintenance and rearrangement, a small, hand-operated pallet truck was selected to allow one man to move and store the modular units.

The addition of a variable lighting system was a necessary part of the cathe-dral remodeling. The architects knew the cathedral needed a lighting system that could adapt to the varied arrangements within the space, if the facility was to be truly flexible. The existing fixtures were preserved, but they needed to be supplemented by a more flexible and powerful lighting system. Below the church's clerestory windows on each side of the sanctuary, the architects added a narrow balcony that provides a continuous lighting track on which any number of spotlights can be placed at any point and aimed in any di-rection. Control for the units is from a master switch in the rear balcony; maintenance and arrangement of the lights are conveniently handled by one person. Other elements that were a part of the stretching process at Christ Church were the improvement of both the main and side entrances. The cleaning of the walls of the entry developed a more inviting front entrance; the side entrance was refurbished with a new doorway, and the construction of a walk with an integral ramp provided convenient access for elderly and handicapped individuals.

As with many other churches, there could have been a host of rationalizations for the members of Christ Church to avoid these alterations. It could have been argued that as the oldest church west of the Mississippi, they should preserve their historic traditions. The question is, however, which historic traditions. In the latter part of the nineteenth century, the church had been considered radical when it decided to build on its present site. Many critics considered it to be too far from the center of the town. But these pioneers did well. The location proved an overwhelming success as St. Louis continued to grow, and indeed the principal difficulty now is that the metropolitan area is still growing. The foresight of the early members of Christ Church demonstrated that change is not a phenomenon limited to the present. Many churches are active today because of clergy and members who were willing to make changes in the past and to take risks when necessary to meet new challenges.

It could have been argued that as the Episcopal spiritual center of the Diocese of Missouri, the cathedral should preserve formal traditions, letting younger churches develop new worship settings. In part this had already happened. Life does not stand still, and younger families were going to newer churches. It could have been argued that as a recently designated historic landmark of St. Louis, the church should not alter its building in any way. Yet the changes were made, and the architectural integrity of the building was preserved through the sensitive handling of the existing space and materials.

It could have been argued that the project would cost too much and that existing funds need to be conserved as a church membership becomes smaller. The membership of Christ Church elected to meet the challenge of vitality and growth rather than to fearfully hold on to a fading past.

It could have been argued that the money should be used to help the needy rather than for building. The revitalized programs of the cathedral have already assisted the entire urban area with a variety of worthwhile community programs and service projects.

*Flower Sunday*

*Communion Service*

*Concert*

What has been the effect of these changes in the religious environment upon the life of the church? The Dean of Christ Church has written a very enlightening article entitled "The Flexible Cathedral." Dean Blair points out that there were times of confusion, fear, and rumors during the process of re-modeling; members of the congregation were concerned that the reredos were being completely destroyed and that the entire stonework of the cathedral was being whitewashed. The church survived these early doubts. Near the time of completion, new questions were heard. Would the cathedral work? Was it worth the money? Dean Blair answers:

> It was an act of faith, the congregation risking all that was dear to it in this great change. In a very real way, the cathedral was engaged in a gamble upon which its very life depended.
>
> The first day in the "new" cathedral was All Saints Day 1969. It began with a great service in the morning, followed by a "Festival of Creation" that lasted through late afternoon. The church proved to be splendid for worship. There was great space in the chancel. With nothing to distract the eye, the reredos and the high altar stood out as never before. You could see and you could hear. The sound of music was greatly enhanced, increasing the possibilities for real congregational participation.[21]

After the morning services, the portable altar and lectern were moved, and a day-long "Festival of Creation" began. The program included every facet of the performing arts, including an organ recital, contemporary jazz, madrigal singers, drums, and ballet. The church, encouraged by the enthusiastic response, planned an Advent series entitled "Christmas in the Cathedral" for the office-workers and shoppers who make up a good part of the downtown population on weekdays. Several hundred people attended each of these events. A new series, "Spring in the Cathedral," took place during Lent, as well as a Sunday afternoon music series late in the summer. The Alpha and Omega Dramatic Players have appeared twice, and there have also been small concerts and recitals. Other groups, both religious and secular, have used the space for various programs. The most spectacular, dramatic event was the production of Berlioz's *Te Deum*, presented with a full chorus and symphony orchestra. In the words of Dean Blair:

> Actually, only a bit more than a year has passed since the changes were made in the cathedral. And the congregation of Christ Church Cathedral

believes that it has done the right thing. The present indications are that the gamble was won. It was a leap of faith, a leap in the dark, but apparently a leap in the right direction. The building itself says what the church is here to say, a word of light, of beauty, of life and joy. The space speaks for itself, a word of good news.

The program which takes place, involving the cathedral with the contemporary scene, says that God is not dead, nor is he alive just in the distant past. He is the lord of this age in the midst of the change and the revolution which surges throughout society.

The "flexible cathedral" appears as an outward and visible sign of the inward and spiritual new life which is surging into the Christian church today, going before it and calling it into a new ministry to a new world.[22]

Christ Church Cathedral refused to die or to become another tired dragon cluttering the spaces of our major cities. The church was willing to look honestly at the realities of life around it and was willing to face those realities with a new commitment. Christ Church breathed deeply and stirred. The church was able to stretch its architectural perimeters to meet its needs. The potential for revitalization was there in the leadership and the membership, but it required the expertise of a qualified and interested architect to help translate these new ideas into the reality of the cathedral's structure. The thorough evaluation of space, materials, features, color, and lighting led to many innovations that can be applied to other churches facing similar problems. The flexibility of the movable seating, pulpits, and chancel furnishings was balanced with the preservation of many elements. This blend of creative innovation and respect for the integrity of the existing building has made Christ Church Cathedral a most successful example of church remodeling.

# NEW DIRECTIONS

## COOPERATION

**A**s churches explore new possibilities of organization and environmental development, they must be willing to seek new forms of adaptability and harmony. The most important opportunities lie in cooperative relationships with other elements in society.

The need for cooperation can be seen in the case history of another tired dragon, the railroads. Railroads, like the churches, were a dominant feature on the landscape late in the nineteenth century and early part of this century. Because they were the principal means of transportation, railroads wielded great power. Impressive structures gave evidence of their influence. Railroad terminals in every major city expressed in their design a nostalgia at the cultural heritage of Europe. These buildings emulated the forms of the Renaissance, which had been inspired by the ancient Greeks and Romans. Typical of this eclecticism was Pennsylvania Station in New York City, copied after the Baths of Caracalla, built in A.D. 200. There were occasional exceptions, but, in general, every major city had at least one grand railroad station.

From the grandeur of the turn of the century to the present time, the gradual decline of railroad passenger service is no secret to the railroad buff, the commuter, or the average traveler. The railroads were unable to adapt to increased competition from the automobile and the airlines, which significantly altered the travel orientation of most Americans. In addition, the railroads' decline was further hastened by increased wages, restrictive legislation, and outmoded procedures.

This decline is expressed in the architecture of the railroad stations. Ticket counters are styled like old-fashioned bank-tellers' cubicles, with little peepholes that create the illusion that clerks are handling gold shipments instead of passenger train tickets. Similar protective attitudes exist in handling baggage, with endless ticket checks and counterchecks to be sure that baggage is prop-

213

erly identified. These ponderous patterns of railroad service are in vivid contrast to the efficient service of airlines. The airline ticket counter, instead of resembling a bank vault, looks like a quick sale counter where people spend hundreds of dollars as if making an insignificant purchase. Ticketing is automated, and cooperation among the airlines is standard procedure. Baggage is handled with a concern for identification, but a general acceptance of individual trustworthiness, resulting in a vastly improved system of baggage handling. Some of the procedural limitations of the railroads were influenced by the restrictions of railroad station architecture. The grills at the ticket counters, the placement of the luggage room, fostered these slow-paced patterns. Many railroads realized the difficulty but acted too late. By the time old buildings were remodeled and procedures changed, there had already been a decline in public confidence.

In addition to the problems of the building and competition, the railroads could not work out effective means of cooperation. There were some mergers and cooperative relationships but not enough to solve the growing problems. Only now, in a last gasping effort, has passenger rail service, particularly at the regional and local level, emerged with new possibilities. At the national level, new forms of organization, such as Amtrak, may be able to renew public confidence in rail service. Even more promising are regionally supported public corporations that will provide new forms of mass transit. These rail services will not follow the patterns of the past, but the essential form of high-speed cars moving over fixed rails will remain and in the future provide once again a major source of transportation.

The railroads are an example of a large national institution that did not alter its patterns and cooperate within itself or with others and was almost forced to extinction. Many churches operate much like the railroads. Other churches are seen as insidious rivals; pennies are looked upon as dollars; minor expenses are regarded as major catastrophes; buildings are seen as valuable baggage that must be protected with every possible safeguard. The churches should consider that all these security methods have not protected the railroads from continued decline.

Religious denominations in this country have always had a varied history of cooperation. The relationships can be generally characterized as more competitive than cooperative. At the national level, the Federal Council of Churches was formed early in this century but was relatively ineffective in preventing competition between denominations. Not until the formation of the National Council of Churches of Christ was there a more concerted effort to encourage cooperative efforts. The council, a federation of over thirty Protestant and Eastern Orthodox denominations, represents over forty million members. Since its inception in 1950, the council has played an important role in the ecumenical movement, working toward greater cooperation among Protestants, Eastern Orthodox churches, and ultimately all Christians.

At the local level, community councils of churches have been established for many years and have worked cooperatively in planning occasional joint services and engaging in modest community projects. In more recent years, with the growth of ecumenism, greater cooperative efforts at the national level, and the inclusion of the Catholic churches for the first time, many of these local councils have reached new levels of spirit and cooperation, working together in facilities planning and meaningful community service projects. These changes have not come easily, and in the 1960's the most vigorous programs were not without their critics.

Beyond the cooperation of the councils of churches, a more inclusive form of cooperation has been the merging of various denominations. Since the merger of the Congregational Christian Churches and the Evangelical and Reformed Church in 1957 to create the United Church of Christ, there have been three significant mergers. In 1958 the United Presbyterian Church in the United States of America was formed; in 1960, the United Lutheran Church; and in 1962, the Lutheran Church of America. The most discussed and promising of all mergers began in 1962 as the Consultation of Church Union, a study of the merger of nine denominations to form the Church of Christ Uniting. Participating churches include the African Methodist Episcopal Church, the African Methodist Episcopal Zion Church, the Christian Church (Disciples of Christ), the Christian Methodist Episcopal Church, the Episcopal Church, the Presbyterian Church in the United States, the United Church of Christ, the United Methodist Church, and the United Presbyterian Church in the United States of America.

If the merger is achieved, church historian, Edwin Gaustad has speculated, "It is conceivable, then, that in the next decade Protestantism in America would have three major divisions: Baptists, Lutherans, and a 'United

Church.' " [1] Such a simplification of the denominational structure would have a significant impact upon churches and their facilities at the local level. Already one of the most successful and unheralded forms of cooperation has been the mergers of churches in many rural communities throughout the country. Small towns often bring into focus complex issues; shifting populations and obvious duplications of staff and facilities motivated many rural congregations to join in various forms of merged and federated churches. Case histories of some recent mergers have been documented in *Grassroots Ecumenicity* by Horace Sills. The opening chapter describes the background of these churches.

> The major thrust of the missionary endeavors of denominational groups in this land was directed primarily toward a rural-oriented constituency. Churches were located at the crossroads of barter and trade, in hamlets of some economic possibilities, and in the open country where farm families could gather easily for worship and fellowship. Large groups of persons were not necessarily the only criterion for the establishment of a particular congregation. Often a congregation was established because of an ethnic heritage or language preference, or because of the means of travel available at that time, or because there was no congregation already established, or because of factions and fractions within a congregation that led some to withdraw and start another congregation of the same denomination in the same community. Whatever the reason, the early churching of America was thorough. [2]

The lessons of the rural churches and the increased awareness of common bonds has led to a growth of cooperation and joint endeavors among denominations. Herbert Schneider predicted in the early 1950's the changes taking place within denominational structures and more specifically individual churches:

> There has been a steady growth of Protestant community churches or federated churches, which cut across denominational lines. They are especially popular in college communities and suburban towns. More widespread and significant is the growth of "comity" among denominations, which aims at avoiding useless competition within a community. If the members can agree on a mode of public worship, other issues are apt to be regarded as "unessential." The strength of many of the denominational lines is dependent on the fact that they reflect European communities and nationalities which still preserve some vitality in America. Dif-

ferent kinds of Lutherans come from different parts of Europe. The Scottish connections are still important in Presbyterians, and the English to Episcopalians and Congregationalists. Surrounded by such churches, the Baptists and Methodists are apt to feel like 110 per cent Americans. Local Roman Catholic churches, too, are apt to be less Roman than they are Italian, Irish, Polish, Mexican, and so on. These cultural differences, reflecting the cultural pluralism of the American people, are probably the most powerful cause for the variety and vigor of our churches. No doubt, the European backgrounds are gradually receding, and European visitors are able to detect better than we ourselves the emergence of a "typically American form of Christian worship." [3]

The plea for new reconciliation and cooperation is expressed in the introductory words of the Consultation on Church Union Study, *A Plan of Union.*

The church is one.

Yet the disunity of the visible companies of Christian people obscures this reality. In a world of repression and anarchy, a renewed church is called to a new unity. This oneness in the church is required for the credibility and effectiveness of Christ's mission. The characteristics that are God's gifts to the church can be only as the church becomes visibly one. As the world looks at us now, it is unimpressed by our claim to love one another for it sees how we are fractured and divided by lesser loyalties.[4]

A more personal plea was made many years ago by H. Richard Niebuhr in his *The Social Sources of Denominationalism.* In the concluding passages he states:

The road to unity which love requires denominations, nations, classes, and races to take is no easy way. There is no short cut even to the union of the churches. The way to the organic, active peace of brotherhood leads through the hearts of peace-makers who will knit together, with patience and self-sacrifice, the shorn and tangled fibers of human aspirations, faiths, and hopes, who will transcend the fears and dangers of an adventure of trust.[5]

This trust will need to be expressed in new directions of cooperation among churches in all forms of shared activities and religious environments. Churches will need to leave their present positions of isolation and become centers of community activity, joining with others to bring new programs of social service. In every dimension the church is entering a period of cooperation that can signify a new religious maturity.

## NATURE

The new sense of cooperation requires of churches an ethical and spiritual commitment to a greater understanding and appreciation of the natural elements. Much of Western history has been a record of man's domination of natural life. Western tradition has fostered the belief that the earth was made for man and all other living creatures were created for man's pleasure. We believed other organisms were created to enhance human life, never thinking these creatures have a right to their own lives. This divorce from the natural environment was in part fostered by the need to separate Christian beliefs from pagan concepts of multiple gods and of spirits residing in living objects. The Judeo-Christian tradition presented a transcendent omnipotent God.

Lynn White, Jr., a professor of history at the University of California at Los Angeles, writes:

> Especially in its Western form, Christianity is the most anthropocentric religion the world has seen. As early as the second century both Tertullian and Saint Irenaeus of Lyons were insisting that when God shaped Adam he was foreshadowing the image of the Incarnate Christ, the Second Adam. Man shares, in great measure, God's transcendence of nature. Christianity, in absolute contrast to ancient paganism and Asia's religions (except, perhaps, Zoroastrianism), not only established a dualism of man and nature but also insisted that it is God's will that man exploit nature for his proper ends.[6]

The tension between Christianity and the natural environment is further explained by Albert Camus in *The Rebel*:

> It consummates twenty centuries of abortive struggle against nature, first in the name of a historic god and then of a deified history. Christianity, no doubt, was only able to conquer its catholicity by assimilating as much as it could of Greek thought. But when the Church dissipated its Mediterranean heritage, it placed the emphasis on history to the detriment of nature, caused the Gothic to triumph over the romance, and destroying a limit in itself, has made increasing claims to temporal power and historical dynamism. When nature ceases to be an object of contemplation and

admiration, it can then be nothing more than material for an action that aims at transforming it. These tendencies—and not the concepts of mediation, which would have comprised the real strength of Christianity— are triumphing in modern times, to the detriment of Christianity itself, by an inevitable turn of events.[7]

The reign of domination is coming to an end, and in the future the church will need to seek a more cooperative relationship with the natural environment.

In this country from the time of the early settlers to the present time of accelerated technology, we have been engaged in a long and constant battle with natural forces and have only recently realized we were winning the battle but losing the war. We now have the capability to construct or level a mountain, build or destroy a lake, but have no philosophy or spiritual direction on which to base our decisions. One of the dilemmas of our time, of which young people are particularly aware, is the lack of a consistent, positive theory or attitude toward our environment.

The Christian tradition, with rare exceptions such as Saint Francis, has encouraged domination over nature as a means of maintaining the purity of the spirit against the corruptness of the flesh. In contrast, the respect for nature inherent in Eastern religions is one of many reasons for its current popularity. The location of Western churches atop imposing hills expresses domination of the natural environment, whereas Eastern temples stand near quiet ponds and wooded glens.

We need a new direction in our attitude toward nature. A spiritual basis must be developed to change the world view and ethics of the Christian tradition from a position of domination to cooperation and appreciation. This does not mean worshiping trees and seeking absolution in rivers. We do not need to "return to nature," which is an unrealistic reversal of today's needs; nor do we need to "love nature," which implies an unrealistic romanticizing of the many potentially destructive natural forces. We do need to respect and care for the living elements of the natural world. A more cooperative attitude will take the form not only of actively working to decrease the pollution of our air and water but also of visually enhancing our urban and rural environments. This concern will be expressed in long-range attitudes and goals related to environmental problems and more specific applications within the life of the church. No matter how cosmopolitan and sophisticated urban man becomes, he still has deep within him primitive impulses. Activity in natural surroundings provides a release for some of this energy. Urban dwellers are increasingly aware that living elements are a necessary part of a fully satisfying environment. Concrete plazas and monumental fountains are not enough; people need areas of intimacy and privacy in natural surroundings.

The desire to participate in nature is expressed in the growing trend in leisure activities. On the ski slope or in a boat, people can feel free of the constant time demands and sterile walls of the work environment. Because the church in the past has denied the importance of nature as a source of spiritual harmony, increased numbers of people find themselves estranged from religion. Parishioners should not have to choose between sailing under the open sky and sitting in the rigid pews of a darkened church.

In previous eras men worked all day, every day, most often in fields under the sun. The work was often dirty and backbreaking, and Sunday morning worship provided a welcome change. The family came to worship to secure the blessings of a successful harvest and the courage for upright living. On Sunday the farmer and his wife could discard their coveralls and don their best clothes. The farmer's daily work was demanding, but did allow some self-regulation. The situation is completely the opposite for people today. Factory and office workers spend five days a week in isolated environments largely disciplined by corporate and hierarchical forces. Hours are regulated; vacations are given; relaxation and lunch breaks are scheduled. Under these pressures, people need to spend their leisure in unstructured, more inspiring settings. The natural environment is a welcome respite from the rigid patterns of corporate and social management. Where the churches in the past provided dignity and social regulation for orderliness and predictability, in today's society we need a more relaxed, personal encounter to provide spiritual regeneration from the automations of corporation engineering.

Churches have paid lip service to nature with an occasional outdoor service, usually on Easter morning for those hardy souls who can rise before six o'clock, or with conferences and retreats in natural settings, most of which have been youth oriented. Both sunrise services and youth camps are inadequate expressions of the natural environment within religion; nature needs to become part of religious teachings and activities throughout the year and to find expression in church settings. Many churches have outdoor chapel areas that have deteriorated into grass fields or outdoor pulpits that are unused; some churches are adjacent to natural ponds or beautiful streams but have turned their back on them and function as if these delightful natural elements do not exist. Ministers and congregations are often reluctant to have outdoor services because they think they will be too much trouble. Moving chairs and equipment can be cumbersome; in some locations bugs and mosquitoes can be annoying; in other areas the sun is too hot; rain can wash out all plans. However, church members should be willing to take some risks. Outdoor worship requires an acceptance of outdoor problems as well as outdoor wonder. We need to accept some natural variations; a distracting sound, flying insects, unexpected rain are all part of daily life. In religion, we should not always try to protect ourselves.

For alive human beings, life, ethics, and beauty do not exist in a pure state. Each is always modified by the variations of practical considerations and by forces that alter our ideal projected possibilities. In all the arts, there is an increased desire to incorporate the world of daily living into art forms. John Cage, composer and musical theorist, has conducted a number of experiments that have broadened the definition of musical sounds to include what were previously considered noises. Cage contends that the present form of musical concerts, such as the performance of a symphony, is in reality a wide mixture of sounds. Coughing, shuffling, outside noises are all a part of the concert that we have learned to accept. John Cage would like to see a broader concept of music, including more of the sounds heard throughout the day, in order to awaken people to the music that is a part of their ordinary existence. Similarly, outdoor services could broaden the definition of religious worship and might lead to a better transference from Sunday to the remainder of the week.

Outdoor services require advanced planning. The congregation should understand the intention and purpose of the outdoor service. Living with nature's variations does not mean going out during the rainy season into a mosquito-ridden swamp. The service should be scheduled for seasons of moderate weather with such practical considerations as facing people away from the sun. Alternative indoor locations should be planned in advance. A shorter service is generally advisable, with informal singing and music, a short sermon, and extended periods of prayer and silence; each of these elements will take on a special meaning in the context of natural surroundings. Trying to conduct an outdoor service with indoor formality can be deadly. Outdoor sounds and visual interest require a more free-form service. Outdoor services do not need to be limited to the grounds of the church. Many areas have nearby parks, mountains, or lakes that can provide beautiful and quiet settings for worship. Those participating in outdoor services usually agree that the fellowship of the united church activity, combined with the beauty of the setting in the context of a religious service, creates a very meaningful and enjoyable experience. Such experiences show that worship and nature can be combined to provide the ancient function of spiritual replenishment and satisfy the contemporary need for relaxing and natural surroundings.

If we genuinely want to integrate our natural environment in our spiritual life, we need to give this attitude direct expression in our religious facilities. Churches do not need to run off and buy a camp or immediately build an outdoor chapel, but there should be a concerted effort to improve existing buildings to better utilize available natural resources. Many urban churches have grounds that are undeveloped or poorly maintained, areas that could easily be developed into relaxing terraces for midday conversation, for services, and as oases of calm beauty in the hectic rush of city life. Many suburban churches have similar natural potential on their properties. If new buildings are to be constructed, consideration should be given to sites that are not necessarily on the busiest street corner or atop the highest hill. Natural beauty should increasingly be a major consideration; sites can be found in which trees can be preserved, ponds enhanced, and hillsides developed.

At the present time, many churches foolishly try to maintain extensive formal gardens and acres of lawn. Large areas of grass are one more expression of the need to dominate the land; we seem to feel that natural life is inadequate and the earth must be overcome with our cultivated products. In the cities, concrete is our dominating material; in suburbia it is grass. Hardly an inch of ground is left in natural form; everywhere are expressions of our order and control. Only a new spiritual enlightenment can help us realize that a natural hill or a growing tree can be as important as a bulldozed site barren of all growing life except green blades of the family Gramineae. To substitute for time-consuming, expensive, unused lawns, a visual focus could be developed at the church as a center of outdoor activity. Similar to the interior full-functioning environment, the outdoor areas should have an active value to the church membership and in some cases the larger community. A small, well cared-for terrace, garden, play area, or fountain can provide an interesting center of activity. Small gardens with occasional benches are delightful for quiet sitting, and with appropriate easily cared-for plants, maintenance can be at a minimum. Some churches, such as the Orangethorpe United Methodist Church in Fullerton, California, have used donated plants to contribute living memorials to the church in contrast to the more static lifeless gifts of the past. The creation of a small garden or park through voluntary efforts can develop a significant spirit of congregational accomplishment and fellowship.

Terraces are excellent areas of focus, as well as practical settings for outdoor gatherings. In new buildings, terraces should be developed as a part of the initial design, considering such factors as sun, wind, and noise. In existing buildings, new terraces will require the careful consideration of the architect and the planning committee to determine appropriate locations. A terrace can be relatively inexpensive and may involve only the addition of a doorway, a modest amount of paving, or perhaps a fence. If the area is properly used, the investment will be worthwhile. Typical of the modest terrace additions that are successful is the new paved patio at Christ Church, in Washington, D.C. The church remodeled an existing parish house and added as part of the total project an enclosed terrace with a surrounding wall, plantings, and shade trees. The area, located directly outside the main body of the church, has been used for weddings, worship, and fellowship gatherings before and after services.

Small reflecting pools are one of the most economical and beautiful features in any outdoor design. Throughout the world, water is used as an important design element. In warm climates, it has been known for centuries that even the smallest trickle of water can create a refreshing, cooling atmosphere. The city spaces of Europe have a long tradition of fountains and waterways at the center of their plazas. Until recently, water was largely neglected as a source of delight in this country. When water was used, it was in relation to civic monuments that tended to be overpowering. Only in recent years have commercial centers changed this trend, utilizing water in fountains and pools for pleasure and decoration rather than because of their somber impressiveness. City and commercial plazas are turning to fountains as a focus of open-space designs. Unfortunately, many of these plazas are still designed to impress, and the water does not serve as a calming influence but as a giant-scale design feature related more to surrounding skyscrapers than to people. The plaza fountains are symbols of water power rather than water beauty.

Churches have the potential of using modest water designs to create a human and peaceful setting. A church courtyard with a reflecting pool or a slowly bubbling fountain can be inducive to a relaxing calm. An important dimension of the beauty in the gardens at the Cloisters in New York City is the gentle sound of water from the fountains in contrast to the muffled noises from the city streets. Some church committees and architects have avoided using water because they feel it will present an undesirable maintenance problem. A reflection pool can be quite shallow, allowing easy cleaning; in the winter months in cold climates it can be filled with a thin layer of white gravel. A small garden with a reflecting pool can be more serviceable than acres of unused lawn, and certainly easier and less expensive to maintain.

Churches, especially in crowded urban areas, should not develop grounds for their use alone but should explore possibilities of service to the community. Many churches could make an important contribution by developing their property into pleasant sitting areas or creating safe playgrounds for neighborhood children. In *Playgrounds for City Children* M. Paul Friedberg emphasizes that city children are deprived of the advantages of open spaces and a natural environment for exploration and growth:

> The deficiencies of today's playgrounds, as well as of the street and sidewalk, are most clearly defined when contrasting the activities of a child in a natural environment. For here he is exposed to a wealth of experiences —stepping stones across a stream, a slide down or a climb up a hill, balancing on a fence, digging in the earth, climbing a tree, throwing a rock.[8]

He later states:

> There is much to be learned from the world nature provides for the child. It is the environment—not the facilities—to which the child responds. When the play situation is transposed from country to city, the experience of nature is lost and in its place is fabricated for the child an artificial, stultifying play situation.
>
> The obvious need of children is not just a place to play—a circumscribed area with three or four pieces of equipment, swing by sandbox, slide by teeter-totter, side by side—but a total world to which he can respond.[9]

An example of the types of play environments that can be created for children of all ages is the playground of St. Ann's Episcopal Church in the Morrisania section of the Bronx, in New York City. Father Henry D. Moore, Jr.,

*Playground, St. Ann's Episcopal Church*

the pastor of the church, organized the effort to develop the church property. The architect, Charles Jacob, and the landscape architect, George Cushine, designed a three-level playground with funding provided by the church and private foundations. The top level is devoted to handball and basketball courts; the middle level is a scrambling area with wooden climbing equipment; and the lowest level contains simple climbing equipment and a spray pool where preschool children are supervised by neighborhood mothers in the community center's day-care program. The church, significantly, welcomed the involvement of area residents in planning and operating the playground, and avoided stereotyped, rigid equipment in favor of an imaginative play environment.

Awareness of and cooperation with nature will be a more integral part of religion in the future. This concern will be expressed in the involvement of churches in ecological issues and changes in the church environment. Whether the congregation gathers on a terrace, around a pond, or in a wooded glen for an outdoor service, a picnic supper, or a community hike, the members will become increasingly more sensitive to the possibilities and beauty of the natural surroundings.

## COMMUNITY

The new directions of the church will require increased cooperative relationships with the community. Involvement is not limited to social action but should extend to a wide range of concerns. The commitment of the church to the community is more a return to previous practices than a radical departure; the church has at many times in its history been the focus of community life.

The church as the center of community activity has been well documented by J. G. Davis, professor of theology at the University of Birmingham, in his *The Secular Use of Church Buildings*. Dr. Davis traces the varied uses of church facilities, which in many ecclesiastical periods were considered natural extensions of the life of the church. Many of these activities are now designated as secular, in contrast to sacred, but such a dichotomy did not always exist:

> For something like 1,800 years churches were used for almost every conceivable secular activity. Such practices, as we have noted, were under constant fire from the ecclesiastical authorities; bishop after bishop condemned, on an inadequate theological basis, what they considered to be

acts of desecration, but their efforts had little immediate effect. It is only within the last two centuries that the battle has been largely won, with the consequence that to many a church appears to be totally irrelevant to their secular and daily life. The Christian appeal to tradition is often heard; here then is a lay tradition that is overwhelmingly in favour of the secular use of church buildings, and we must also take notice of the fact that in at least one country this tradition has never been broken.

Many of the buildings of the Reformed Churches in the Swiss Cantons are still in regular use for secular activities. They are the scenes of village assemblies, when all the voting members of the community discuss matters of local concern. They are used for elections, for concerts and for plays and films, the last two being of all kinds and not restricted to the "religious." Extramural university classes take place in them, as well as brass band rehearsals and, if there is no alternative accommodation, schools also are found within them.[10]

Dr. Davis shows with considerable supporting data the historical uses of church facilities. He discusses the absence of churches in the first two hundred years of Christianity, reviews the formative period of religious structures when they were used for healing, sanctuary, and lodgings for travelers, and describes in extensive detail the development of the cathedral in the Middle Ages:

> In the Middle Ages, the nave of the church, according to G. M. Trevelyan, was "the village hall" for most communal purposes. The correctness of this description has been amply demonstrated by this survey of non-liturgical activities within churches which have a continuous history from the patristic period, although some of them have been elaborated and extended as the centuries passed. The size of many medieval parish churches now becomes understandable. They were frequently far too spacious to accommodate the normal worshipping congregation from the immediate locality, but their dimensions are to be understood, not simply in terms of devotional display, but as the necessary means of providing for the multitude of activities which took place within them.[11]

The medieval church provided a broad range of services to the community, including healing of the sick, sanctuary from legal prosecution, lodging for poor travelers, and feasts, especially in celebration of the sacraments of marriage and baptism. The church was a setting for dance presentations, yearly fairs, meetings of ecclesiastical councils, sessions of parliaments and city councils, elections, discussions, and debate, financial transactions, education and libraries, academic ceremonies, the storing of individual valuables and possessions, and the publishing of notices—one of the principal communications of the period. During the Middle Ages new social activities and institutions were devised, including the distribution of relief to the poor, game playing in the Feast of Fools, dramatic presentations, and military defense; the church had a part in all these. The medieval church was an all-purpose building, but this in no way interfered with the sacredness of the worship services:

> In all, there was no conscious irreverence. The church was a home away from home, where people could sleep, live, eat, drink, play, act and meet. It was part and parcel of everyday life; it was there to be used and used it was. Its decorations reflected the pursuits and home life of the parishioners, as when carvings represented a quarrel between husband and wife, or the ugly spectacle of a bear-baiting. The style might change from Romanesque to Gothic and churches might grow larger as aisles and chapels were added to them, but their use was constant and increasing. There was ample space for every activity, since it was only towards the end of the period under review that fixed pews on any large scale were introduced. Sacred and secular were united and while excesses were perpetrated, what made them condemnable was not the place but the excesses themselves. We are bound to conclude therefore that a knowledge of the liturgy alone is insufficient to describe the use of medieval churches—this was one important facet, but only one of many activities in these multipurpose buildings.[12]

In the nineteenth and twentieth centuries the growth of industrialism and the resulting increase of specialization in labor and institutions led to the gradual replacement of the church as the center of community life. The church has become increasingly removed from secular activities. It was not too long ago that many colleges in this country were supported and administered by religious institutions; similarly, hospitals, recreational facilities, social service programs, and general counseling were under the auspices of a church.

Over the years, each of these institutions has separated itself from its religious origin. Colleges have retained some of their historic ties but have become broad-based private institutions operating under independent control in order to serve a larger constituency and be in a more equitable position for community, foundation, and governmental support. Proximity, cost, and quality of the school became more important than denominational affiliation in the process of college selection. The same influences were important in the increasing secularization of hospitals, recreational centers, and social agencies. Broad-based community support could best provide the funds necessary for expanded facilities and the rising costs of more technically competent personnel. While many churches still maintain activities in these areas, most church-supported educational and medical facilities are straining under the pressures of limited income and rising costs. Many churches are active in various forms of counseling, neighborhood centers, and assistance to the disadvantaged, but these services are increasingly operated in conjunction with secular agencies. If the church is to remain relevant to the lives of people, it must relate to daily living and the total spectrum of community life. The church needs to relate to both the advantaged and the disadvantaged, and its facilities should serve both the slick urban skyscraper complex and the deteriorating dwellings of the slum areas. If the church is to return to the mainstream of activity, it will need broader concepts of the nature of the religious environment.

The church in the community will not assume a dominating position but will serve a humble role in a more practical setting. There will be a moving away from the traditional image of separate ecclesiastical facilities, of each denomination standing apart from home and business. Some churches have already located adjacent to a shopping center; the worshipers use the vacant parking facilities on Sundays, and the church is a part of these centers of activity during the remainder of the week. With more churches drawing members from an extended geographical area, the shopping center, usually located near major traffic patterns, provides a convenient location. Churches may also rent space within the center itself. The Christian Scientists have been pioneers in this field, providing reading rooms and missionary stations throughout the country in shopping centers and commercial buildings. Other denominations are beginning to explore these possibilities.

Shopping center locations are no longer limited to the suburbs; churches will also acquire space in the large complexes presently under construction in most major cities. Typical of these large commercial ventures is the Prudential Center in Boston. Within this enormous marketplace the Franciscan friars are successfully demonstrating the value of a religious presence by their Saint Francis Chapel. Worship services are conducted every day of the week; there are five masses a day, attended by employees and customers of the center, residents of the nearby apartment complexes, and others who come from surrounding areas. In addition, counseling and confessionals are available throughout the week. In this location, the chapel shares all the advantages that make the center a commercial success, including its convenient location near a major highway, a dense local population, ample and convenient parking, and spacious malls with water displays and seating areas. Of course, all these amenities are not inexpensive, and the friars pay the full commercial rent for their space.

Activity in the marketplace is costly, and churches in these locations need to modify their operating procedures to justify the high cost of space. These rentals force the churches to face the realities of space costs in urban areas; the present tax-exempt status of many churches on prime property has lulled them into inefficient facilities and procedures. Large, unused sanctuaries and vacant classrooms are impossible at commercial rental rates. Saint Francis Chapel has effectively used its center by fully using the chapel throughout the day, seven days a week. Rent is high, but because the space is limited and efficiently used, other expenses such as insurance, maintenance, and utilities have been considerably reduced. As commercial complexes increase in importance in metropolitan life, the church will need to devise new means of operating to provide a religious presence in these centers of activity.

Churches are developing closer ties with public educational institutions. Some communities have had clergymen at the high school on a scheduled basis to assist in a counseling program. These programs are ecumenical in format, allowing the young people to visit with the clergyman of their choice. The book *Focus: Building for Christian Education*, by Mildred Widber and Scott T. Ritenour, surveys such developments as adult and high school religious education programs conducted by a nearby college and having a common format of lectures and presentations followed by small group discussions led by community clergymen.[13] This type of experimentation in community educational programs will have a continuing influence upon future plans for religious education facilities. One of the most dramatic concepts of community educational outreach is the cooperative efforts of the churches of Bennington, Vermont, which have developed the Bennington Religious Education Foundation (BREF) as a means of providing a "periodic released time" religious education during the academic day. The foundation, composed of four Roman Catholic parishes, two United Church of Christ, one United Methodist, one Episcopal, and one Church of God, has developed a program of cooperation with the high school and provides informal religious classes in both denominational and ecumenical courses. These classes are conducted in a small house purchased by the foundation across the street from the high school. William Abernethy, the minister of the Congregational Church in Bennington, writes:

> With older models of religious education increasingly recognized as inadequate to the complexity of modern life, BREF provides at least one new model of what can be done. BREF does not solve all problems; it, too, is limited. The Bennington Religious Education Foundation provides a structure through which the religious community can provide quality religious education, when that community is stimulated to see the need for such education and to take that need seriously.[14]

The idea of "periodic released time" is being explored on a larger scale by other churches, but the full legal arrangements and restrictions will need further investigation. The plan does, however, suggest a significant relationship with the larger community and a sharing of facilities.

In all such arrangements cooperative efforts among churches are an important prelude to cooperative relationships with the community. Most public organizations or institutions are more responsive to coordinated activity with religious groups when they feel the churches are working together toward a common goal.

Another move being made to bring the church to the mainstreams of daily living is the increased emphasis upon small religious gatherings and worship in the houses of members. This trend is occurring in all denominations and religions. The Catholic church has encouraged experiments in home masses in such different locations as New York City and the state of Oklahoma. In other areas, home worship has continued in spite of lack of official approval. The home setting allows a more personal and intimate gathering of people and brings the act of worship and communion back into the patterns of home life. Home worship eliminates the need for elaborate church facilities and resulting expenses, even though many of the experimental groups continue to feel some kinship with existing established churches. The principal difficulty with home groups is their limited size and transient location, which can make them ingrown and unstable.

The mainstreams are not limited to shiny new commercial centers, colleges, or homes but must include the lusterless back streets of society. The increased separation of institutional social services and church life dulled much of the

ethical thrust of religion, so that in the 1960's many people became confused
and disenchanted when the church, and particularly the clergy, became involved in action for social change. Parishioners could understand the orderly
services to the community or hospital contributions or charity donations for
the poor, but the concept of disorderly conduct to call attention to larger social
ills was more than they could comprehend. For the first time since the social
gospel of the 1930's, the church was involved in a significant way in its concern for the disadvantaged. Some religious leaders made predictions of completely altering society through the united efforts of the churches, but these
claims were unfounded, and in some cases the most radical advocates went
beyond the limits necessary to maintain a relatively cohesive church organization. These were the learning years of contemporary church involvement. In
the past few years, the churches have been more modest, and perhaps more realistic, in their involvement within the community. The church has prudently
turned to smaller-scaled projects in order to bridge the gap between human
problems and social and governmental response. Just as the church is no longer
the sole patron of the arts, it can no longer pretend to be sole healer of the sick
or disadvantaged, but it can fulfill a needed human dimension in social services.

In recent years many new churches have had a much more pronounced emphasis on providing facilities for community service. One of the most outstanding of these is St. Mark's Church in Kansas City, Missouri. It is an ecumenical venture formed to serve the people of the inner city in an area
dominated by low-income housing, with approximately eight thousand residents within a six-block radius. The origins of the project grew from the decline of two churches, one Presbyterian and one United Church of Christ, located in an area of population shift. The clergy became painfully aware of the
insignificance of their immersion in routine tasks and unsuccessful efforts to
preserve these dying churches while all around them were immense problems
of poverty and despair. The churches decided that a more cooperative effort
would provide a stronger congregation and a more successful organization to
work on the problems of the area. Both churches sold their existing properties
in order to gather the resources to build a new worship and community center. As the project developed the Roman Catholics and Episcopalians joined
the Congregationalists and Presbyterians. St. Mark's is not a merger, but a
single building jointly staffed and supported and used as a center of mission to

*St. Mark's Church*

serve the community. Rev. William Hayes, the administrative director of the church, emphasizes that "St. Mark's is not a merger, for the four communions mutually recognize and respect any real differences in church structure, doctrinal belief, or sacramental life that may exist among them." [15] He goes on to say:

> St. Mark's represents ecumenicity with a purpose. The four groups did not come together simply out of a passion for church union but out of a desire to render a more effective service to the inner city. They saw problems: spiritual lostness, apathy, powerlessness, which concerned them all. They understood the complexity of community problems like housing, education, welfare, racial injustice, etc., and realized that a strong coalition would be necessary to make even a dent in them.
>
> We are not here to play ecumenical games. We are not experimenting on the community. Our primary purpose is to serve the unmet needs, religious and social, of this inner city community. The building, beautiful as it may be, is not an ornament to decorate this corner, but an instrument to help us serve people.[16]

The building expressed the emphasis upon community service. The exterior is a blending of texturized concrete and inviting open areas and plazas for community use. Inside, the facility is divided into three areas, including an administrative suite for the participating clergy, community spaces, and a worship center. The most active area is the first floor spaces designed for community programs. A preschool has been conducted for several years and will become a kindergarten if community needs warrant. The first floor also has a crafts and shop room, providing a major element in the full-functioning environment. The most popular and versatile room is a multipurpose area used for a range of programs and community groups including the PTA, welfare rights group, parents organizations, a tutoring program, special events, general recreation, and suppers. The worship area is located upstairs. The sanctuary uses flexible, individual seating and colorful banners designed and made especially for the space by Sister Jeanne d'Arc and Sister Maria Edward from Hartford, Connecticut. The worship area is pleasant but appears to be too large, considering the constant use of the full-functioning community areas on the first floor and the limited use of the sanctuary space.

With increased community and cooperative experience, the church facility might now be built with a more adaptable worship area. But even with a few design limitations, St. Mark's has made a significant contribution to the improvement of human services in the area. The principal difficulty with a project such as St. Mark's is that almost all funds for its operation come from outside the area, and as total church funds become limited, these projects are in danger of being forced to accept a minimum budget, which can curtail the effectiveness of the staff and the full utilization of the building. It is, therefore, important that even ecumenical community-service church structures be limited in scope through the use of a full-functioning environment in order to maintain complete operations without constant concern for the costs of building maintenance.

The staff and congregation of St. Mark's are determined not to be captives of the building. Rev. Orris Walker, a participating Episcopal clergyman, states:

> We believe the Church should go where the action is. The vital decisions that affect community life are not made in churches but in City Halls, Boards of Education, in board rooms of business institutions, in political caucuses, and in neighborhood organizations. If the Church is to be relevant, it must be there.[17]

There is a tendency for churches to make considerable expenditures on their buildings, rationalized by the concept of providing space for community services. Churches have built large halls or extensive classroom wings with the justification that these would be used by the community during the week, only to learn that the spaces were not suitable or that their own building policies severely restricted community use. One church in Vermont built an elaborate hall with the stated intention of serving the assembly and concert needs of the community. They built a space large enough to meet the area requirements in order to make concerts economically feasible, but found that the room was much too large for their own worship and assembly, and was extremely expensive to maintain. To further aggravate the situation, the musicians were not satisfied with the quality of the space and sound. As a result, the large hall was seldom used by the community or the church.

In providing spaces for the community, churches must be honest with themselves and not justify excessive building programs with rationalization of community concern. Churches should only build spaces that are genuinely compatible with their own needs and resources, and that can be used by both the church and the community.

Church building concerns will have to be more responsive to the needs of others. This will entail a realignment of assets. Elaborate unused worship spaces will be redesigned, and church-owned parsonages may be eliminated as ministers and their families increasingly desire to live in homes of their own choosing. Community nurseries, day-care centers, clinics, local advocacy and service organizations will increase as part of the concerns and facilities of the contemporary church. Even the sale of existing church properties should give consideration to community needs and possible uses of the building for service-oriented goals.

One contemporary extension of church facilities has been the recent participation of religious organizations in providing housing for those with low and moderate income. These projects exemplify the unique role the church can serve in the community. Through cooperative enterprises with other organizations, agencies, and governmental bodies, the church can bring together people and programs at the local level. The federal government provides the source of financing and some expertise, and the churches provide the concerned citizens to implement the program. Many of the churches described here have participated in these federal programs. The Melrose Congregational Church has built a substantial facility for the elderly, and the Interfaith Center in Columbia, Maryland, has built low- and moderate-income housing. Churches have also worked cooperatively with other churches and community groups to sponsor projects that provide much more than a building but an active program of counseling, activities, and events. The Melrose elderly housing unit is only half a block from the church, providing a convenient programing location. In Palo Alto, California, a church has provided a housing unit for the elderly on land adjacent to the church, pleasantly connected over a wooden walking bridge on a small waterway.

One of the most innovative housing programs was developed in Oakland, California, through the coordinated planning of the Council of Churches of Oakland. Instead of one or more churches constructing one large facility, the Oakland project provides smaller units to be built in a variety of locations in residential areas throughout the city near sponsoring churches. The program is organized separately as Satellite Senior Homes, Inc., and has a board composed of representatives of the twenty participating groups, including seventeen churches, one synagogue, a federation, and a foundation. One core unit has been built in a central location within the city composed of 150 units and auxiliary facilities for recreation and meals. The satellite units have been built in outlying areas with individual church sponsors; these include the cooperative efforts of the Plymouth United Church of Christ of Oakland and the large Piedmont Community Church cosponsoring sixty-six units, and the Durant Avenue Presbyterian Church of Oakland with only 158 members sponsoring the construction of forty-four units. Each church also takes on the responsibility of providing programs and assistance to the residents of their satellite. The total project has constructed six buildings totaling 402 units, and several more buildings are in various stages of development. Regardless of the form of organization or the building, these churches and many others have not limited their environmental thinking to their own facilities but have seen the value of cooperative effort to create needed housing projects. Through these efforts many people of all ages with modest income are living satisfying lives in pleasant environments.

Housing is only one form of cooperative community service requiring broader concept of church involvement. Churches have participated in a wide variety of community projects, including teenage drop-in centers and numerous local service organizations. Some of these groups have used church facilities; others have used donated, rented, and purchased quarters separate from the church building. An excellent example of this type of project is the 29th and Sedgely Playpark in Philadelphia. An unsightly, dangerous lot filled with old cars owned by the Most Precious Blood Church was transformed into an appealing play area by the cooperative efforts of the volunteer architects of the Philadelphia Workshop working with mothers from the Most Precious Blood and from the Clara Baldwin House Association, with Gino's restaurant chain providing the funds. The church alone could not develop the property, but through cooperative planning and funding a new park was created.

There are many possibilities for such joint ventures. The Philadelphia Workshop is one of many community design centers active in every major city, developing small projects and feasibility studies on larger structures, which have included remodeling and solutions of construction problems. If a church has limited funds and would like to change its present environment to a full-functioning facility, property that can be developed into a community park, or an idea for a service project or housing unit, community design centers can help define, with skilled technical assistance, the feasibility of the project. The centers can be contacted through the local chapters of the American

Institute of Architects. In addition to design assistance, financial assistance is available in most communities. Many businesses, foundations, and other organizations are willing to cooperate with churches in worthwhile community endeavors. Just as the local church needs only a little imagination to implement the full potential of its present building, an idea to improve the community can become a reality with little more than the desire and persistence of the congregation.

One church that has experimented with a combination of facilities somewhere between the home and areas of need is the Christ Church, Presbyterian, of Burlington, Vermont. The church was formed in the mid-1950's in a rapidly growing suburb. At first everything about the church looked typical. Early in its development it purchased a temporary facility and adjacent building site. Plans were discussed for the first phase of a building program, and a sign placed on the property designated the site as the future home of yet another Protestant church. If Christ Church had followed the expected pattern, an architect would have been hired for preliminary studies, a financial campaign begun, and a host of committees organized to begin the programs of the typical suburban church. However, under the leadership of the minister, William Hollister, the church moved in a different direction. There are no committees formed around property maintenance and fund raising; instead, committees are formed for missionary service in the community. Under Mr. Hollister's direction, the church has been actively engaged in the moral issues of the community, and in recent years the church has been a prime mover in the development of the Burlington Ecumenical Action Ministry, which operates a drug counseling center and a house for runaways. Mr. Hollister has been twice elected to the Vermont legislature and works actively in many areas of social concern, with special emphasis in the reforms of correctional procedures in the state. In the mid-1960's, as a further expression of the emphasis upon activity and community involvement, the church eliminated weekly Sunday morning worship and replaced it with a once-a-month, day-long Sunday program with lunch called the Festival Day. The members feel strongly that the day is not intended as a giant Sunday morning worship service that carries the congregation for the remainder of the month: "Our Sunday gatherings are thought of as home base. Every action of the church should center on the places in the world where we are called to serve as God's agents of peace, justice and reconciliation." [18] The Festival Day holds the missionary activities together. In a report on the church, Eliot A. Daley wrote:

> They like the monthly Festival Day, a day-long, no-necktie, bring-the-kids-and-dogs celebration. It is not just a celebration for the sake of celebrating, but it is a celebration of something—a celebration of their being the church, a celebration of their common calling, a celebration of their interdependent ministries which constitute the real life of the church all month long. Festival-goers chatter excitedly about ministries on school boards, in unions, at the coffee house, in tutorial projects, and other spare-time involvements; doctors, telephone linemen, professors, and state employees animatedly engage one another in interpretation of their ministries within their full-time occupations. The conversational theme is the ministries of the members during the month, and the mood is one of informality, enthusiasm, and mutual enjoyment. A four-year-old boy crawling under a row of chairs during the Communion celebration is not glared at and despised as a distraction; someone reaches down and tickles him as he goes by.[19]

Through its history Christ Church has had to fight against typical institutional expectations. The church has not grown rapidly but has always been characterized by a high sense of membership commitment both spiritual and financial. In the 1960's the church was reviewed by the Presbytery of Northern New England to determine if the church was adequately meeting the needs of the region and passed the appraisal with a new sense of Presbytery support.

If the church had followed normal patterns, it would probably now own a half-million dollars' worth of real estate, with a sanctuary, religious education wing, and staff offices—and be in the midst of a financial crisis trying to pay for these structures. Instead, the church still meets in the television repair shop and boat showroom the congregation converted into a meeting hall over ten years ago. The facility is not an imposing religious edifice; it is a series of spaces designed to implement the goals of the church. There are no towering steeples and electronic carillons, but simple rooms for the religious community and its mission. The members do not see the church environment as one location but as a series of places:

> We believe it to be the primary job of the church to seek where God is at work and to follow him there in obedient service. We believe that God is

at work in Burlington  . . .  in our homes, our places of work, our jail, our city hall, our slums, our playground, our schools, and our churches.[20]

The corridors of the jails, the lounge of Lund Home for unwed mothers, and the legislative halls in Montpelier are all extensions of their place of worship. The church facilities extend to the coffeehouse bookstore called the Loft, a rented halfway house for ex-offenders called the Reach, and their joint sponsorship in the Ecumenical Ministry in operating a drug counseling center called the Place and a house for runaways called the Shac. Everything the church sponsors does not have to be literally within its four walls, and the church does not need to own every facility it uses. In view of the rapidly changing needs in any community today, it may be more prudent for many smaller churches with community concerns to have a modest center facility with a variety of shared and rented spaces for community programs. The members of Christ Church do not advocate this structure for all churches, but it is the pattern that has allowed them to worship and work most effectively. Most congregations would find the central meeting space at Christ Church uninspiring and unattractive, and many larger churches would need more space for clerical and staff organization. The significance of Christ Church in Burlington is not only that it avoided the edifice complex and entered the mainstream of concern but that it has developed an alternative to the tradition of single location religious architecture. The church is a series of spaces throughout the community, owned, rented, or shared with other organizations. Christ Church is just one experiment among many; in the future, there will be increased experimentation in a wide variety of religious environments for worship and community service.

## SHARED FACILITIES

One of the most important new directions for the church will be the implementation of the ideals of cooperation within the realities of religious environments. The first step in cooperation has already occurred in many areas, from the development of joint planning in the location of new church structures to the merging of existing groups. Religious institutions, from seminaries to college chapels to local parishes, are actively engaged in various forms of ecumenical programs of community service and cooperative use of staff and facilities. Seminaries are developing cooperative experiments as the only means of survival as the cost of higher education rapidly increases. Everywhere seminaries are gathered, they are exploring possibilities for cooperation. One of the leaders in this movement is the Graduate Theological Union in Berkeley, California. It is composed of Alma College, Berkeley Baptist Divinity School, Church Divinity School of the Pacific (Episcopal), Pacific Lutheran Theological Seminary, Pacific School of Religion, St. Patrick's College (Roman Catholic), San Francisco Theological Seminary (Presbyterian), and Thomas Starr King School for the Ministry (Unitarian Universalist). As the program develops, each of the participating schools becomes more involved in the economic and educational advantages of extended cooperative effort. Coordinated class scheduling, a cross-indexed central library, and utilization of the total existing facilities have led to an improved, more practical seminary program for all participants.

Closely related to this direction for seminaries is the trend at universities to develop ecumenical centers rather than continue patterns of competitive denominationalism. On most campuses, the challenge is not to outdo other denominations but to decrease the apathy of students toward traditional forms of institutional religion. The real task is to work cooperatively to seek ministries that have validity in the lives of the young people. The rejection of denominationalism by the young is understandable; denominational origins are usually based on national and ethnic differences that have limited influence upon second and third generations. Many denominations were formed because of doctrinal differences, geographical locations, or personality conflicts, which have little relevance to the contemporary religious situation. Many church members have accepted these historical patterns, but the young see no reason to continue these denominational differences.

At the local church level, many of the old divisions persist. The ecumenical spirit is always easiest at the abstract and verbal level; the real test of cooperative action is the implementation of specifics into the daily life of the members and the programs of the church. In this regard, the most successful cooperative efforts and mergers are those providing a specific practical advantage to each of the participating parties. Some churches have not cooperated or merged because they do not see the potential in such efforts. They have based their evaluation on past difficulties rather than on future benefits. Too often vital decisions related to the future of the church are determined by personal wishes that reach the proportions of selfish desires, rather than by a fair consideration of the larger factors related to the total concerns of church community. Whether pertaining to changes within the church building or to working co-operatively with other churches, decisions should be based not upon nostalgia or present needs alone but on a greater concern for the future. Backward decision-making instead of forward projection has led to much of the tiredness in present-day churches. Young people will not be drawn into rigid church environments or meaningless denominational battles; neither will they contribute large sums of money to maintain obviously superfluous facilities that serve limited purposes.

Denominational and interfaith rivalries are evident throughout the country. In the smallest town, there are often more churches than houses in the village center, and in suburbia the new buildings located at the crossroads are a constant reminder not only of the lack of cooperation but of the aggressive competition to woo newcomers. One of the saddest examples of the failure of churches to work cooperatively has been described by John Morse, formerly chairman of church planning and architecture for the National Council of Churches. On the windward side of Oahu, Hawaii, a landowner assigned a strip of land two blocks long for churches, offering free sites to those agreeing to build. More than seven denominations have already built separate, competing structures, and, as Mr. Morse comments, "there is nothing so disillusioning and reminiscent of ruthless denomination competition as to drive by this 'church row' and read the shopping-center-type signs inviting the customer to pick his brand of Christianity." [21]

The same problem applies to older urban churches. In one area of Boston there are nine churches within a one-block radius. Most of them are old and oversized; each church has an average seating capacity in the worship spaces of a thousand, with one church large enough to accommodate sixteen hundred. The average attendance in all the churches runs under three hundred on an average Sunday. There is a lot of vacant space: seven hundred seats per church are empty during the period of supposed peak usage, to say nothing of the emptiness during the remainder of the week. Only some form of cooperative endeavor and a plan of modified facilities can get these churches back on their feet again. The most promising churches could be remodeled to provide a full-functioning environment; the others could be rented, leased, or sold as a means of supporting a more united inner-city ministry. If there is a disadvantage to the successful remodeling at Christ Church Cathedral in St. Louis, it is the uniqueness of the effort. If every urban church remodeled its facilities in a similar manner, it would be a waste of resources. In the future, shared facilities will be a necessity at the local level to allow total resources to be used constructively. Christ Church Cathedral could easily accommodate other urban churches on some cooperative basis and with additional funds could provide an increased program of outreach into the community.

Cooperative use of church buildings has been successful in the past in limited ways but will need to increase through the broadening of arrangements. Churches can share buildings on a rental basis, join together to form church campuses, create special nonprofit corporations for cooperative building use, or merge. The first possibility, church rentals, has been in existence for many years as a form of building sharing. It has been particularly popular among Protestant churches that use the building on Sundays and rent to Jewish and Seventh Day Adventist congregations that meet on Friday evenings and Saturdays. There is now an increased exploration of greater sharing with rental arrangements among Protestant denominations and with Roman Catholics. Rental arrangements have always been considered temporary alternatives until the renting congregation became large enough to finance its own structure. Now we can see that these arrangements do not need to be limited and can provide practical long-range solutions to the problems of church structures. In the past, many rental relationships were arranged casually, with the renting congregation subject to the whims of the host church. Longer range cooperative building use will require more formal leases, which will provide more stable and equitable arrangements, protecting the host church against damages and the renting church against the idiosyncrasies of the leasing congregation.

Long-term sharing can have beneficial results for both congregations. In the mid-1950's in New York City, the Brotherhood Synagogue joined with the Village Presbyterian Church to share a building. At first, the association was awkward, but under prudent leadership the two faiths have come together to provide family counseling services and work with retarded children, as well as to share in services and exchange pulpits. Both clergy feel the Jewish service has remained strongly Jewish and the Christian service strongly Christian, but in the meantime, both congregations have experienced a deeper understanding and mutual respect.

An intermediate solution between renting and merger is the development of a cooperative church campus. The potential of this arrangement has never been fully explored. Separate churches have built church campus complexes, but the cooperative building of a complex is rare. One of the most successful projects was developed on the college campus at Brandeis University in Waltham, Massachusetts, where an ecumenical complex of Protestant, Catholic, and Jewish chapels was built around a small pond. The situation at Brandeis was somewhat unique because the university was able to coordinate the development of the total center. The sensitive handling of the natural setting enhances the visual expression of church cooperation. The broad terraces, curving walkways, and delicate plantings, combined with the harmonious use of materials and design, make the grounds of the center very attractive and a pleasant environment for walking, study, and sitting.

A more recent attempt at a similar type of complex at the Kennedy International Airport in New York is not so successful. Unlike the careful placement of chapels at Brandeis, the Tri-Faith Chapels at Kennedy are all in a straight line and seem more like three jumbo jets waiting for takeoff than three chapels for meditation and worship. As at Brandeis, the unifying design motif at Kennedy is water, but instead of creating an inviting atmosphere, the pond appears so sterile that it is more like a small community reservoir restricted from public use than a place for people. Where Brandeis had one architect coordinating the entire design, creating variety but still maintaining a total unit, the Tri-Faith Chapels were designed by different architects with unrelated materials. Where the Brandeis complex creates a feeling of compatibility and underlying harmony among the three faiths, at Kennedy, the feeling is one of lined-up competition.

Campus complexes require a sensitive handling of the exterior spaces and grounds to create an environment of relaxing beauty similar to that of the Brandeis center rather than the regimented stance of the chapels at Kennedy Airport. Campus plans offer excellent possibilities for the cooperative development of a full-functioning environment. Churches could have separate worship spaces but shared facilities for church programs, religious education, and administration. In the past, general lack of interest and the inability of churches to coordinate the timing of their building plans have limited campus plan considerations, but in the future, imaginative concepts will be developed to create various unified campus structures.

One of the most successful solutions in the cooperative use of church structures in the campus plan has been devised by the United Church of the Applewoods, United Church of Christ, and the Jefferson Unitarian Church in Golden, Colorado. These groups formed the Church Campus Corporation as a means of sharing church and religious education facilities. Both churches were faced with building problems. The United Church had a good office and worship space but no religious education facilities and little prospect of being able to afford an addition in the near future. The Jefferson Unitarian Church owned property but was unable to raise enough funds for a building adequate to meet its needs. The first talks between the congregations explored the possibilities of joint building ownership. This concept was discarded because it required the Unitarians to assume responsibility for the United Church mortgage as well as build an additional structure. Later the present innovative plan of church sharing was devised. The two churches formed the Church Campus Corporation; it has a board of six people, three representatives from each church. The Unitarians purchased a two-acre site adjacent to the existing building of the Congregationalists and constructed a religious education and program facilities building. The United Church participated in forming the design requirements, and the architectural firm of Roger, Nagel, and Langhart skillfully selected materials and designed the building to match the existing Congregational structure.

In a unique arrangement, each congregation leases its building to the Church Campus Corporation, and the corporation leases both buildings back to the congregations. The corporation is responsible for the maintenance of both buildings, payment of all utilities and insurance, and scheduling. The separate congregations pay the corporation on a formula basis for the use of the buildings. The first forty percent of expenses are shared equally, and the remainder is prorated according to the number of contributing units. The corporation format was devised in order to avoid the "your" and "our" concept in relation to the separate buildings. Both churches stress that this is not a merger, for each church wants to maintain its own ministry, worship, and programs. This separateness of identity, yet cooperative use of buildings, is expressed in the bylaws of the Church Campus Corporation:

> The Congregations of the Jefferson Unitarian Church and the United
> Church of the Applewoods, searching for new patterns of church devel-
> opment that would free more of our energies for the responsibilities of
> our respective churches, agree to the joint use of our land and buildings.
> It is the intent of this corporation to enable each of our churches to

serve the needs of its own Congregation and the larger community through joint use of buildings and lands.

We affirm the validity of separate identities and separate programs; respect the uniqueness and distinction of one another's traditions; and expect each Congregation to evolve its total program without regard to the religious philosophy, program goals or growth pattern of the other Congregation.[22]

This type of cooperative merger is not without its potential problems. If one church grew at a much faster rate, or if one faltered, this would put additional strains on the venture. Even with these potential problems, the church campus corporation concept will need to be more fully explored and developed. Leon Hopper, minister of the Unitarian church, summarized the advantages of the arrangement to their church:

> As for the benefits—financial is a significant one for us. Our mortgage will be about $35,000. While we will have 9,500 square feet of space available for our use, we could not have built this on our own. If we had built on our own, we would have had about 5,500 square feet and a mortgage of $80,000.
>
> We believe that there is a need to conserve land, and make the maximum use of church facilities, a good portion of which is unused most of the week. We believe that it is better to put our funds with programs than toward building—money for people rather than edifice. We believe that, given the tremendous costs of building today—and the amount of time a church building in toto is used—we owe it to ourselves to come up with some new patterns and forms.[23]

Mergers are the most important source of building consolidation. Many articles have been written about the recommended steps toward uniting churches. One of the best has been developed by the Illinois Council of Churches, through its Commission on Church Planning and Development, entitled, "Suggested Procedures for Uniting Churches." The suggestions of the document are specific and have been developed from the experiences of assisting in the consolidation of more than twenty congregations. A shorter summary of much the same recommendations appeared in the *Christian Century* in the article "Church Union" by Rev. Philip Weiler, minister of the United Church of Two Harbors, Minnesota, itself the product of a merger.

Reviewing his experiences with merger, Mr. Weiler emphasizes that there must be a concrete concern such as declining attendance or membership, limited finances, or building deterioration, for which merger can provide a solution. Mr. Weiler recommends a middleman who can objectively work with both parties, clergy and denominational support, consultation with others who have experienced merger, and the judicious pacing of the process, allowing the congregation to become familiar with each major development. Lastly, referring to his own experience, he states:

> There was trust at the bottom. Basic to any contract is good faith. In any negotiations such as ours, where countless verbal agreements and understandings must precede any formal agreement, implicit trust and mutual respect are absolutely essential. Each of the pastors had, over a period of several years, built strong relationships of trust within his congregation. The pastors had full faith in each other. These bonds were strong enough to survive the initial outburst of hostility on the part of a few members, as well as the succeeding ripples of rumor which circulated periodically.[24]

One of the most dramatic proposals of church merger has been suggested by Stephen Rose in *The Grass Roots Church*. Mr. Rose proposes a decrease in denominational organization and an increase in cooperation in local areas. In presenting this proposal, he discusses a hypothetical example of ten churches in a given area that decide to pool their resources to form a cooperative ministry. He assumes each of the churches would have a budget of $30,000 and an active membership of 250 adults. With the emphasis upon the coordination of church facilities, Mr. Rose suggests selecting one building, having a worship area with a seating capacity of five hundred or more, and a supplemental small chapel to serve as the center for a chaplaincy ministry for the entire community. This building would be called the Central House. The staff of Central House would be composed of two preachers, a director of music, a secretary, and a maintenance man. The total annual budget for the House would be $60,000. Three of the remaining buildings would be selected to house teaching ministries, one for young children including two weekday nurseries, a second for youth, and a third for adult education. Each teaching center could operate on a budget of $30,000, for a total of $90,000. One additional building would be selected as an administration and counseling center at a budget of $50,000 per year. Mr. Rose concludes:

We began our hypothetical model with ten congregations, ten buildings, and a combined annual budget of $300,000. We assumed a total membership of 2,500 adults. At this point we have at least five remaining church buildings to do with as we choose, an extra $100,000 which we have not budgeted, and more than two thousand laymen who are as yet uninvolved. In other words we have flexibility.

Take first the five remaining buildings. We can sell them, if we choose, and use the proceeds to buy or rent facilities that are more appropriate for the ministries of abandonment. We can hire specialized professionals to serve as resource persons in the task of involving the laity in direct service ministries. We can use the unbudgeted income to support local community organization projects, city-wide specialized ministries, or less affluent cooperative ministries in other areas.[25]

Mr. Rose's assumptions may be optimistic and his ideas would require a substantial amount of reorganization to obtain the degree of coordination he recommends, but the principle of increased cooperation of funds, staff, membership, and buildings is forcefully presented.

The recent formation of the United Parish in Brookline, Massachusetts, represents a more modest expression of this concept of cooperation. St. Mark's Methodist Church, the Baptist Church in Brookline, and the Harvard Congregational Church (United Church of Christ) joined to form the United Parish. The churches, all located in an affluent suburb of Boston, shared the characteristics of declining membership caused by population shifts, lack of new young families, depressed morale, and buildings that were becoming a financial burden. Through the leadership of the ministers and the support of the congregations, these churches explored various forms of cooperation, including shared facilities and joint programs and worship. In time the churches officially merged as the United Parish. As in similar arrangements, there were some initial problems, but the eventual benefits made the early difficulties seem of little consequence. The United Parish now operates a team ministry, with one clergyman responsible for worship and adult teaching, one for religious education and youth work, and one primarily involved with community programs. With their new vitality they have begun a family service and a youth service to supplement more traditional worship services. The merged church now uses one substantial facility, the former Harvard Congregational, for the conducting of worship and the programs of the church rather than trying to maintain three partially used unsatisfactory buildings, which can now be rented or sold to provide funds to further the work of the new United Parish.

The merger of some churches will require a new building to meet the needs of the combined groups and to implement their goals as a church community. Such an example is the Emmanuel Presbyterian Church located on the South Side of Chicago. Three small churches, two Methodist and one Presbyterian, dying as religious institutions and ineffective in meeting the problems of the community, elected to merge into one strong congregation. They were joined by the United Church of Christ through its Board of National Missions. The area around Emmanuel Presbyterian is not decayed, but it is neglected and serves as a melting pot for Appalachian whites, Afro-Americans, Latin Americans, and Puerto Ricans. At other times, the same area has served as the port of entry for people from Germany, Ireland, and Czechoslovakia.

Emmanuel Presbyterian is the only remaining Protestant congregation in an area of over thirty thousand people and therefore serves every segment of Christianity, including Methodist, Baptist, Pentecostal, Lutheran, Congregationalist, Church of God, Catholic, and Presbyterian. The largest percentage of the people now living in the area are of Mexican descent, and Spanish is as common as English. One of the ministers is originally from Mexico and serves the Spanish-speaking people in the congregation and the community. The working goal of the church is to bring the diverse peoples together into a united congregation. This has been successfully achieved, with individuals from all backgrounds participating in positions of responsibility in the church. In adapting to the needs of the area, Spanish is spoken in one of the worship services each Sunday. They also realized language could become a dividing element, so they hold joint bilingual services of communion. The choir, directed by a former music teacher from Mexico, performs at all services in Spanish and English.

People from Emmanuel have been active in the local community organization and helped form and have consistently held decision-making positions in a federal credit union, which has worked toward better housing, more play space, and better library facilities. The church serves the community directly through its store-front library, sponsorship of scouting groups, and, with the help of volunteers, a tutorial and study program for local children. A preschool nursery is also in operation in partnership with the local settlement house in the Neighborhood Service Organization. The merger of the churches and the

*Emmanuel Presbyterian Church*

combining of facilities has not only developed a more secure base for the church's mission but has freed the ministers from the separate details of building administration that would have been continued in three separate and deteriorating churches. The combined staff of three clergymen may now put their emphasis in reaching out into the community to work with people.

The Emmanuel Presbyterian building successfully reflects both the social needs of the area and the goals and programs of the church. In an urban area of asphalt and concrete, with limited green spaces, the church provides a respite with a small planted area in the front. Within the budget limitations, the architect has been particularly successful in using brick and wood to create a building of interest and imagination. The exterior of the building respectfully acknowledges its setting but is not dull or squalid. In a prosaic environment, it is poetic; it is neither pretty nor sweet but represents vigor and vitality. Emmanuel Presbyterian is one of many examples showing that each merger has its own story and its own solution to the problems of excessive buildings.

In the future, the combination of ecumenical idealism and practical realities will necessitate an increased emphasis upon shared facilities. Every aspect of the full-functioning environment is best achieved through the cooperative sharing of buildings, whether the arrangement is a rental, an imaginative campus complex, or a merger. Expensive duplication of facilities cannot continue. The new direction in church architecture requires a more innovative, cooperative relationship among religious organizations.

## INTERFAITH CENTER

The Interfaith Center in Columbia, Maryland, embodies all the qualities represented by the new directions of the church. At Columbia there has been cooperation among all faiths, development of outdoor and natural areas, integration with the total community, as well as service to the disadvantaged, and, most significantly, the development of a shared facility. The creation of the center has required cooperation not only among religious groups but also with secular organizations, namely the Rouse Company, which is predominantly responsible for the development of Columbia. The city is located on gently rolling wooded hills between the metropolitan areas of Washington, D.C., and Baltimore, in one of the fastest growing areas in the nation. On a site of over fifteen thousand acres James Rouse has created a new city with the goal

of providing the best environment possible for the growth and maturing of
people. Rouse believes that by bringing together a staff skilled in community
development, the free enterprise system can provide through careful planning
a better environment. He stated:

> There is absolutely no dialogue in the United States today between the
> people who have developed knowledge about people—the teachers, the
> ministers, psychiatrists, sociologists—and the people who are designing
> and building our cities. We are not asking the right questions, and so, we
> are not getting the right answers.[26]

William Finley, Columbia's director of development, described the high-
minded goals for the city of Columbia:

> To set aside permanent open-space land for "the lungs of the city."
> To provide opportunities for new institutions that will better meet
> human needs than the older established ones.
> To establish communities that provide for a high degree of human
> communication, for freedom of movement, freedom from fears, freedom
> from the depressing aspects of the older cities. . . .
> To provide the ability to get around; to avoid the slavery of the second
> car, of the "mother chauffeur"; to allow a system of transportation from
> the first day for the children, the aged, the infirm, the mother-in-
> law. . . .
> To achieve a democratic social balance, to provide a wide range of
> housing by type, style, and price. Housing open to all. Housing available
> to every person employed in the community.[27]

These goals are being implemented through a design concept based on small
villages clustered around a downtown center. The pivotal planning decision
for Columbia was the acknowledgment that learning is the basic foundation
for a human community, a concept supported by such prognosticators as Marshall McLuhan and Buckminster Fuller. The schools are, accordingly, a focal
point of community life. Each neighborhood with from three hundred to five
hundred families will have an elementary school and each village, from three
thousand to five thousand families or approximately twelve thousand people,
will have a secondary school. All the schools will be within easy walking distance of the areas they serve. Schools are only the beginning, for each village
center also has a major food store, auxiliary shops, community meeting places,

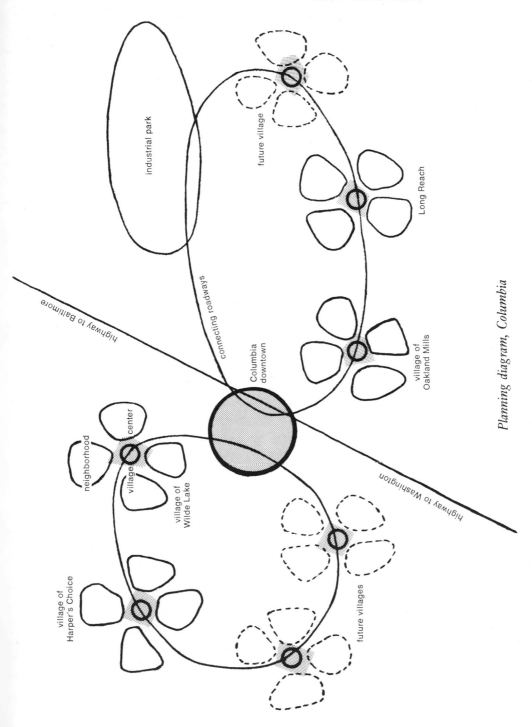

industrial park

future village

Long Reach

connecting roadways

village of
Oakland Mills

highway to Baltimore

Columbia
downtown

neighborhood

village center

village of
Wilde Lake

highway to Washington

village of
Harper's Choice

future villages

*Planning diagram, Columbia*

a library, a day-care center, and recreational facilities, including a swimming pool and tennis and basketball courts. Each village is also conceived as a spiritual center, and religious facilities are an integral part of the village complex.

Early in the total planning, major portions of land were set aside adjacent to the village centers for use by the churches. Mr. Rouse, an elder in the Presbyterian church, saw these future churches with the same imagination that has characterized the development of Columbia and approached the National Council of Churches to explore the possibilities of the cooperative use of the church sites. The council was excited by the possibilities and designated the area as a pilot project to develop new forms of cooperatively planned ecumenical ministries. Dr. Stanley Hallett was commissioned by the council in 1964 to study the possibilities.

In his report, "Working Papers in Church Planning, Columbia, Maryland," Dr. Hallett wrote the following statement about the attitudes toward all institutional problems at Columbia; it describes the framework of social thinking that led to the development of the Interfaith Center:

> Planning for Columbia started with the effort to throw out all preconceptions about "the way it has to be done." Instead of looking at the health of the people as a problem of medical care, the question was framed, "How can we develop a healthy community?" Instead of assuming that the libraries must be separate units, the question was "How can the total library needs be met?" The development of a multi-purpose library at the village center serving the lower and upper schools plus adults was proposed. Instead of assuming that profitable recreation facilities (golf courses, tennis courts and bowling alleys) should be operated by private enterprises, and other recreation facilities (bicycle paths, participating art programs, etc.) should be tax or donation supported, it was proposed that profitable programs be undertaken by a community service corporation and the resources used to support whatever other programs the community desires.
>
> These illustrations seek to indicate the kind of solutions to problems of building a community which are at least conceivable when the starting point is the basic task to be done, and the design of organizational structures, facilities, resources, and land-use is developed around these tasks.[28]

Dr. Hallett explored every aspect of the proposed ecumenical venture, projecting various alternative developments, their costs, size, and levels of cooperation including shared facilities, a cooperative ministry, shared-time religious education, an ecumenical institute, pastoral counseling center, metropolitan and world mission program, and a national conference and retreat center. The following year a steering group, the Mission Development Committee, representing the Maryland Council of Churches and the National Council of Churches, was formed and adopted two of Dr. Hallett's proposals, the development of the Cooperative Ministry and the Religious Facilities Corporation. Thirteen denominations established the Columbia Cooperative Ministry including the American Baptist; American Lutheran Church; Baltimore Yearly Meeting of Friends; Christian Churches (Disciples of Christ); Church of the Brethren; Church of God, Anderson, Indiana; Episcopal Church; Lutheran Church in America; Lutheran Church, Missouri Synod; Presbyterian Church, U.S.; United Church of Christ; United Methodist Church; and United Presbyterian Church, U.S.A.

Local Lutheran, Episcopal, Presbyterian, and Methodist churches also entered the covent.

In 1966, the Cooperative Ministry began with Rev. Clarence Sinclair as executive minister. Since its inception the Cooperative Ministry has stressed the development of a team ministry, touching upon some of the special services emphasized in Dr. Hallett's report with new forms of religious education, comprehensive counseling, and youth programs.

The most important breakthrough in cooperative planning was the development of the Interfaith Center under the auspices of the Religious Facilities Corporation. In order to widen the ecumenical basis of the center, the Columbia Interfaith Planning Council was formed. It is composed of the Cooperative Ministry and the Archdiocese of Baltimore with associate members, the Baptist Convention of Maryland, the Howard County Jewish Council, and the Unitarian Universalist Society of Howard County. The Archdiocese also joined and became a full participant in the Columbia Religious Facilities Corporation, broadening the center's program to include facilities for use by Roman Catholics. The first structure to be built was planned for the village of Wilde Lake. The firm of Huygens and Tappé was selected to be the coordinating architects. This young firm had not previously designed a religious facility but had successfully designed a wide variety of institutional and commercial buildings. The firm of Gaudreau, Inc., of Baltimore was added to share in the general planning and supervision and, in particular, to design the interior of the Roman Catholic space. The architects were an instrumental part of the development process and fully participated in the programing of the Interfaith Center as well as the design and construction of the building. A. Anthony Tappé, partner in charge of the project, explained the process:

> This planning process became an important venture in interfaith cooperation. As highlights of this cooperation, several of the many important points of the program should be mentioned, which set the stage for the architectural concept: 1. The basic idea was that all religious facilities should be clustered together on one common site. 2. From this idea developed the concept that all church facilities should be in one building. 3. A common entrance court and foyer became an expression of interfaith cooperation. 4. The idea of sharing suggested a common baptistry. 5. Office and service spaces were to be shared. 6. Careful scheduling should enable the sharing of worship spaces.[29]

Each of these points has been successfully integrated into the Interfaith Center, which has a design concept of an inviting pavilion for religious activity, with plentiful open spaces for human activity. Mr. Tappé said of the building:

> Expressing the diversity of its function in the community, the building provides a flexible framework within which the interfaith principle may flourish. This non-traditional concept has been given a non-traditional form without clichés or shallow symbolism. It is a building of dignity and restraint with a lightness and openness to the world. Its non-static quality encourages experimentation with new liturgies and their physical expressions.[30]

To understand the design of the Interfaith Center, it is necessary to see it in the total context of the area. Columbia, with all its planning ideals and excellent design, has a certain quality that implies a predetermined living pattern. William Whyte describes new towns in *The Last Landscape:*

> American planners tend to overplan, even where the constraints of reality are great, and when they are given a clean slate to work with, the temptation to overplan can be irresistible. There are exceptions, but physically the most striking thing about the plans for the ideal new towns is their finality. Everything is in its place: There are no loose ends, no question marks, and it is this completeness of the vision, more than the particulars of it, that stirs recalcitrance. It is one thing to be beckoned

down the road to a distant utopia, quite another to be shown utopia itself
in metes and bounds and all of it at once.[31]

At Columbia the physical environment is everything the planners promised,
but it all comes together as almost too much of a good thing, as if everyone is
acting out everyone else's dream of what the good life should be. Some of
these feelings may result from the affluent suburbanness of the setting or the
pristine newness of everything from television antennas to fire hydrants. The
planning ideas are all sound, but the real test will be their actual value in the
lives of people as the area grows and mellows.

In this setting of suburban homes and the village center, designed in what
Tappé calls pseudo-ranch style, the Interfaith Center seems out of character.
The design task was difficult in itself because requirements for the center required a building larger in scale than most of those already in the village. In
addition, the architects felt a meaningful religious building should not be more
pseudo-ranch, but a direct and positive architectural statement. The selected
design with strong stark lines of brick and glass seems incongruous with the
area. It is questionable whether the architects achieved their design objective;
one almost feels the same integrity of design could have been achieved with
materials more compatible with the remainder of the village. However, much
of the harshness of the present building may be modified in the future as small
plants and trees are added to the surrounding areas.

The entrance to the building does express the design goal of encouraging all
people to enter its doors. Unlike the usual cramped entrances to most
churches, the Interfaith Center has large glass areas leading to an open foyer
that is accented with changing religious and art displays. The foyer is the
entry to all the major areas in the building, making it both the symbolic and
practical focus of the center's activities. It is conceived as a broad, enclosed
atrium where people of various faiths may gather before and after their individual worship services and as a continuous open meeting place for all members of the religious community. A liturgical symbol of this sense of sharing is
the central baptismal font, placed in the foyer between the Protestant and
Catholic worship spaces and used by all participating churches. The surrounding space is large enough so that the usual problems of crowding at the font
are avoided, and a small or large congregation can be comfortably gathered
around the font. At the end of the foyer, a comfortable lounge area with tables

*Protestant worship space*

*Catholic worship space*

and soft chairs provides a relaxing meeting place. Hopefully, in time, the entrance walks and foyer will be filled with potted plants and flowers to help fulfill the architect's initial concept of a gracious entrance area.

The Protestant worship space is located in the center of the building, directly off the foyer. The room is square and is designed to seat three hundred fifty people. Tappé described the possibilities of the room:

> Flexibility is at the heart of the program for the use of this space. Within the square, the liturgical focus can be located in a corner, on a side, or in the center. Each of these arrangements has different characteristics.
>
> A corner liturgical focus with its strong direction and formality is also easily adaptable to conventional still and motion picture projection techniques.
>
> With a central liturgical focus, the congregation gathers around the chancel to participate in worship. Three hundred and sixty degree seating can present a challenge to the planning of the service, and less conventional techniques would come into their own with this space use. Multi-screen total environment presentations, sometimes as part of the new liturgy, could be developed.
>
> The more traditional axial liturgical focus allows the gathering of the congregation around the chancel, combining some of the formal qualities of the corner focus with the participating congregation aspects of the central chancel arrangement.[32]

The Catholic worship area, designed by the associate architectural firm of Gaudreau, Inc., is the largest space in the building, with a seating capacity for six hundred people. The room can be divided into two separate areas, each seating three hundred people, by opening a large wood-paneled motorized folding door. The architect of the interior, William Gaudreau, described the design:

> In 1966, the descriptive, "multi-celebration," was first introduced to explain a concept of design for places of worship in the future. The concept means that churches can be designed for a multitude of functions or celebrations: liturgical, social, educational, and theatrical. All are by choice and these functions become a specific part of program decisions.
>
> In 1967 at the earliest stages of program development for the Columbia Religious Facilities Center, the Catholic community discussed in depth and were unanimous in their agreement that the proposed place of worship for Catholics in the new center should express this concept. Of prime concern was the visual and audible success of the programmed

functions chosen to be performed in the proposed space. A modified arena design with a center-stage effect and sloping floors was found to satisfy this concern.[33]

To provide for the Reservation of the Eucharist, a small, quiet meditation chapel is located off the main foyer, near the entrance to the Catholic meeting space.

Both the Catholic and the Protestant worship spaces express the principles of a full-functioning environment. The spaces provide an opportunity for worship of celebration and participation, and the flexible seating allows a wide variety of arrangements for worship services and other programs and activities within the area. Both churches have used semi-circular seating surrounding the altar as the most effective means of expressing the centrality of communion and community. The Protestant space has a multisectional movable platform; both worship areas use movable pulpits and altars. Singing during the services is led by choirs seated within the congregation; the choir members participate fully in the worship service and lead the congregation in singing. Both churches freely use a variety of musical forms, depending upon the nature of the service. The areas are actively used for worship. The Catholic church conducts a series of masses on Saturday and Sunday, including one folk mass each weekend, and mass every morning throughout the week. The Protestant space is used at nine o'clock by the Lutherans and at eleven o'clock by the St. John United Methodist–United Presbyterian Church. Both worship areas are also active during the week with weddings, funerals, and other occasions. The worship spaces are designed and designated for one denomination, but there has been an agreement from the beginning that all spaces will be used interchangeably by the participating churches for both worship and special events. For the building dedication service, in which participants of the three major faiths spoke, the Catholic space was used; during Rosh Hashanah observances the Jewish congregation used the large Catholic and Protestant rooms. During the week, community forums, suppers, and church meetings are held in the Protestant room; drama and large gatherings are particularly well suited to the Catholic space.

There are a variety of smaller spaces in the building used by the other participating congregations. One central area reached directly from the foyer can seat one hundred fifty people. This area is one of the most popular meeting and conference rooms in the building and is used by St. John's Baptist Church as a worship area on Sunday. A small area, seating seventy people, also di-

*Before, Christ Church*

*After, terrace, Christ Church*

rectly off the foyer, is used by two separate Jewish congregations. All the smaller auxiliary rooms are active during the week because of their ideal size for conferences, small gatherings, clubs, youth groups, and other organizational meetings. In light of the heavy demands on the auxiliary rooms, it appears that the larger Catholic and Protestant rooms should have been designed to be more adaptable to smaller groups during the week. With hindsight, it is easy to say that the large Protestant space should be more flexible for smaller groups, since the larger Catholic space is available for most larger meetings. However, at the time of its initiation, it was a daring innovation to have the churches meeting in the same building.

No extensive religious education facilities were planned for the Interfaith Center. The Catholics have implemented a successful program of religious education after school in members' homes. Small groups of ten students are led by trained parents in a program coordinated by the resident sisters. The Protestant groups rent facilities from an adjacent public school for Sunday morning classes. Some consider this lack of education space a weakness of the center because the participating churches pay not only for religious space at the center but also at the schools. They feel the money spent on the larger foyer and other areas might have been better used in developing more classroom spaces. This problem may take care of itself as the village and congregations grow, easing the financial burden of the initial groups. The concept of the large unifying foyer is essential to the ecumenical quality of the design, but it might have been modified to be more usable for classes during the peak period on Sunday morning. Some of the office spaces should also be used on Sunday. Other additions to make the center more serviceable are a more secluded adult program lounge and an unfinished room or media room for young people. On the whole, however, considering the wide range of community service already available at the village center, the home-study program and supplemental space rental, the avoidance of a large amount of religious education space was very sensible. The Interfaith Center is not the ideal embodiment of the full-functioning environment, but it comes so close that its apparent flaws in appearance and flexibility can be readily accepted.

The Interfaith Center at Columbia is moving in new directions in every aspect of its development. The level of cooperation among the Protestant denominations, the Catholics, and the Jews is unprecedented, and the Interfaith Center building is unique as a successful religious shared facility. The center goes beyond these achievements to express the concepts of increased environ-

*Exterior, Interfaith Center*

mental and community awareness. Harmony with the natural environment is an integral part of the design of the city of Columbia, with preserved open green belts of the original landscape between villages and the downtown area. The Interfaith Center has made its contribution to these efforts through the economical use of land. The initial plans called for several church sites at the village center; this was later reduced to one site of ten acres and further reduced to seven and a half acres by using cooperative parking arrangements with the community shopping plaza. In a typical suburban situation, just one church could easily take this much land. The center not only saves money but also frees more land for open space. In a combination of outdoor orientation and community cooperation, the church, located at one edge of the village center, can share in the use of the community plaza with its terraced open spaces, sitting and play areas.

The center has not limited community involvement to its own facilities but has reached out with a broader concept of buildings and service to organize a separate corporation to develop low- and moderate-income housing within Columbia. The Interfaith Housing Corporation was formed by the Cooperative Ministry, the Roman Catholic Archdiocese of Baltimore, and representatives of the Jewish Council of Howard County. A total of three hundred units on five separate sites have already been constructed and financed through the Federal Housing Administration. Working on the Interfaith Housing Corporation not only provided a needed community service, but the Interfaith Council reports that involvement in a common concern was an important part of developing cooperative church relationships.

The Interfaith Center has its problems as well as its successes, but many of these difficulties are inevitable in light of the unprecedented nature of the project. Because there were very few families in Columbia at the inception of the building program, the initial members of the Religious Facilities Corporation were representatives from outside Columbia. As the population of the village of Wilde Lake and the surrounding areas grew and the building was completed, there were some tensions between the desires of the growing local congregations and the existing board. Many of these difficulties have been resolved with the increased participation of representatives of the local churches in decision-making bodies.

The Interfaith Center in the village of Wilde Lake, even with some of its design flaws, is a major step forward in new directions of church cooperation and the development of shared facilities. Other villages at Columbia have church groups experimenting in a variety of religious formats, including lay-man-led gatherings and a coffeehouse church. In the nearby village of Oak-land Mills, a cooperative congregation of United Church of Christ and the Church of the Brethren are temporarily meeting in rented facilities and in time may build or not build the next village religious center, based on the ex-perience of the Interfaith Center and the desires of the local membership. Many of the design features at the center at Wilde Lake are related to the spe-cifics of the particular place and time of the planning and construction, but we can still learn by their experiences and apply the basic principles of sharing and cooperation to other locations. Anthony Tappé evaluated the center:

> The idea of Columbia and the interfaith venture proposed here required a new answer to the question as to what the appropriate forms of religious life in a new community should be. This building, not a church in the traditional sense, creates a stimulating environment which permits, and indeed encourages, new patterns of worship and community life. In the final analysis, it falls to the people to create their spiritual community. This building intends to assist them.[34]

The clergy and members of each of the participating faiths have indicated their enthusiasm for the process of creating a meaningful religious community. The Right Reverend Lawrence Shehan, Archbishop of Baltimore, is affirma-tive and optimistic:

> The opening of the new Interfaith Center at Columbia provides a unique opportunity for long-time growth in ecumenism and brotherly spirit. Hopefully, under the roof of the Center, the congregations, each with its own place of worship, will continue to strive for new ecumenical experi-ences, will encourage joint biblical study, and will cooperate as far as is feasible in religious education.
> The mutual ownership of land and facilities and the sharing of space, administrative personnel and costs, and the development of coordinated programming, will testify to the good stewardship of the resources God has given these congregations to administer. This will be further high-lighted in the multi-use nature of the large spaces in the Center, which when not needed for worship, will be available for a wide variety of com-munity and personal needs and activities.[35]

Siegfried Rowe, the president of the Jewish Council of Howard County, de-scribed the experience of the Interfaith Center for the Jewish congregation:

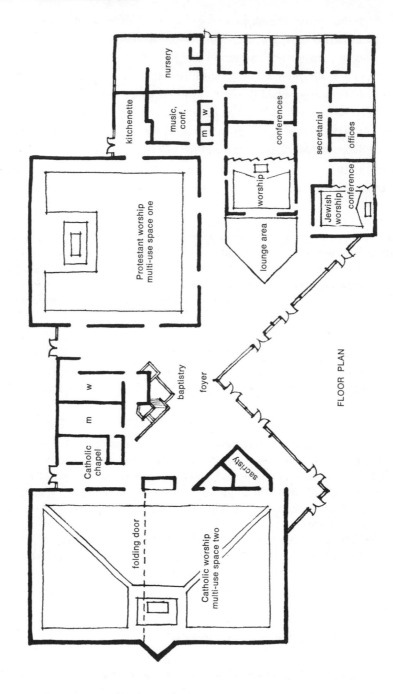

*Floor plan, Interfaith Center*

We're getting used to seeing nuns with their habits walking around and greeting you and Protestants saying hello to you down the hill. We Jews have traditionally been suspicious of Gentiles. Because of past experience, we have had a difficult time learning how to trust. Now, partially because of what is happening here in the center, we're beginning to enjoy each other and learning how to trust.[36]

David Luecke, pastor of the Lutheran congregation, discerns a whole new dimension of ecumenical relationships between the faiths at the center. He finds that the joint efforts have led not to a watered-down super-religion of sterile efficiency but rather to a slow human understanding with a respect for honest differences and a sharing of mutual concerns:

Being together has its advantages. . . . In an interfaith context, one makes decisions only after a thorough examination of the "whys" and the priorities involved. So you do not make fast, expedient decisions. But it's in this process that you really get to know one another.[37]

With an active schedule of worship services and a full range of church and community programs, the Interfaith Center is a vital church facility, responsive to the religious needs and aspirations of the people of Columbia.

## ALIVE AND WELL

Many religious spaces are deteriorating as society moves and changes, but there are others that have been adapted and are alive and well. The process of renewal is not easy; there will be conflicts, but these are the price of vitality. The church has always had to grapple with beliefs and values and their expression in the physical world and the tension between idealized aspirations and their fulfillment in daily activities. The church will need to balance a relevance to contemporary living and its forms of expression but not lose sight of its concern for the deeper sanctities of life that transcend every age. The church will need "to outgrow the past but not extinguish it, to be progressive but not raw." [38] Its buildings will need to be flexible but not formless, gracious but not sterile.

The church is people and it is place. Joseph Sittler has stated, "No place is holy, but the presentation of the holy never occurs without a place." [39] People and buildings are interrelated. Religious structures reflect religious values; reli-

*Festival Day, Christ Church, Presbyterian*

gious attitudes are shaped by the environment. A religious building can never exist for itself but should always be conceived as a place of human activity, whether for the sanctity of worship, the stimulation of discussion, or opportunities for community service.

A religious environment that is alive and well is a space for people. It is a gathering of adults talking, laughing, listening in a conversations group in the adult program lounge of the First Congregational Church in Melrose, Massachusetts.

It is a young family attracted to the variety and dignity of worship services at the remodeled Christ Church Cathedral in St. Louis.

It is lively youngsters splashing in the wading pool on a hot summer day at the playground of St. Ann's Church in the Bronx.

It is young people gathered for a folk service in evening candlelight at the Catholic Chapel at Brandeis University.

It is a day laborer singing with full voice in both Spanish and English in the choir of the Emmanuel Presbyterian Church on the South Side of Chicago.

It is a high schooler in trouble stopping in at the Place, the rented drop-in center sponsored by Christ Church, Presbyterian, in Burlington, Vermont.

It is a lonely elderly woman at Saint Francis Chapel in the Prudential Center in Boston in sorrowful prayer over the death of a loved one.

It is the gathering of people of all ages at an arts festival on the terrace of Christ Church in Washington, D.C.

It is the neighborhood parents at St. Mark's Church in the urban residential area of Kansas City, Missouri, attending a meeting to improve community services.

It is the gathering of the religious community around the fireplace at the First Unitarian Society on a snowy, winter Sunday morning in Milford, New Hampshire.

It is the newcomer meeting the members of the church after the morning service in the pleasant surroundings of the fellowship hall at the Hope United Presbyterian Church in Creve Coeur, Missouri.

It is an elderly couple enjoying dignified living in Oakland, California, in the housing units built through the joint efforts of the Plymouth United Church of Christ and Piedmont Community Church.

It is the members of the United Parish of Brookline, Massachusetts, coming together in formal session to discuss the program and direction of their team ministries.

It is those "who hurry by to dance, to act, to pray, to hang a canvas, to sing, to place a sculpture, to dream, to proclaim or to listen—all offerings, if worthy at all, to community and to God.[40] It is all these people passing in the foyer of the Interfaith Center in Columbia.

Churches are a place for people. The architecture is the means, the setting; but the individual people bring a church to life. The building can help or it can hinder each experience. The members of the church must care enough to create a meaningful religious environment that will truly meet the needs of the gathered community.

# NOTES

## FRESH AIR

1. John A. T. Robinson, *Honest to God* (Philadelphia: Westminster Press, 1963); Harvey Cox, *The Secular City* (New York: Macmillan, 1965); Pierre Berton, *The Comfortable Pew* (Philadelphia: Lippincott, 1965).

2. Marshall McLuhan, *Understanding Media: The Extensions of Man* (New York: McGraw-Hill, 1964), p. 21.

3. Paul Tillich, *The Courage to Be* (New Haven: Yale University Press, 1952), p. 47.

4. Rollo May, "The Significance of Symbols," in *Symbolism in Religion and Literature*, Rollo May, ed. (New York: Braziller, 1960), p. 25.

5. Quoted by Norman Cousins in *Saturday Review* (January 19, 1963), p. 20.

6. Henry Adams, *Mont Saint Michel and Chartres* (Boston: Houghton Mifflin, 1905), p. 87.

7. Alvin Toffler, *Future Shock* (New York: Random House, 1970), p. 1.

8. Ibid., p. 11.

9. Buckminster Fuller and John McHale, *World Design Science Decade 1965–1975*, quoted in Toffler, *Future Shock*, p. 51.

## FULL FUNCTIONING

1. Children's Bureau, *Daytime Programs for Children* (Washington, D.C., U.S. Department of Health, Education, and Welfare, 1967), p. 4.

2. E. Belle Evans, Beth Shub, and Marlene Weinstein, *Day Care: How to Plan, Develop and Operate a Day Care Center* (Boston: Beacon Press, 1971), p. 42.

3. Ronald W. Haase, "Space Which Allows," *Housing for Early Childhood Education*, Sylvia Sunderlin, ed. (Washington, D.C.: Association for Childhood Educational International, 1968), p. 7.

4. Ruth E. Jefferson, "Indoor Facilities," ibid., p. 41.

5. John Hancock Callender, ed., *Time Savers Standards* (New York: McGraw-Hill, 1966), p. 959.

6. Marshall McLuhan, "Explorations in the New World, Part II," in *McLuhan: Hot and Cool*, Gerald E. Stearn, ed. (New York: New American Library, 1969), p. 120.

7. Von Ogden Vogt, *Art and Religion* (Boston: Beacon Press, 1948), p. 26.

## STIRRING

1. John Scotford, "Innovations in the Lord's Supper," *Your Church* 15, no. 5 (1969): 26.

2. Harvey Cox, *The Feast of Fools* (Cambridge, Mass.: Harvard University Press, 1969), p. 11.

3. Edward Sinnott, *Meetinghouse and Church in Early New England* (New York: Bonanza Books, 1963), p. 7.

4. Paul Tillich, "Contemporary Protestant Architecture," in *Modern Church Architecture: A Guide to the Form and Spirit of Twentieth Century Religious Buildings,* Albert Christ-Janer and Mary Mix Foley, eds. (New York: McGraw-Hill, 1962), p. 123.

5. Plato, *Republic,* Book 4, in *The Dialogues of Plato,* B. Jowett, trans. (New York: Random House, 1920), p. 687.

6. Scotford, "Innovations in the Lord's Supper," p. 26.

7. Ibid., p. 31.

8. John E. Morse, *To Build a Church* (New York: Holt, Rinehart and Winston, 1969), p. 97.

9. James White, *Protestant Worship and Church Architecture* (New York: Oxford University Press, 1964), p. 143.

10. Ibid.

11. Benjamin Elliott, cited in Edward Sovik, "Comment on Multi-Purpose Worship Spaces," *Faith and Form* 2 (April 1969): 21.

## STRETCHING

1. Harvey Cox, *The Secular City* (New York: Macmillan, 1965), p. 47.

2. James D. Morgan, "Design for Merchandising," *Architectural Record* (February 1971), p. 99.

3. Pietro Belluschi, "Eloquent Simplicity in Architecture," *Architectural Record* (July 1963), pp. 131–35.

4. Staff of the Department of Architecture, Norman G. Boyer, Executive Director, *Preliminary Planning* (Philadelphia: National Division of the Board of Admissions of the Methodist Church, 1965).

5. Bruno Zevi, *Architecture as Space* (New York: Horizon Press, 1957), p. 24.

6. Geoffrey Scott, *The Architecture of Humanism* (New York: Scribners, 1924), pp. 168, 6.

7. Ibid., p. 168.

8. Frank Lloyd Wright, *The Natural House* (New York: Horizon Press, 1954), p. 44.

9. Zevi, *Architecture as Space,* pp. 22–23.

10. Wright, *The Natural House,* p. 53.

11. Belluschi, "Eloquent Simplicity in Architecture," pp. 131–35.

12. Frank Lloyd Wright, "The Nature of Materials," in Edgar Kaufman and Ben Raeburn, eds., *Writings and Buildings* (Cleveland: World, 1960), p. 224.

13. Eugene Ruskin, *Architectural Speaking* (New York: Dell, 1954), p. 91.

14. Ibid., p. 93.

15. Albert O. Halse, *The Use of Color in Interiors* (New York: McGraw-Hill, 1968), p. 21.

16. Alexander Eliot, *Sight and Insight* (New York: Dutton, 1960), p. 9.

17. Le Corbusier, quoted in *Modern Church Architecture: A Guide to the Form and Spirit of Twentieth Century Religious Buildings,* Albert Christ-Janer and Mary Mix Foley, eds. (New York: McGraw-Hill, 1962), p. 103.

18. Robert Sowers, "Stained Glass: A Dialogue—The Artist's Position," in *Faith and Form* 1 (April 1968): 14.

19. Thom W. Blair, "The Flexible Cathedral," *The Cathedral Age* 46, no. 1 (1971): 7.

20. Karl Landberg, ibid., p. 4.

21. Blair, ibid., p. 9.

22. Ibid., p. 10.

# NEW DIRECTIONS

1. Edwin S. Gaustad, "America's Institutions of Faith," in *The Religious Situation 1968*, Donald K. Cutler, ed. (Boston: Beacon Press, 1968), p. 846. One of a number of articles in this extensive survey of religious ideas and trends in the late sixties.

2. Horace S. Sills, *Grassroots Ecumenicity* (Philadelphia: United Church Press, 1967), p. 2. A series of detailed case studies of rural churches working together to form cooperative churches.

3. Herbert Wallace Schneider, *Religion in 20th Century America* (New York: Atheneum, 1964), pp. 187–188. An overview of religious practices and trends in the early fifties seen in the perspective of historical changes since the turn of the century.

4. *A Plan of Union* (Princeton, New Jersey: Consultation of Church Union, 1970), p. 10. The widely distributed statement of the plan for church union stating objectives and organizational considerations.

5. H. Richard Niebuhr, *The Social Sources of Denominationalism* (New York: Meridan Books, Inc., 1957), p. 284. An excellent historical review of the sources of denominationalism in this country.

6. Lynn White, Jr., "The Historical Roots of Our Ecological Crisis," *Science*, vol. 155 (March 10, 1967), pp. 1203–07. A good article presenting a survey of Western religions attitudes toward the environment. Mr. White proposes in the conclusion that St. Francis become the patron saint of ecologists.

7. Albert Camus, *The Rebel* (New York: Vintage Book, Alfred Knopf, Inc., 1956), p. 299. One of the most eloquent and profound statements upon the historical and philosophical roots of contemporary society.

8. M. Paul Friedberg, *Playgrounds for City Children* (Washington, D.C.: Association for Childhood Educational International, 1969), p. 7.

9. Ibid., p. 12.

10. J. G. Davies, *The Secular Use of Church Buildings* (New York: The Seabury Press, 1968), p. 241–42. A thorough historical review of the many uses of church buildings based on extensive original documents.

11. Ibid., p. 78.

12. Ibid., p. 96.

13. Mildred C. Wilder and Scott T. Ritenour, *Focus: Building for Christian Education* (Philadelphia: United Church Press, 1969), p. 112. This beautiful book is full of helpful information about religious education. The principal difficulty is its premise that new buildings are designed solely for religious educational purposes, and it does not deal adequately with the needs for full utilization of existing buildings.

14. William Abernethy, "The Bennington Religious Education Foundation: A Contemporary Model of Quality Religious Education," *Religious Education* (January–February 1970), (New York: Religious Education Association), p. 43.

15. Rev. William Hayes, *St. Mark's Church* (Kansas City, Missouri: St. Mark's Church, 1969), p. 1.

16. Ibid.

17. Ibid., p. 4.

18. Eliot A. Daley, "Where the Mission Is the Church," in *Presbyterian Life*, vol. 21, no. 6 (March 15, 1968), p. 6. This article describes the full development of Christ Church, Presbyterian, in Burlington, Vermont.

19. Ibid.

20. Ibid., p. 5.

21. John E. Morse, *To Build a Church* (New York: Holt, Rinehart, and Winston, 1969), p. 67.

22. Bylaws of the Campus Corporation, United Church of the Applewoods and the Jefferson Unitarian Church, Golden, Colorado, 1967.

23. Leon Hopper, unpublished report on the Campus Corporation, 1968.

24. Philip J. Weiler, "Church Union," *The Christian Century* (November 25, 1970), p. 1423.

25. Stephen C. Rose, *The Grass Roots Church* (Nashville: Abingdon Press, 1966), p. 81. A provocative book demanding changes in the structure of institutional religion as a means of creating a renewal within the Protestant church.

26. James Rouse quoted in A. Anthony Tappe, "The Religious Facilities Center," in the *Journal of the American Society for Church Architecture*, vol. 10 (April 1970), p. 51. The *Journal* is a semi-annual publication on church architecture published by the American Society for Church Architecture.

27. William Finley quoted in James Bailey, *Architectural Forum* (November 1967), p. 46.

28. Stanley J. Hallett, *Working Papers in Church Planning, Columbia, Maryland* (New York: National Council of Churches of Christ in the USA, 1964), p. 5.

29. Tappe, op. cit., p. 54.

30. Ibid., p. 55.

31. William H. Whyte, *The Last Landscape* (Garden City, New York: Doubleday and Company, 1968), p. 228. A book about our larger sense of environment written with the same reason and wit that have characterized William Whyte's other writings.

32. Tappe, op. cit., pp. 56–57.

33. Columbia Interfaith Planning Council, *Interfaith Center, 1970*, dedication brochure, Columbia Religious Facilities Corporation (September 20, 1970), p. 6.

34. Tappe, op. cit., p. 37.

35. Columbia Interfaith Council, op. cit., p. 11.

36. Wes Yamaka, "Three Faiths Under One Split-Level Roof," in *Columbia Today*, vol. 4, no. 1 (January 1971), p. 16.

37. Ibid., p. 17.

38. William Sullivan, "To Outgrow the Past," in *Hymns for the Celebration of Life* (Boston: Beacon Press, 1964), No. 496.

39. Joseph Sittler, "Highlights of Sessions and Seminars," in *Revolution, Place and Symbol*, Rolfe Lanier Hunt, ed. (New York: International Congress on Religious Architecture and the Visual Arts, 1969), p. 250.

40. Columbia Interfaith Council, op. cit., p. 8.

*Drawings*

Edwin Charles Lynn

*Photographs*

vi Courtesy Trinity Episcopal Church, New York City
12 Alinari, Florence, Italy
13 Arthur Mazmanian, Worcester, Massachusetts
14 Alinari, Florence, Italy
69 Courtesy First Unitarian Universalist Church, Burlington, Vermont
121 Courtesy Burk and Landberg, Architects, St. Louis, Missouri
125 Courtesy John Sinclair, architect, Farmington, Connecticut
197 Courtesy Burk and Landberg, Architects, St. Louis, Missouri
199 Courtesy Design Furnishing Company, Cleveland, Ohio
202 Courtesy Burk and Landberg, Architects, St. Louis, Missouri
203 Courtesy Burk and Landberg, Architects, St. Louis, Missouri
204 Courtesy Burk and Landberg, Architects, St. Louis, Missouri
207 Courtesy Burk and Landberg, Architects, St. Louis, Missouri
208 Courtesy Burk and Landberg, Architects, St. Louis, Missouri
209 Courtesy Burk and Landberg, Architects, St. Louis, Missouri
224 Donald Wood, architect, New York City
233 Courtesy Charles Steele, architect, Kansas City, Missouri
250 Studio 601/Cabandan, Chicago, Illinois
258 Courtesy the Rouse Company, Columbia, Maryland
259 Courtesy the Rouse Company, Columbia, Maryland
262 Courtesy Philip Ives, architect, New York City
263 Courtesy Philip Ives, architect, New York City
270 Noonan Photography, Burlington, Vermont

All other photographs by Edwin Charles Lynn